# The SPARC Architecture Manual

*Version 8*

Revision SAV080SI9308

# The SPARC Architecture Manual

*Version 8*

## SPARC International, Inc.
*Menlo Park, California*

Upper Saddle River, New Jersey 07458

Copyright © 1992 SPARC International, Inc.

 Published by Prentice-Hall, Inc.
A Simon & Schuster Company
Upper Saddle River, New Jersey 07458

**The publisher offers discounts on this book when ordered in
bulk quantities. For more information, write: Special
Sales/Professional Marketing, Prentice Hall, Professional &
Technical Reference Division, Englewood Cliffs, NJ 07632.**

Printed in the United States of America

10  9  8  7  6  5  4

ISBN  0-13-825001-4

PRENTICE-HALL INTERNATIONAL (UK) LIMITED, *London*
PRENTICE-HALL OF AUSTRALIA PTY. LIMITED, *Sydney*
PRENTICE-HALL CANADA INC., *Toronto*
PRENTICE-HALL HISPANOAMERICANA, S.A., *Mexico*
PRENTICE-HALL OF INDIA PRIVATE LIMITED, *New Delhi*
PRENTICE-HALL OF JAPAN, INC., *Tokyo*
SIMON & SCHUSTER ASIA PTE. LTD., *Singapore*
EDITORA PRENTICE-HALL DO BRASIL, LTDA., *Rio de Janeiro*

# Contents

Contents — *Continued*

# Tables

# Figures

# Preface

**About SPARC International, Inc.**

SPARC International, Inc., a not-for-profit consortium for providors of SPARC® products and services, directs the evolution and standardization of the SPARC microprocessor architecture and systems operating environment. Through its committee structure, SPARC International documents this evolution through two primary vehicles: *The SPARC Architecture Manual* and the *SPARC Compliance Definition (SCD)*. These two documents tell vendors of chips, systems, applications, and add-in/add-on hardware how to comply with SPARC International standards, and how to ensure binary level compatibility with all other SPARC products.

To give buyers of SPARC products that same assurance, SPARC International provides compliance testing services to members and grants vendors of SPARC Compliant™ products the right to use the SPARC Compliant trademark. The SPARC Compliant trademark lets buyers know their products have been independently tested for compliance. SPARC International calls the SPARC Compliant trademark the mark of user confidence.

**The SPARC Architecture Committee**

*The SPARC Architecture Manual: Version 8* is a product of the SPARC International Architecture Committee, which at this printing included representatives from Amdahl Corporation, Fujitsu Limited, ICL, LSI Logic, Matsushita, Philips International, Ross Technology, Sun Microsystems, and Texas Instruments.

This committee is open to executive members of SPARC International. Every executive member is investing heavily in the SPARC architecture and applying its best architectural talent to include the features most demanded by customers, and to ensure that every SPARC architecture implementation maintains binary compatibility at the application level.

**SPARC Open Licensing**

As a result of the Sun Microsystems vision of a truly open standard computing environment, the SPARC architecture has reached a level of openness heretofore unimagined in the computer industry. Not only are a wide range of compatible SPARC chip implementations available from a variety of merchant SPARC licensees, but today anyone can obtain a license to the SPARC architecture for a small fee. To receive an information package, simply sign and return the reply card at the back of this manual to SPARC International. You will receive detailed information, including a license to sign and return with a payment of $99.00 (U.S. dollars).

This open licensing policy is further evidence of the SPARC standard's radical departure from current business practices. Until the advent of the SPARC standard, large microprocessor concerns maintained exclusive ownership of their standard architectures, and as a result, wielded substantial control over entire technology bases and markets developed around their products.

Today, semiconductor customers all the way through to end-users will realize the benefit of greatly accelerated innovation created by the open SPARC microprocessor standard. As a rapidly-broadening base of engineers implement the SPARC architecture, the base of compatible and complementary SPARC microprocessor products will expand as well to the advantage of both vendors and users.

Note: Rights to specific SPARC microprocessor implementations are the property of their respective developers.

**Version 8 Specification**

This book specifies Version 8 of SPARC, the Scalable Processor ARChitecture. It supersedes the Version 7 SPARC document, which has evolved for over three years. Since the publication of Version 7, several commercial sources have released SPARC processors. All of them conform to the Version 7 architecture.

Upward Compatibility

SPARC Version 8 is upward-compatible from Version 7; all Version 7 conformant software will run on Version 8 conformant processors with one minor exception discussed in a following section. The Version 8 changes are enhancements to the architecture; the most obvious is the addition of Integer Multiply and Divide instructions. For a detailed list of changes, refer to the *What's New? – Architecture* section that follows.

**Audience for this Manual**

Audiences for this specification include implementors of the architecture and developers of SPARC system software (simulators, compilers, debuggers, and operating systems, for example). Software developers who need to write SPARC software in assembly language will also find this information useful.

**Where to Start?**

If you are new to the SPARC architecture, read Chapters 1 and 2 for an overview. Then look into the following chapters and appendixes for more details on your areas of interest.

If you are already familiar with Version 7, you will want to review the list of changes at the end of the Preface. For additional detail, review Appendix B for each of the new or changed instructions, read Chapter 6 (*Memory Model*), Chapter 7 (*Traps*), and Appendixes J (*Programming with the Memory Model*) and K (*Formal Specification of the Memory Model*).

**Manual Contents**

The first chapter describes the background, design philosophy, and high-level features of SPARC, and reviews the typographic conventions used in the manual. Chapter 2 is an overview of the SPARC architecture: its organization, instruction set, and trap model. Subsequent chapters describe the SPARC data types, registers, instructions, memory model, and traps in detail.

Appendixes follow the chapters and include the following:

◻ Appendix A, *Suggested Assembly Language Syntax,* defines syntactic conventions used in the appendixes for the suggested SPARC assembly language. It also lists "synthetic instructions" that may be supported by SPARC assemblers for the convenience of assembly language programmers.

◻ Appendix B, *Instruction Descriptions,* contains definitions and all instructions for the SPARC assemblers for the convenience of assembly language programmers, including tables showing the recommended assembly language syntax for each instruction.

◻ Appendix C, *ISP Descriptions,* defines the architecture using a formal algorithmic (Instruction Set Processor, or ISP) notation.

◻ Appendixes D, E, and G, respectively, contain general SPARC software considerations, SPARC ABI software considerations, and example multiplication/division algorithms.

◻ Appendix F contains tables detailing all opcodes and condition codes.

◻ Appendixes G through N contain the Reference MMU architecture, programming with the SPARC memory model, a formal description of the SPARC memory model, and characterizations of existing SPARC implementations.

**What's New? — Architecture**

Changes to the SPARC architecture since Version 7 are in four main areas: the memory model, trap model, data formats, and instruction set.

**Enhanced Memory Model**

Version 8's memory model is an upward-compatible extension of the Strong Consistency model implicitly assumed in Version 7. The new model allows building of higher-performance memory systems in either uniprocessor or shared-memory multiprocessor SPARC applications.

**Enhanced Trap Model**

Trap categories have been renamed since Version 7; the correspondence is as follows:

| SPARC Version 7 | | SPARC Version 8 |
|---|---|---|
| Synchronous Trap | $\rightarrow$ | Precise Trap |
| Asynchronous Trap | $\rightarrow$ | Interrupting Trap |
| Floating-Point/Coprocessor Trap | $\rightarrow$ | Deferred Trap |

The Version 8 trap model enhancements give SPARC implementors more latitude in their designs. The privileged and essentially user-code-transparent trap architecture includes some new trap types. It also allows for new, implementation-specific traps.

A given trap may be implemented as either "precise" or "deferred", although each implementation must provide a way to handle traps precisely. Chapter 7 describes the enhanced trap model in detail.

| | |
|---|---|
| Data Formats | Quad (128-bit) precision data format replaces the Extended (96-bit)-precision format. No existing SPARC application code uses Extended-precision floating-point arithmetic. So, although this one change is not strictly upward-compatible with SPARC Version 7, the impact is insignificant. |

Instruction Set

Version 8 modifies the definitions of some SPARC instructions as follows:

- Extended-precision floating-point operations are now Quad-precision operations
- IFLUSH has been renamed FLUSH; its definition has expanded to encompass multiprocessor systems and processor implementations with separate instruction and data memories.

A few instructions have been added to the Version 8 architecture:

- Store Barrier instruction (STBAR)
- Integer Multiply instructions (SMUL, SMULcc, UMUL, UMULcc)
- Integer Divide instructions (SDIV, SDIVcc, UDIV, UDIVcc)
- Floating-point Multiply Single to Double (FsMULd)
- Floating-point Multiply Double to Quad (FdMULq)
- Ancillary State-Register access instructions (RDASR, WRASR), of which RDY/WRY and STBAR are subcases
- NOP ("promoted" from being a pseudo-instruction)

FQ Optional

The floating-point queue (FQ) is now optional for SPARC implementations that choose to make floating-point traps precise instead of deferred.

New FSR.*ftt* Value

A new value, invalid_fp_register, is defined for the FSR.*ftt* field. Use of the new value is optional. If implemented, its use indicates attempted execution of an instruction that refers to an invalid floating-point register number.

**What's New? — the Manual**

The SPARC Architecture Manual itself has changed since Version 7.

- Text has been clarified throughout and known errors corrected.
- The index has been considerably expanded.
- A table of synthetic instructions has been added to Appendix A (*Suggested Assembly Language Syntax*).
- Appendix D (*Software Considerations*) and Appendix F (*Opcodes*) have been enhanced.
- Appendixes G through N are completely new.

**Acknowledgments**

Architecture Definition

The SPARC Version 7 instruction set was defined by a team of individuals at Sun Microsystems that included Anant Agrawal, Fayé Briggs, Will Brown, Robert Garner, David Goldberg, David Hough, Bill Joy, Steve Kleiman, Tom Lyon, Steven Muchnick, Masood Namjoo, David Patterson, Joan Pendleton, Wayne Rosing, K.G. Tan, and Richard Tuck.

The following additional people contributed to Version 8 of the architecture: Michel Cekelov, David Ditzel, Jean-Marc Frailong, Peter Hsu, Eric Jensen, Mike Powell, and Pradeep Sindhu.

Authors

The bulk of the manual was written by Robert Garner of Sun Microsystems. Appendixes were contributed as follows: Appendixes A and G: David Weaver; Appendixes B, C, L, and M: Robert Garner; Appendix D: Richard Tuck and David Weaver; Appendix E: Richard Tuck; Appendix F: Robert Cmelik; Appendix H: Steve Kleiman and David Ditzel; Appendix I: Robert Garner and Ed Kelly; Appendixes J and K: Pradeep Sindhu; and Appendix N: David Hough.

Editors

Robert Garner, Steve Kleiman, Steven Muchnick, and Mike Bechler have served as editors of the SPARC Architecture specification. The editor for the Version 8 specification was David Weaver.

Reviewers

The thoughtful criticisms and suggestions of many colleagues have added much to the readability, completeness, and accuracy of this manual. The editors would like to particularly thank employees at SPARC International member companies, too numerous to list here, for their valuable suggestions and feedback on earlier versions of this document.

Book Production

The production editor for the book edition of this specification was Bobbie Madsen. SPARC-generated computer images on the cover were provided by Sun Microsystems, Inc.

Special Appreciation

Special appreciation is extended to Robert Garner, Bill Joy, Dave Patterson, and Anant Agrawal, who guided and gave form to the definition of SPARC. Robert served as principal architect, and also invested copious amounts of time and energy in the development and enhancement of Versions 0 (9/84) through 7 (10/87) of this document.

# 1

Introduction

This document specifies Version 8 of the Scalable Processor **AR**Chitecture, or **SPARC**.

## 1.1. SPARC Attributes

SPARC is a CPU **instruction set architecture** (ISA), derived from a reduced instruction set computer (RISC) lineage. As an architecture, SPARC allows for a spectrum of chip and system **implementations** at a variety of price/performance points for a range of applications, including scientific/engineering, programming, real-time, and commercial.

### Design Goals

SPARC was designed as a target for optimizing compilers and easily pipelined hardware implementations. SPARC implementations provide exceptionally high execution rates and short time-to-market development schedules.

### Register Windows

SPARC, formulated at Sun Microsystems in 1985, is based on the RISC I & II designs engineered at the University of California at Berkeley from 1980 through 1982. the SPARC "register window" architecture, pioneered in UC Berkeley designs, allows for straightforward, high-performance compilers and a significant reduction in memory load/store instructions over other RISCs, particularly for large application programs.

For languages such as C++, where object-oriented programming is dominant, register windows result in an even greater reduction in instructions executed. Note that supervisor software, not user programs, manages the register windows. A supervisor can save a minimum number of registers (approximately 24) at the time of a context switch, thereby optimizing context switch latency.

One difference between SPARC and the Berkeley RISC I & II is that SPARC provides greater flexibility to a compiler in its assignment of registers to program variables. SPARC is more flexible because register window management is not tied to procedure call and return (CALL and JMPL) instructions, as it is on the Berkeley machines. Instead, separate instructions (SAVE and RESTORE) provide register window management.

## 1.2. SPARC System Components

The architecture allows for a spectrum of input/output (I/O), memory management unit (MMU), and cache system sub-architectures. SPARC assumes that these elements are optimally defined by the specific requirements of particular systems. Note that they are invisible to nearly all user application programs and the interfaces to them can be limited to localized modules in an associated operating system.

### Reference MMU

The SPARC ISA does not mandate that a single MMU design be used for all system implementations. Rather, designers are free to use the MMU that is most appropriate for their application — or no MMU at all, if they wish. A SPARC "Reference MMU" has been specified, which is appropriate for a wide range of applications. See Appendix H, "SPARC Reference MMU Architecture," for more information.

### Supervisor Software

SPARC does not assume all implementations must execute identical supervisor software. Thus, certain supervisor-visible traits of an implementation can be tailored to the requirements of the system. For example, SPARC allows for implementations with different instruction concurrency and different exception trap hardware.

### Memory Model

A standard memory model called Total Store Ordering (TSO) is defined for SPARC. The model applies both to uniprocessors and to shared-memory multiprocessors. The memory model guarantees that the stores, FLUSHes, and atomic load-stores of all processors are executed by memory serially in an order that conforms to the order in which the instructions were issued by processors. All SPARC implementations must support TSO.

An additional model called Partial Store Ordering (PSO) is defined, which allows higher-performance memory systems to be built.

Machines (including all early SPARC-based systems) that implement Strong Consistency (also known as Strong Ordering) automatically satisfy both TSO and PSO. Machines that implement TSO automatically satisfy PSO.

## 1.3. SPARC Compliance Definitions

An important SPARC International Compatibility and Compliance Committee function is to establish and publish SPARC Compliance Definitions (SCDs) and migration guidelines between successive definitions. SCD use accelerates development of binary-compatible SPARC/UNIX systems and software for both system vendors and ISV members. SPARC binaries executed in user mode should behave identically on all SPARC systems when those systems are running an operating system known to provide a standard execution environment.

AT&T and SPARC International have developed a standard Application Binary Interface (ABI) for the development of SPARC application code. Software conforming to this specification will produce the same results on every SPARC ABI-compliant system, enabling the distribution of ''shrink-wrapped'' SPARC software. Although different SPARC systems will execute programs at different rates, they will generate the same results.

The formulation of SPARC Compliance Definitions (SCD 1.0 and SCD 2.0) by SPARC International allows member companies to verify compliance of a broad base of SPARC/UNIX products through openly agreed-upon, standard definitions. SCD 2.0 is a superset of the SPARC ABI.

SCD 1.0 compliance is the formal beginning of migration to SCD 2.0, based on the industry-standard UNIX System V Release 4 operating system from AT&T and the OPEN LOOK graphical user interface. SPARC International's Compatibility and Compliance Committee works to make this migration as smooth and as representative of the members' interests as possible.

The System V ABI from AT&T consists of two components: the processor independent generic specification and the processor (SPARC)-specific supplement. (Consult the AT&T manuals for strict adherence to the SCD 2.0 binary interface conventions.)

SPARC International participates in all ABI specification reviews, and tests for ABI compliance as part of the SCD 2.0 verification process. For more details on SCD 2.0, contact SPARC International, 535 Middlefield Road, Suite 210, Menlo Park, California 94025.

## 1.4. SPARC Features

SPARC includes the following principal features:

- A linear, 32-bit address space.

- Few and simple instruction formats — All instructions are 32 bits wide, and are aligned on 32-bit boundaries in memory. There are only three basic instruction formats, and they feature uniform placement of opcode and register address fields. Only load and store instructions access memory and I/O.

- Few addressing modes — A memory address is given by either "register + register" or "register+immediate."

- Triadic register addresses — Most instructions operate on two register operands (or one register and a constant), and place the result in a third register.

- A large "windowed" register file — At any one instant, a program sees 8 global integer registers plus a 24-register window into a larger register file. The windowed registers can be described as a cache of procedure arguments, local values, and return addresses.

- A separate floating-point register file — configurable by software into 32 single-precision (32-bit), 16 double-precision (64-bit), 8 quad-precision registers (128-bit), or a mixture thereof.

- Delayed control transfer — The processor always fetches the next instruction after a delayed control-transfer instruction. It either executes it or not, depending on the control-transfer instruction's "annul" bit.

- Fast trap handlers — Traps are vectored through a table, and cause allocation of a fresh register window in the register file.

- Tagged instructions — The tagged add/subtract instructions assume that the two least-significant bits of the operands are tag bits.

□   Multiprocessor synchronization instructions — One instruction performs an atomic read-then-set-memory operation; another performs an atomic exchange-register-with-memory operation.

□   Coprocessor — The architecture defines a straightforward coprocessor instruction set, in addition to the floating-point instruction set.

## 1.5. Conformability to SPARC

An implementation that conforms to the definitions and algorithms given in this document is an implementation of the SPARC ISA.

The SPARC architecture is a **model** which specifies unambiguously the behavior observed by **software** on SPARC systems.  Therefore, it does not necessarily describe the operation of the **hardware** in any actual implementation.

An implementation is **not** required to execute every instruction in hardware.  An attempt to execute a SPARC instruction that is not implemented in hardware generates a trap.  If the unimplemented instruction is nonprivileged, then it must be possible to emulate it in software.  If it is a privileged instruction, whether it is emulated by software is implementation-dependent. Appendix L, "Implementation Characteristics," details which instructions are not in hardware in existing implementations.

Compliance with this specification shall be claimed only by a collection of components which is capable of fully implementing all SPARC opcodes, through any combination of hardware or software.  Specifically, nonprivileged instructions which are not implemented in hardware must trap to the software such that they can be implemented in software.  For the implementation to be complete, by default the implementation must trap and report all undefined, unimplemented, and reserved instructions.

Some elements of the architecture are defined to be implementation-dependent. These elements include certain registers and operations that may vary from implementation to implementation, and are explicitly identified in this document.

Implementation elements (such as instructions or registers) that appear in an implementation but are not defined in this document (or its updates) are not considered to be SPARC elements of that implementation.

Note that a "SPARC Architecture Test Suite" and a "SPARC Architectural Simulator" (SPARCsim) are available.

## 1.6. Fonts in Manual

In this manual, fonts are used as follows:

□   *Italic* is used for register names, instruction fields, and register status fields. For example: "The *rs1* field contains the address of the *r* register."

Italic is also used for references to sections, chapters, and appendices.

□   `Typewriter` font is used for literals throughout the appendixes.

□   **Bold** font is used for emphasis and the first time a word is defined.  For example: "A **precise trap** is induced by a particular instruction...".

SPARC International, Inc.

□ UPPER CASE items may be either acronyms, instruction names, or register mode fields that can be written by software. Some common acronyms appear in the glossary in this chapter. Note that names of some instructions contain both upper case and lower case letters.

□ Underbar characters join words in register, register field, exception, or trap names. For example: "The integer_condition_code field..."

□ Square brackets [ ] indicate an addressed field in a register or a numbered register in a register file. For example: "r[0] is zero."

## 1.7. Notes

This manual provides three types of notes: ordinary notes, programming notes, and implementation notes.

□ Programming notes contain incidental information about programming using the SPARC architecture; they appear in a reduced size font.

□ Implementation notes contain information which may be specific to an implementation, or which may differ in different implementations. They also appear in a reduced size font.

## 1.8. Glossary

The following paragraphs describe some of the most important words and acronyms used in this manual:

Coprocessor Operate (CPop) instructions
Instructions that perform coprocessor calculations, as defined by the CPop1 and CPop2 opcodes. CPop instructions do not include loads and stores between memory and the coprocessor.

Current window
The block of 24 *r* registers to which the Current Window Pointer points.

Floating-Point Operate (FPop) instructions
Instructions that perform floating-point calculations, as defined by the FPop1 and FPop2 opcodes. FPop instructions do not include loads and stores between memory and the FPU.

Ignored
Used to describe an instruction field, the contents of which are arbitrary, and which has no effect on the execution of the instruction. The contents of an "ignored" field will continue to be ignored in future versions of the architecture. See also *reserved* and *unused*.

Implementation
Hardware or software that conforms to all the specifications of an ISA.

Instruction Set Architecture (ISA)
An ISA defines instructions, registers, instruction and data memory, the effect of executed instructions on the registers and memory, and an algorithm for controlling instruction execution. An ISA does not define clock cycle times, cycles per instruction, data paths, etc.

Next Program Counter (nPC)

Contains the address of the instruction to be executed next (if a trap does not occur).

Privileged

An instruction (or register) that can only be executed (or accessed) when the processor is in supervisor mode (when PSR[S]=1).

Processor

The combination of the IU, FPU, and CP (if present).

Program Counter (PC)

Contains the address of the instruction currently being executed by the IU.

*rs1, rs2, rd*

Specify the register operands of an instruction. *rs1* and *rs2* are the source registers; *rd* is the destination register.

Reserved

Used to describe an instruction or register field which is reserved for definition by future versions of the architecture. A reserved field should only be written to zero by software. A reserved register field should read as zero in hardware; software intended to run on future versions of SPARC should not assume that the field will read as zero. See also *ignored* and *unused*.

Supervisor Mode

A processor state that is active when the S bit of the PSR is set (PSR[S] = 1).

Supervisor Software

Software that executes when the processor is in supervisor mode.

Trap

A vectored transfer of control to supervisor software through a table whose address is given by a privileged IU register (the Trap Base Register (TBR)).

Unused

Used to describe an instruction field or register field that is not currently defined by the architecture. When read by software, the value of an unused register field is undefined. However, since an unused field could be defined by a future version of the architecture, an unused field should only be written to zero by software. See also *ignored* and *reserved*.

User Mode

A processor state that is active when the S bit of the PSR is not set (when PSR[S] = 0).

User Application Program

A program executed with the processor in user mode. Also simply called "application program". [Note that statements made in this document regarding user application programs may be inapplicable to programs (for example, debuggers) that have access to privileged supervisor state (e.g., as stored in a core dump)].

## 1.9. References

For additional information, see:

R. B. K. Dewar and M. Smosna [1990]. *Microprocessors: A Programmer's View*, McGraw-Hill, Inc.

R. B. Garner [1988]. "SPARC: The Scalable Processor Architecture", *SunTechnology*, vol. 1, no. 3, Summer, 1988, and M. Hall and J. Barry (eds.), *The Sun Technology Papers*, Springer-Verlag, 1990, pp. 75-99.

R. B. Garner, A. Agrawal, F. Briggs, E. W. Brown, D. Hough, W. N. Joy, S. Kleiman, S. Muchnick, M. Namjoo, D. Patterson, J. Pendleton, K. G. Tan, and R. Tuck [1988]. "The Scalable Processor Architecture (SPARC)", *33rd Annual IEEE Computer Conference (COMPCON)*, Feb., 1988, San Francisco, CA.

J. Hennessy and D. Patterson [1990]. *Computer Architecture: A Quantitative Approach*, Morgan Kaufman Publishers, Inc, San Mateo, CA.

IEEE Standard for Binary Floating-Point Arithmetic, ANSI/IEEE Std 754-1985, IEEE, New York, NY, 1985.

M. Katevenis [1983]. Reduced Instruction Set Computer Architectures for VLSI, Ph.D. dissertation, Computer Science Div., Univ. of California, Berkeley, 1983. Also published by M.I.T. Press, Cambridge, MA, 1985.

S. Kleiman and D. Williams [1988]. "SunOS on SPARC", *33rd Annual IEEE Comp. Conf. (COMPCON)*, Feb., 1988, San Francisco, CA, also appeared in M. Hall and J. Barry (eds.), *The Sun Technology Papers*, Springer-Verlag, 1990, pp. 13-27.

S. Muchnick [1988]. "Optimizing Compilers for SPARC", *Sun Technology*, summer 1988, pp. 64-71; also appeared in W. Stallings (ed.), *Reduced Instruction Set Computers* (2nd edition), IEEE Computer Society Press, 1990, pp. 160-173, and M. Hall and J. Barry (eds.), *The Sun Technology Papers*, Springer-Verlag, 1990, pp. 41-68.

D. Patterson [1985]. "Reduced Instruction Set Computers", *Communications of the ACM*, vol. 28, no. 1, Jan. 1985.

# 2

# Overview

SPARC is an instruction set architecture (ISA) with 32-bit integer and 32-, 64-, and 128-bit IEEE Standard 754 floating-point as its principal data types. It defines general-purpose integer, floating-point, and special state/status registers and 72 basic instruction operations, all encoded in 32-bit wide instruction formats. The load/store instructions address a linear, $2^{32}$-byte address space. In addition to the floating-point instructions, SPARC also provides instruction set support for an optional implementation-defined coprocessor.

## 2.1. SPARC Processor

A SPARC processor logically comprises an integer unit (**IU**), a floating-point unit (**FPU**), and an optional coprocessor (**CP**), each with its own registers. This organization allows for implementations with maximum concurrency between integer, floating-point, and coprocessor instruction execution. All of the registers — with the possible exception of the coprocessor's — are 32 bits wide. Instruction operands are generally single registers, register pairs, or register quadruples.

The processor can be in either of two modes: **user** or **supervisor**. In supervisor mode, the processor can execute any instruction, including the privileged (supervisor-only) instructions. In user mode, an attempt to execute a privileged instruction will cause a trap to supervisor software. "User application" programs are programs that execute while the processor is in user mode.

### Integer Unit (IU)

The IU contains the general-purpose registers and controls the overall operation of the processor. The IU executes the integer arithmetic instructions and computes memory addresses for loads and stores. It also maintains the program counters and controls instruction execution for the FPU and the CP.

An implementation of the IU may contain from 40 to 520 general-purpose 32-bit *r* registers. This corresponds to a grouping of the registers into 8 *global r* registers, plus a circular stack of from 2 to 32 sets of 16 registers each, known as **register windows**. Since the number of register windows present (NWINDOWS) is implementation-dependent, the total number of registers is implementation-dependent.

At a given time, an instruction can access the 8 *global*s and a register **window** into the *r* registers. A 24-register window comprises a 16-register set — divided into 8 *in* and 8 *local* registers — together with the 8 *in* registers of an adjacent register set, addressable from the current window as its *out* registers.

SPARC International, Inc.

The current window is specified by the current window pointer (CWP) field in the processor state register (PSR). Window overflow and underflow are detected via the window invalid mask (WIM) register, which is controlled by supervisor software. The actual number of windows in a SPARC implementation is invisible to a user-application program.

When the IU accesses an instruction from memory, it appends to the address an **address space identifier**, or **ASI**, which encodes whether the processor is in supervisor or user mode, and whether the access is to instruction memory or to data memory.

**Floating-point Unit (FPU)**

The FPU has 32 32-bit floating-point $f$ registers. Double-precision values occupy an even-odd pair of registers, and quad-precision values occupy a quad-aligned group of 4 registers. Thus, the floating-point registers can hold a maximum of either 32 single-precision, 16 double-precision, or 8 quad-precision values.

Floating-point load/store instructions are used to move data between the FPU and memory. The memory address is calculated by the IU. Floating-Point **operate** (FPop) instructions perform the actual floating-point arithmetic.

The floating-point data formats and instruction set conform to the IEEE Standard for Binary Floating-point Arithmetic, ANSI/IEEE Standard 754-1985. However, SPARC does not require that all aspects of the standard, such as gradual underflow, be implemented in hardware. An implementation can indicate that a floating-point instruction did not produce a correct ANSI/IEEE Standard 754-1985 result by generating a special floating-point unfinished or unimplemented exception. Software must emulate any functionality not present in the hardware.

If an FPU is not present, or if the enable floating-point (EF) bit in the PSR is 0, an attempt to execute a floating-point instruction will generate an fp_disabled trap. In either of these cases, software must emulate the trapped floating-point instruction.

**Coprocessor (CP)**

The instruction set includes support for a single, implementation-dependent coprocessor. The coprocessor has its own set of registers, the actual configuration of which is implementation-defined but is nominally some number of 32-bit registers. Coprocessor load/store instructions are used to move data between the coprocessor registers and memory. For each floating-point load/store in the instruction set, there is an analogous coprocessor load/store instruction.

If a CP is not present, or the enable_coprocessor (EC) bit in the PSR is 0, a coprocessor instruction generates a cp_disabled trap.

## 2.2. Instructions

Instructions fall into six basic categories:

1) Load/store

2) Arithmetic/logical/shift

3) Control transfer

4) Read/write control register

5) Floating-point operate

6) Coprocessor operate

**Load/Store**

Load/store instructions are the only instructions that access memory. They use two $r$ registers or an $r$ register and a signed 13-bit immediate value to calculate a 32-bit, byte-aligned memory address. The IU appends to this address an ASI that encodes whether the processor is in supervisor or user mode, and that it is a data access.

The destination field of the load/store instruction specifies either an $r$ register, $f$ register, or coprocessor register that supplies the data for a store or receives the data from a load.

Integer load and store instructions support byte, halfword (16-bit), word (32-bit), and doubleword (64-bit) accesses. There are versions of integer load instructions that perform sign-extension on 8 and 16-bit values as they are loaded into the destination register. Floating-point and coprocessor load and store instructions support word and doubleword memory accesses.

**Alignment Restrictions**

Halfword accesses must be **aligned** on 2-byte boundaries, word accesses must be aligned on 4-byte boundaries, and doubleword accesses must be aligned on 8-byte boundaries. An improperly aligned address in a load or store instruction causes a trap to occur.

**Addressing Conventions**

SPARC is a "**big-endian**" architecture: the address of a doubleword, word, or halfword is the address of its most significant byte. Increasing the address generally means decreasing the significance of the unit being accessed. Addressing conventions are illustrated in Figure 5-2.

**Load/Store Alternate**

There are special, privileged versions of the load/store integer instructions, the **load/store alternate** instructions, which can directly specify an arbitrary 8-bit address space identifier for the load/store data access. The privileged load/store alternate instructions can be used by supervisor software to access special protected registers, such as MMU, cache control, and processor state registers, and other processor or system-dependent values.

**Separate I&D Memories**

Most specifications in this manual are written as if store instructions write to the same memory from which instructions are accessed. However, an implementation may explicitly partition instructions and data into independent instruction and data memories (caches), commonly referred to as a "Harvard" architecture or "split I & D caches". If a program includes self-modifying code, it must issue FLUSH instructions (or supervisor calls that have an equivalent effect) for the addresses to which new instructions were written. A FLUSH instruction ensures that the data previously written by a store instruction is seen by subsequent instruction fetches from the given address.

**Arithmetic/Logical/Shift**

The arithmetic/logical/shift instructions perform arithmetic, tagged arithmetic, logical, and shift operations. With one exception, these instructions compute a result that is a function of two source operands; the result is either written into a destination register, or discarded. The exception is a specialized instruction, SETHI, which (along with a second instruction) can be used to create a 32-bit constant in an $r$ register.

Shift instructions can be used to shift the contents of an $r$ register left or right by a given distance. The shift distance may be specified by a constant in the instruction or by the contents of an $r$ register.

The integer multiply instructions perform a signed or unsigned $32 \times 32 \rightarrow 64$-bit operation. The integer division instructions perform a signed or unsigned $64 \div 32 \rightarrow 32$-bit operation. There are versions of multiply and divide that set the condition codes. Division by zero causes a trap.

The tagged arithmetic instructions assume that the least-significant 2 bits of the operands are data-type "tags". These instructions set the overflow condition code bit upon arithmetic overflow, or if any of the operands' tag bits are nonzero. There are also versions that trap when either of these conditions occurs.

**Control Transfer**

Control-transfer instructions (**CTIs**) include PC-relative branches and calls, register-indirect jumps, and conditional traps. Most of the control-transfer instructions are delayed control-transfer instructions (**DCTIs**), where the instruction immediately following the DCTI is executed before the control transfer to the target address is completed.

The instruction following a delayed control-transfer instruction is called a **delay** instruction. The delay instruction is always fetched, even if the delayed control transfer is an unconditional branch. However, a bit in the delayed control-transfer instruction can cause the delay instruction to be annulled (that is, to have no effect) if the branch is not taken (or in the branch always case, if the branch is taken).

Branch and CALL instructions use PC-relative displacements. The jump and link (JMPL) instruction uses a register-indirect target address. It computes its target address as either the sum of two $r$ registers, or the sum of an $r$ register and a 13-bit signed immediate value. The branch instruction provides a displacement of ± 8 Mbytes, while the CALL instruction's 30-bit word displacement allows a control transfer to an arbitrary 32-bit instruction address.

**State Register Access**

The Read/Write Register instructions read and write the contents of software-visible state/status registers. There are also read/write "ancillary state register" instructions that software can use to read/write unique implementation-dependent processor registers. Whether each of these instructions is privileged or not is implementation-dependent.

**Floating-Point/Coprocessor Operate**

Floating-point operate (FPop) instructions perform all floating-point calculations. They are register-to-register instructions which operate upon the floating-point registers. Like arithmetic/logical/shift instructions, FPop's compute a result that is a function of one or two source operands. Specific floating-point operations are selected by a subfield of the FPop1/FPop2 instruction formats.

Coprocessor operate (CPop) instructions are defined by the implemented coprocessor, if any. These instructions are specified by the CPop1 and CPop2 instruction formats.

**2.3. Memory Model**

The SPARC **memory model** defines the semantics of memory operations such as load and store, and specifies how the order in which these operations are issued by a processor is related to the order in which they are executed by memory. The model applies both to uniprocessors and shared memory multiprocessors. The standard memory model is called **Total Store Ordering (TSO)**. All SPARC implementations must provide at least TSO. An additional model called **Partial Store Ordering (PSO)** is defined to allow higher performance memory systems to be built. If present, this model is enabled via a mode bit, for example, in an MMU control register. See Appendix H, "SPARC Reference MMU Architecture."

Machines that implement Strong Consistency (also called Strong Ordering) automatically support both TSO and PSO because the requirements of Strong Consistency are more stringent. In Strong Consistency, the loads, stores, and atomic load-stores of all processors are executed by memory serially in an order that conforms to the order in which these instructions were issued by individual processors. However, a machine that implements Strong Consistency may deliver lower performance than an equivalent machine that implements TSO or PSO.

Programs written using single-writer-multiple-readers locks will be portable across PSO, TSO, and Strong Consistency. Programs that use write-locks but read without locking will be portable across PSO, TSO, and Strong Consistency only if writes to shared data are separated by STBAR instructions. If these STBAR instructions are omitted, then the code will be portable only across TSO and Strong Consistency.

The guidelines for other programs are as follows: Programs written for PSO will work automatically on a machine running in TSO mode or on a machine that implements Strong Consistency; programs written for TSO will work automatically on a machine that implements Strong Consistency; programs written for Strong Consistency may not work on a TSO or PSO machine; programs written for TSO may not work on a PSO machine.

Multithreaded programs where all threads are restricted to run on a single processor will behave the same on PSO and TSO as they would on a Strongly Consistent machine.

**Input/Output**

SPARC assumes that input/output registers are accessed via load/store alternate instructions, normal load/store instructions, coprocessor instructions, or read/write ancillary state register instructions (RDASR, WRASR). In the load/store alternate instructions case, the I/O registers can only be accessed by the supervisor. If normal load/store instructions, coprocessor instructions, or read/write Ancillary State Register instructions are used, whether the I/O registers can be accessed outside of supervisor code or not is implementation-dependent.

The contents and addresses of I/O registers are implementation-dependent.

Definitions of "real memory" and "I/O locations" are provided in Chapter 6, "Memory Model".

## 2.4. Traps

A **trap** is a vectored transfer of control to the operating system through a special trap table that contains the first 4 instructions of each trap handler. The base address of the table is established by software in an IU state register (the trap base register, TBR). The displacement within the table is encoded in the type number of each trap. Half of the table is reserved for hardware traps, and the other half for software traps generated by trap (Ticc) instructions.

A trap causes the current window pointer (CWP) to advance to the next register window and the hardware to write the program counters into two registers of the new window. The trap handler can access the saved PC and nPC and, in general, can freely use the 6 other local registers in the new window.

A trap may be caused by an instruction-induced **exception**, or by an external **interrupt request** not directly related to a particular instruction. Before executing each instruction, the IU checks for pending exceptions and interrupt requests. If any are present, the IU selects the one with the highest priority and causes a corresponding trap to occur.

**Trap Categories**

An exception or interrupt request can cause either a precise trap, a deferred trap, or an interrupting trap.

A **precise trap** is induced by a particular instruction and occurs before any program-visible state is changed by the trap-inducing instruction.

A **deferred trap** is also induced by a particular instruction, but unlike a precise trap, it may occur after program-visible state is changed by the execution of one or more instructions that follow the trap-inducing instruction. A deferred trap may occur one or more instructions after the trap-inducing instruction is executed. An implementation must provide sufficient supervisor-readable state (called a **deferred-trap queue**) to enable it to emulate an instruction that caused a deferred trap and to correctly resume execution of the process containing that instruction.

An **interrupting trap** may be due to an external interrupt request not directly related to any particular instruction, or may be due to an exception caused by a particular previously executed instruction. An interrupting trap is neither a precise trap nor a deferred trap. An implementation need not necessarily provide sufficient state to emulate an instruction that caused an interrupting trap.

User-application programs do not "see" traps unless they install user trap handlers for those traps (via calls to supervisor software). Also, the treatment of implementation-dependent "non-resumable machine-check" exceptions can vary across systems. Therefore, SPARC allows an implementation to provide alternative trap models for particular exception types.

SPARC defines a **default trap** model, which must be present in all implementations. The default trap model states that all traps must be precise except for:

(1) Floating-point or coprocessor traps, which may be deferred.

(2) "Non-resumable machine-check" exceptions, which may be deferred or interrupting.

(3) "Non-resumable machine-check" exceptions on the second access of a two-memory-access load/store instruction, which may be interrupting.

See Chapter 7, "Traps," for a complete description of the default trap model.

# 3

## Data Formats

The SPARC architecture recognizes three fundamental data formats (or types):

□   Signed Integer — 8, 16, 32, and 64 bits

□   Unsigned Integer — 8, 16, 32, and 64 bits

□   Floating-Point — 32, 64, and 128 bits

The format widths are defined as:

□   Byte — 8 bits

□   Halfword — 16 bits

□   Word/Singleword — 32 bits

□   Tagged Word — 32 bits (30-bit value plus 2 tag bits)

□   Doubleword — 64 bits

□   Quadword — 128 bits

The Signed Integer formats encode two's-complement whole numbers.  The Unsigned Integer formats are general-purpose in that they do not encode any particular data type; they can represent a whole number, string, fraction, boolean value, etc.  The Floating-Point formats conform to the IEEE Standard for Binary Floating-Point Arithmetic, ANSI/IEEE Standard 754-1985.  The Tagged formats define a word in which the least-significant two bits are treated as tag bits.

Figure 3-1 illustrates the signed integer, unsigned integer, and tagged formats. Figure 3-2 illustrates the floating-point formats.  In Figure 3-1 and 3-2, the individual subwords of the multiword data formats are assigned names.  The arrangement of the subformats in memory and processor registers based on these names is shown in Table 3-1.  Tables 3-2 through 3-5 define the integer and floating-point formats.

SPARC International, Inc.

Figure 3-1    *Signed Integer, Unsigned Integer, and Tagged Formats*

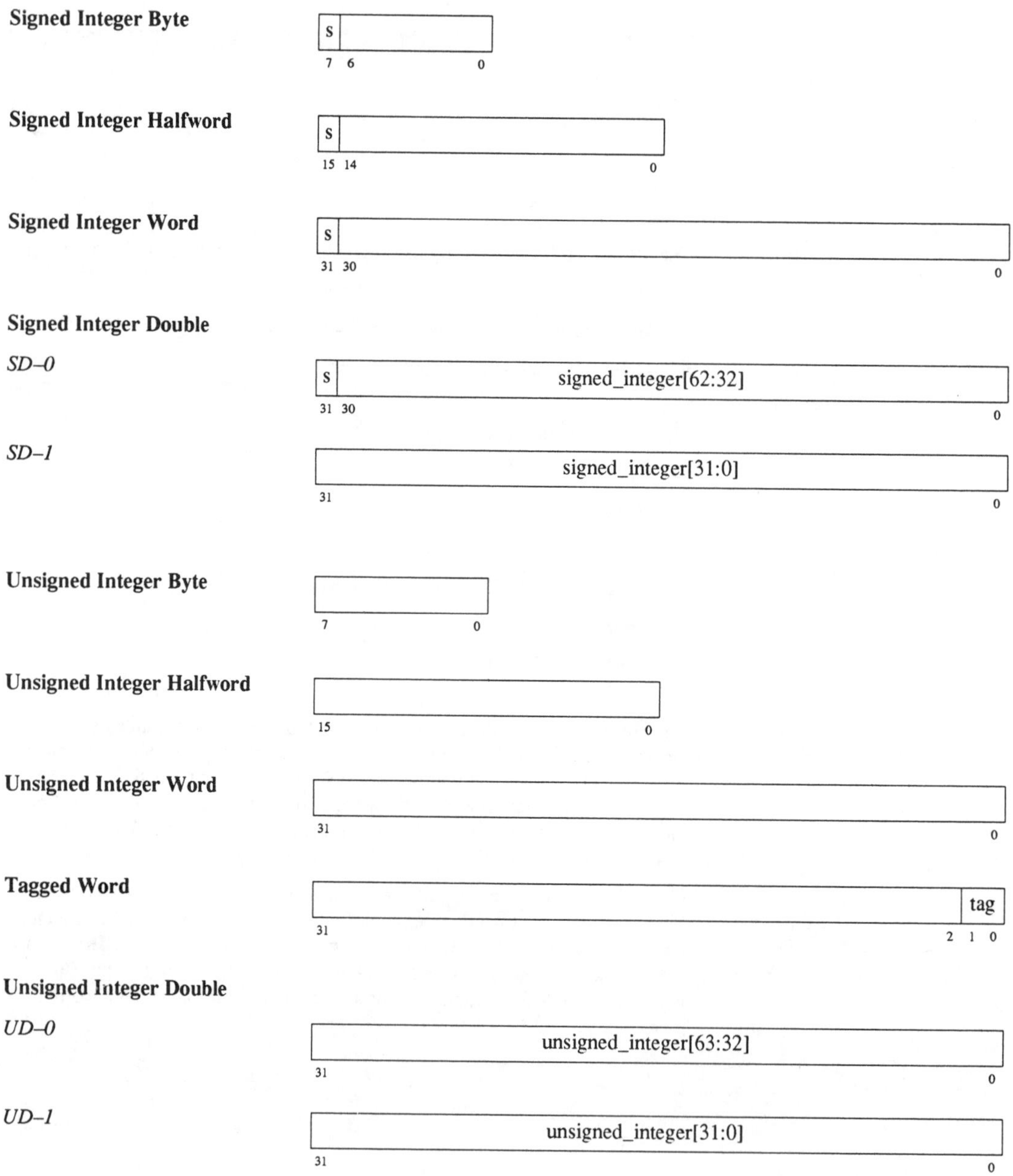

**Signed Integer Byte**

**Signed Integer Halfword**

**Signed Integer Word**

**Signed Integer Double**

*SD–0*

*SD–1*

**Unsigned Integer Byte**

**Unsigned Integer Halfword**

**Unsigned Integer Word**

**Tagged Word**

**Unsigned Integer Double**

*UD–0*

*UD–1*

SPARC International, Inc.

Figure 3-2    *Floating-Point Formats*

**Floating-point Single**

| s | exp[7:0] | fraction[22:0] |
|---|----------|----------------|

31 30                     23 22                                              0

**Floating-point Double**

*FD–0*

| s | exp[10:0] | fraction[51:32] |
|---|-----------|-----------------|

31 30                     20 19                                              0

*FD–1*

| fraction[31:0] |
|----------------|

31                                                                           0

**Floating-point Quad**

*FQ–0*

| s | exp[14:0] | fraction[111:96] |
|---|-----------|------------------|

31 30                              16 15                                     0

*FQ–1*

| fraction[95:64] |
|-----------------|

31                                                                           0

*FQ–2*

| fraction[63:32] |
|-----------------|

31                                                                           0

*FQ–3*

| fraction[31:0] |
|----------------|

31                                                                           0

SPARC International, Inc.

Table 3-1    *Arrangement of Doublewords and Quadwords in Memory & Registers*

| sub-format name | sub-format field | memory address alignment | memory address | register number alignment | register number |
|---|---|---|---|---|---|
| SD-0 | signed_integer[63:32] | 0 mod 8 | $n$ | 0 mod 2 | $r$ |
| SD-1 | signed_integer[31:0] | 4 mod 8 | $n+4$ | 1 mod 2 | $r+1$ |
| UD-0 | unsigned_integer[63:32] | 0 mod 8 | $n$ | 0 mod 2 | $r$ |
| UD-1 | unsigned_integer[31:0] | 4 mod 8 | $n+4$ | 1 mod 2 | $r+1$ |
| FD-0 | s:exp[10:0]:fraction[51:32] | 0 mod 8 | $n$ | 0 mod 2 | $r$ |
| FD-1 | fraction[31:0] | 4 mod 8 | $n+4$ | 1 mod 2 | $r+1$ |
| FQ-0 | s:exp[14:0]:fraction[111:96] | 0 mod 8 | $n$ | 0 mod 4 | $r$ |
| FQ-1 | fraction[95:64] | 4 mod 8 | $n+4$ | 1 mod 4 | $r+1$ |
| FQ-2 | fraction[63:32] | 0 mod 8 | $n+8$ | 2 mod 4 | $r+2$ |
| FQ-3 | fraction[31:0] | 4 mod 8 | $n+12$ | 3 mod 4 | $r+3$ |

Table 3-2    *Signed Integer, Unsigned Integer, and Tagged Format Ranges*

| data type | width (bits) | range |
|---|---|---|
| signed integer byte | 8 | $-2^7$ to $2^7-1$ |
| signed integer halfword | 16 | $-2^{15}$ to $2^{15}-1$ |
| signed integer word | 32 | $-2^{31}$ to $2^{31}-1$ |
| signed integer tagged word | 32 | $-2^{29}$ to $2^{29}-1$ |
| signed integer double | 64 | $-2^{63}$ to $2^{63}-1$ |
| unsigned integer byte | 8 | 0 to $2^8-1$ |
| unsigned integer halfword | 16 | 0 to $2^{16}-1$ |
| unsigned integer word | 32 | 0 to $2^{32}-1$ |
| unsigned integer tagged word | 32 | 0 to $2^{30}-1$ |
| unsigned integer double | 64 | 0 to $2^{64}-1$ |

SPARC International, Inc.

Table 3-3    *Floating-Point Singleword Format Definition*

| | |
|---|---|
| s = sign (1 bit)<br>e = biased exponent (8 bits)<br>f = fraction (23 bits)<br>*u* = undefined | |
| normalized value (0 < e < 255):<br>subnormal value (e = 0):<br>zero (e = 0): | $(-1)^s \times 2^{e-127} \times 1.f$<br>$(-1)^s \times 2^{-126} \times 0.f$<br>$(-1)^s \times 0$ |
| signaling NaN:<br><br>quiet NaN:<br>$-\infty$ (negative infinity):<br>$+\infty$ (positive infinity): | $s = u$; e = 255 (max); f = .0*uu—uu*<br>(at least one bit of fraction must be nonzero)<br>$s = u$; e = 255 (max); f = .1*uu—uu*<br>s = 1; e = 255 (max); f = .000—00<br>s = 0; e = 255 (max); f = .000—00 |

Table 3-4    *Floating-Point Doubleword Format Definition*

| | |
|---|---|
| s = sign (1 bit)<br>e = biased exponent (11 bits)<br>f = fraction (52 bits)<br>*u* = undefined | |
| normalized value (0 < e < 2047):<br>subnormal value (e = 0):<br>zero (e = 0): | $(-1)^s \times 2^{e-1023} \times 1.f$<br>$(-1)^s \times 2^{-1022} \times 0.f$<br>$(-1)^s \times 0$ |
| signaling NaN:<br><br>quiet NaN:<br>$-\infty$ (negative infinity):<br>$+\infty$ (positive infinity): | $s = u$; e = 2047 (max); f = .0*uu—uu*<br>(at least one bit of fraction must be nonzero)<br>$s = u$; e = 2047 (max); f = .1*uu—uu*<br>s = 1; e = 2047 (max); f = .000—00<br>s = 0; e = 2047 (max); f = .000—00 |

Table 3-5    *Floating-Point Quadword Format Definition*

| | |
|---|---|
| s = sign (1 bit)<br>e = biased exponent (15 bits)<br>f = fraction (112 bits)<br>*u* = undefined | |
| normalized value (0 < e < 32767):<br>subnormal value (e = 0):<br>zero (e = 0): | $(-1)^s \times 2^{e-16383} \times 1.f$<br>$(-1)^s \times 2^{-16382} \times 0.f$<br>$(-1)^s \times 0$ |
| signaling NaN:<br><br>quiet NaN:<br>$-\infty$ (negative infinity):<br>$+\infty$ (positive infinity): | $s = u$; e = 32767 (max); f = .0*uu—uu*<br>(at least one bit of fraction must be nonzero)<br>$s = u$; e = 32767 (max); f = .1*uu—uu*<br>s = 1; e = 32767 (max); f = .000—00<br>s = 0; e = 32767 (max); f = .000—00 |

# 4

Registers

A SPARC processor includes two types of registers: general-purpose or "working" data registers and control/status registers. The IU's general-purpose registers are called *r* registers, and the FPU's general-purpose registers are called *f* registers. Coprocessor working registers are coprocessor-implementation dependent.

IU control/status registers include:

- ▫ Processor State Register (PSR)
- ▫ Window Invalid Mask (WIM)
- ▫ Trap Base Register (TBR)
- ▫ Multiply/Divide Register (Y)
- ▫ Program Counters (PC, nPC)
- ▫ implementation-dependent Ancillary State Registers (ASRs)
- ▫ implementation-dependent IU Deferred-Trap Queue

FPU control/status registers include:

- ▫ Floating-Point State Register (FSR)
- ▫ implementation-dependent Floating-Point Deferred-Trap Queue (FQ)

Coprocessor (CP) control/status registers, if present, may include:

- ▫ implementation-dependent Coprocessor State Register (CSR)
- ▫ implementation-dependent Coprocessor Deferred-Trap Queue (CQ)

## 4.1. IU *r* Registers

An implementation of the IU may contain from 40 through 520 general-purpose 32-bit *r* registers. They are partitioned into 8 *global* registers, plus an implementation-dependent number of 16-register *sets*. A register set is further partitioned into 8 *in* registers and 8 *local* registers. See Table 4-1.

SPARC International, Inc.

**Windowed *r* Registers**

At a given time, an instruction can access the 8 *globals* and a 24-register **window** into the *r* registers. A register window comprises the 8 *in* and 8 *local* registers of a particular register set, together with the 8 *in* registers of an adjacent register set, which are addressable from the current window as *out* registers. See Figure 4-1.

The number of windows or register sets, NWINDOWS, ranges from 2 to 32, depending on the implementation. The total number of *r* registers in a given implementation is 8 (for the *globals*), plus the number of sets × 16 registers/set. Thus, the minimum number of *r* registers is 40 (2 sets), and the maximum number is 520 (32 sets).

Table 4-1    *Window Addressing*

| Windowed Register Address | *r* Register Address |
|---|---|
| in[0] – in[7] | r[24] – r[31] |
| local[0] – local[7] | r[16] – r[23] |
| out[0] – out[7] | r[ 8] – r[15] |
| global[0] – global[7] | r[ 0] – r[ 7] |

The current window into the *r* registers is given by the current window pointer (CWP), a 5-bit counter field in the Processor State Register (PSR). The CWP is incremented by a RESTORE (or RETT) instruction and decremented by a SAVE instruction or a trap. Window overflow and underflow are detected via the window invalid mask (WIM) register, which is controlled by supervisor software.

**Overlapping of Windows**

Each window shares its *ins* and *outs* with the two adjacent windows. The *outs* of the CWP+1 window are addressable as the *ins* of the current window, and the *outs* in the current window are the *ins* of the CWP−1 window. The *locals* are unique to each window.

An *r* register with address *o*, where $8 \leq o \leq 15$, refers to exactly the same register as (*o* + 16) does after the CWP is decremented by 1 (modulo NWINDOWS). Likewise, a register with address *i*, where $24 \leq i \leq 31$, refers to exactly the same register as address (*i* − 16) does after the CWP is incremented by 1 (modulo NWINDOWS). See Figure 4-2.

Since CWP arithmetic is performed modulo NWINDOWS, the highest numbered implemented window overlaps with window 0. The *outs* of window 0 are the *ins* of window NWINDOWS−1. Implemented windows must be contiguously numbered from 0 through NWINDOWS−1.

Programming Note

Since the procedure call instructions (CALL and JMPL) do not change the CWP, a procedure can be called without changing the window. See Appendix D, "Software Considerations."

Because the windows overlap, the number of windows available to software is 1 less than the number of implemented windows, or NWINDOWS−1. When the register file is full, the *outs* of the newest window are the *ins* of the oldest window — which still contains valid program data.

No assumptions can be made regarding the values contained in the "local" and "out" regsiters of a register window upon re-entering the window through a SAVE instruction. If, with traps enabled, a program executes a RESTORE followed by a SAVE, the resulting window's *locals* and *outs* may not be valid after the SAVE, since a trap may have occurred between the RESTORE and the

SAVE. However, with traps disabled, the *locals* and *outs* remain valid.

**Doubleword Operands**

Instructions that access a doubleword in the *r* registers assume even-odd register alignment. The least-significant bit of an *r* register address in these instructions is reserved, and for future compatibility should be supplied as zero by software.

An attempt to execute a doubleword load or store instruction that refers to a misaligned (odd) destination register number may cause an illegal_instruction trap.

**Special *r* Registers**

The utilization of four *r* registers is fixed, in whole or in part, by the architecture:

□    If r[0] is addressed as a source operand (*rs1* = 0 or *rs2* = 0, or *rd* = 0 for a Store) the constant value 0 is read. When r[0] is used as a destination operand (*rd* = 0, excepting Stores), the data written is discarded (no *r* register is modified).

□    The CALL instruction writes its own address into register r[15] (*out* register 7).

□    When a trap occurs, the program counters PC and nPC are copied into registers r[17] and r[18] (*local* registers 1 and 2) of the trap's new register window.

**Register Usage**

See Appendix D, "Software Considerations," for a description of conventional usage of the *r* registers.

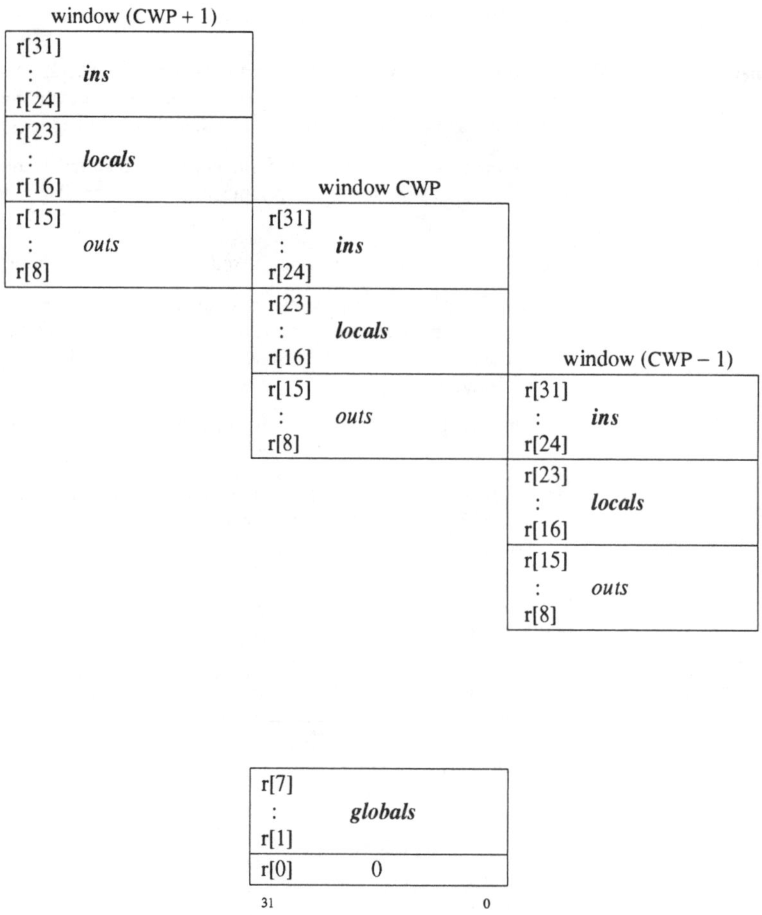

window (CWP + 1)

| r[31] | |
|:--|:--|
| : | *ins* |
| r[24] | |
| r[23] | |
| : | *locals* |
| r[16] | |
| r[15] | |
| : | *outs* |
| r[8] | |

window CWP

| r[31] | |
|:--|:--|
| : | *ins* |
| r[24] | |
| r[23] | |
| : | *locals* |
| r[16] | |
| r[15] | |
| : | *outs* |
| r[8] | |

window (CWP − 1)

| r[31] | |
|:--|:--|
| : | *ins* |
| r[24] | |
| r[23] | |
| : | *locals* |
| r[16] | |
| r[15] | |
| : | *outs* |
| r[8] | |

| r[7] | |
|:--|:--|
| : | *globals* |
| r[1] | |
| r[0] | 0 |

31                                    0

Figure 4-1    *Three Overlapping Windows and the 8 Global Registers*

SPARC International, Inc.

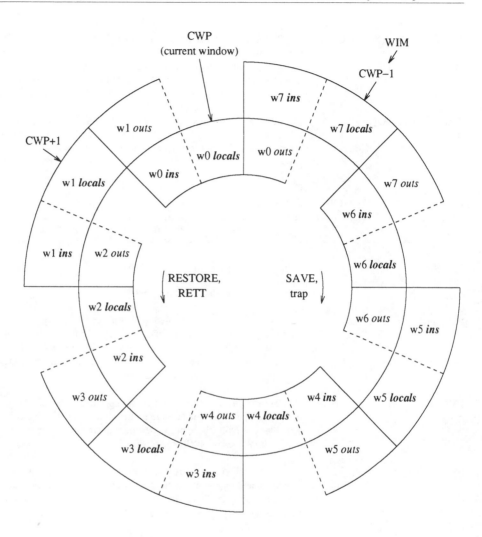

Figure 4-2    *The Windowed r Registers*

In Figure 4-1, NWINDOWS = 8. The 8 *globals* are not illustrated. The register
sets are indicated in bold face. CWP = 0 and WIM[7] = 1. If the procedure using
window w0 executes a RESTORE, window w1 will become the current window.
If the procedure using window w0 executes a SAVE, a window_overflow trap
will occur. The overflow trap handler uses the w7 *locals*.

SPARC International, Inc.

## 4.2. IU Control/Status Registers

The 32-bit IU control/status registers include the Processor State Register (PSR), the Window Invalid Mask register (WIM), the Trap Base Register (TBR), the multiply/divide (Y) register, the program counters (PC and nPC), and optional, implementation-dependent Ancillary State Registers (ASRs) and the IU deferred-trap queue.

**Processor State Register (PSR)**

The 32-bit PSR contains various fields that control the processor and hold status information. It can be modified by the SAVE, RESTORE, Ticc, and RETT instructions, and by all instructions that modify the condition codes. The privileged RDPSR and WRPSR instructions read and write the PSR directly.

Figure 4-3    *PSR Fields*

| impl | ver | icc | reserved | EC | EF | PIL | S | PS | ET | CWP |
|------|-----|-----|----------|----|----|-----|---|----|----|-----|
| 31:28 | 27:24 | 23:20 | 19:14 | 13 | 12 | 11:8 | 7 | 6 | 5 | 4:0 |

The PSR provides the following fields:

PSR_implementation (*impl*)

Bits 31 through 28 are hardwired to identify an implementation or class of implementations of the architecture. The hardware should not change this field in response to a WRPSR instruction. Together, the PSR.*impl* and PSR.*ver* fields define a **unique** implementation or class of implementations of the architecture. See Appendix L, "Implementation Characteristics."

PSR_version (*ver*)

Bits 27 through 24 are implementation-dependent. The *ver* field is either hardwired to identify one or more particular implementations or is a readable and writable state field whose properties are implementation-dependent. See Appendix L, "Implementation Characteristics."

PSR_integer_cond_codes (*icc*)

Bits 23 through 20 are the IU's condition codes. These bits are modified by the arithmetic and logical instructions whose names end with the letters **cc** (e.g., ANDcc), and by the WRPSR instruction. The Bicc and Ticc instructions cause a transfer of control based on the value of these bits, which are defined as follows:

Figure 4-4    *Integer Condition Codes (icc) Fields of the PSR*

| n | z | v | c |
|---|---|---|---|
| 23 | 22 | 21 | 20 |

PSR_negative (*n*)

Bit 23 indicates whether the 32-bit 2's complement ALU result was negative for the last instruction that modified the *icc* field. 1 = negative, 0 = not negative.

PSR_zero (z)

Bit 22 indicates whether the 32-bit ALU result was zero for the last instruction that modified the *icc* field. 1 = zero, 0 = nonzero.

PSR_overflow (v)

Bit 21 indicates whether the ALU result was within the range of (was representable in) 32-bit 2's complement notation for the last instruction that modified the *icc* field. 1 = overflow, 0 = no overflow.

PSR_carry (c)

Bit 20 indicates whether a 2's complement carry out (or borrow) occurred for the last instruction that modified the *icc* field. Carry is set on addition if there is a carry out of bit 31. Carry is set on subtraction if there is borrow into bit 31. 1 = carry, 0 = no carry.

PSR_reserved

Bits 19 through 14 are reserved. When read by a RDPSR instruction, these bits deliver zeros. For future compatibility, supervisor software should only issue WRPSR instructions with zero values in this field.

PSR_enable_coprocessor (EC)

Bit 13 determines whether the implementation-dependent coprocessor is enabled. If disabled, a coprocessor instruction will trap. 1 = enabled, 0 = disabled. If an implementation does not support a coprocessor in hardware, PSR.EC should always read as 0 and writes to it should be ignored.

PSR_enable_floating-point (EF)

Bit 12 determines whether the FPU is enabled. If disabled, a floating-point instruction will trap. 1 = enabled, 0 = disabled. If an implementation does not support a hardware FPU, PSR.EF should always read as 0 and writes to it should be ignored.

Programming Note

Software can use the EF and EC bits to determine whether a particular process uses the FPU or CP. If a process does not use the FPU/CP, its registers do not need to be saved across a context switch.

PSR_proc_interrupt_level (PIL)

Bits 11 (the most significant bit) through 8 (the least significant bit) identify the interrupt level above which the processor will accept an interrupt. See Chapter 7, "Traps."

PSR_supervisor (S)

Bit 7 determines whether the processor is in supervisor or user mode. 1 = supervisor mode, 0 = user mode.

PSR_previous_supervisor (PS)

Bit 6 contains the value of the S bit at the time of the most recent trap.

PSR_enable_traps (ET)

Bit 5 determines whether traps are enabled. A trap automatically resets ET to 0. When ET=0, an interrupt request is ignored and an exception trap causes the IU to halt execution, which typically results in a reset trap that resumes execution at address 0. 1 = traps enabled, 0 = traps disabled. See Chapter 7, "Traps."

PSR_current_window_pointer (CWP)

Bits 4 (the MSB) through 0 (the LSB) comprise the current window pointer, a counter that identifies the current window into the *r* registers. The hardware decrements the CWP on traps and SAVE instructions, and increments it on RESTORE and RETT instructions (modulo NWINDOWS).

SPARC International, Inc.

**Window Invalid Mask Register (WIM)**

The Window Invalid Mask register (WIM) is controlled by supervisor software and is used by hardware to determine whether a window overflow or underflow trap is to be generated by a SAVE, RESTORE, or RETT instruction.

Figure 4-5    *WIM Fields*

There is an active state bit in the WIM for each register set or window in an implementation. WIM[$n$] corresponds to the register set addressed when CWP = $n$.

When a SAVE, RESTORE, or RETT instruction executes, the current value of the CWP is compared against the WIM. If the SAVE, RESTORE, or RETT instruction would cause the CWP to point to an "invalid" register set, that is, one whose corresponding WIM bit equals 1 (WIM[CWP] = 1), a window_overflow or window_underflow trap is caused.

The WIM can be read by the privileged RDWIM instruction and written by the WRWIM instruction. Bits corresponding to unimplemented windows read as zeroes and values written to unimplemented bits are unused. A WRWIM with all bits set to 1, followed by a RDWIM, yields a bit vector in which the implemented windows (and only the implemented windows) are indicated by 1's.

The WIM allows for implementations with up to 32 windows.

SPARC International, Inc.

**Trap Base Register (TBR)**

The Trap Base Register (TBR) contains three fields that together equal the address to which control is transferred when a trap occurs.

Figure 4-6    *TBR Fields*

| TBA | *tt* | zero |
|---|---|---|
| 31:12 | 11:4 | 3:0 |

The TBR provides the following fields:

TBR_trap_base_address (TBA)

Bits 31 through 12 are the trap base address, which is established by supervisor software. It contains the most-significant 20 bits of the trap table address. The TBA field is written by the WRTBR instruction.

TBR_trap_type (*tt*)

Bits 11 through 4 comprise the trap type (*tt*) field. This 8-bit field is written by the hardware when a trap occurs, and retains its value until the next trap. It provides an offset into the trap table. The WRTBR instruction does not affect the *tt* field.

TBR_zero (0)

Bits 3 through 0 are zeroes. The WRTBR instruction does not affect this field. For future compatibility, supervisor software should only issue a WRTBR instruction with a zero value in this field.

See Chapter 7, "Traps," for additional information.

SPARC International, Inc.

**Multiply/Divide Register (Y)**    The 32-bit Y register contains the most significant word of the double-precision product of an integer multiplication, as a result of either an integer multiply (SMUL, SMULcc, UMUL, UMULcc) instruction, or of a routine that uses the integer multiply step (MULScc) instruction. The Y register also holds the most significant word of the double-precision dividend for an integer divide (SDIV, SDIVcc, UDIV, UDIVcc) instruction.

The Y register can be read and written with the RDY and WRY instructions.

**Program Counters (PC, nPC)**    The 32-bit PC contains the address of the instruction currently being executed by the IU. The nPC holds the address of the next instruction to be executed (assuming a trap does not occur).

For a delayed control transfer, the instruction that immediately follows the transfer instruction is known as the delay instruction. This delay instruction is executed (unless the control transfer instruction annuls it) before control is transferred to the target. During execution of the delay instruction, the nPC points to the target of the control transfer instruction, while the PC points to the delay instruction. See Chapter 5, "Instructions."

The PC is read by a CALL or JMPL instruction. The PC and nPC are written to two *local* registers during a trap. See Chapter 7, "Traps," for details.

**Ancillary State Registers (ASR)**    SPARC provides for up to 31 Ancillary State Registers (ASR's), numbered from 1 to 31.

ASR's numbered 1-15 are reserved for future use by the architecture and should not be referenced by software.

ASR's numbered 16-31 are available for implementation-dependent uses, such as timers, counters, diagnostic registers, self-test registers, and trap-control registers. A particular IU may choose to implement from zero to sixteen of these ASR's. The semantics of accessing any of these ASR's is implementation-dependent. Whether a particular Ancillary State Register is privileged or not is implementation-dependent.

An ASR is read and written with the RDASR and WRASR instructions. A read/write ASR instruction is privileged if the accessed register is privileged.

**IU Deferred-Trap Queue**

An implementation may contain zero or more deferred-trap queues. Such a queue contains sufficient state to implement resumable deferred traps caused by the IU. Note that fp_exception and cp_exception deferred traps are handled by the floating-point and coprocessor deferred-trap queues.

An IU deferred-trap queue can be read and written via privileged load/store alternate or read/write ancillary state register instructions.

The contents and operation of an IU deferred-trap queue are implementation-dependent and are not visible to user application programs.

See Appendix L, "Implementation Characteristics," for a discussion of implemented queues.

## 4.3. FPU *f* Registers

The FPU contains 32 32-bit floating-point *f* registers, which are numbered from f[0] to f[31]. Unlike the windowed *r* registers, at a given time an instruction has access to any of the 32 *f* registers. The *f* registers can be read and written by FPop (FPop1/FPop2 format) instructions, and by load/store single/double floating-point instructions (LDF, LDDF, STF, STDF). See Figure 4-7.

Figure 4-7    *The f Registers*

| f[31] |
|:---:|
| f[30] |
| ⋮ |
| f[1] |
| f[0] |

*31*                                    *0*

**Double and Quad Operands**

A single *f* register can hold one single-precision operand. A double-precision operand requires an aligned pair of *f* registers, and a quad-precision operand requires an aligned quadruple of *f* registers. Thus, at a given time, the *f* registers can hold a maximum of 32 single-precision, 16 double-precision, or 8 quad-precision operands.

Instructions that access a floating-point double in the *f* registers assume double alignment. The least-significant bit of a doubleword *f* register address specifier is reserved and should be set to zero by software. Similarly, the least-significant two bits of a quadword *f* register address are reserved and should be set to zero by software. See Table 4-2.

Table 4-2    *Floating-Point Doubles and Quads in f Registers*

| sub-format name | format fields | f register address |
|---|---|---|
| FD-0 | s:exp[10:0]:fraction[51:32] | 0 mod 2 |
| FD-1 | fraction[31:0] | 1 mod 2 |
| FQ-0 | s:exp[14:0]:fraction[111:96] | 0 mod 4 |
| FQ-1 | fraction[95:64] | 1 mod 4 |
| FQ-2 | fraction[63:32] | 2 mod 4 |
| FQ-3 | fraction[31:0] | 3 mod 4 |

It is recommended (but not required) that an attempt to execute an instruction that refers to a mis-aligned floating-point register operand (double-precision operand in a register whose number is not 0 mod 2, or quadruple-precision operand in a register whose number is not 0 mod 4) cause an fp_exception trap with FSR.*ftt* = 6 (invalid_fp_register).

## 4.4. FPU Control/Status Registers

The 32-bit FPU control/status registers include a Floating-point State Register (FSR) that contains mode and status information about the FPU, and an optional, implementation-dependent, floating-point deferred-trap queue (FQ).

**Floating-Point State Register (FSR)**

The FSR register fields contain FPU mode and status information. The FSR is read and written by the STFSR and LDFSR instructions.

Figure 4-8    *FSR Fields*

| RD | u | TEM | NS | res | *ver* | *ftt* | *qne* | u | *fcc* | *aexc* | *cexc* |
|---|---|---|---|---|---|---|---|---|---|---|---|
| 31:30 | 29:28 | 27:23 | 22 | 21:20 | 19:17 | 16:14 | 13 | 12 | 11:10 | 9:5 | 4:0 |

The FSR provides the following fields:

FSR_rounding_direction (RD)    Bits 31 and 30 select the rounding direction for floating-point results according to ANSI/IEEE Standard 754-1985.

SPARC International, Inc.

Table 4-3    *Rounding Direction (RD) Field of FSR*

| RD | Round Toward: |
|----|---------------|
| 0  | Nearest (even, if tie) |
| 1  | 0 |
| 2  | $+\infty$ |
| 3  | $-\infty$ |

FSR_unused (u)

Bits 29, 28, and 12 are unused. For future compatibility, software should only issue a LDFSR instruction with zero values in these bits.

FSR_trap_enable_mask (TEM)

Bits 27 through 23 are enable bits for each of the five floating-point exceptions that can be indicated in the current_exception field (*cexc*). See Figure 4-9. If a floating-point operate instruction generates one or more exceptions and the TEM bit corresponding to one or more of the exceptions is 1, an fp_exception trap is caused. A TEM value of 0 prevents that exception type from generating a trap.

FSR_nonstandard_fp (NS)

Bit 22, when set to 1, causes the FPU to produce implementation-defined results that may not correspond to ANSI/IEEE Standard 754-1985. For instance, to obtain higher performance, implementations may convert a subnormal floating-point operand or result to zero when NS is set. See Appendix L, "Implementation Characteristics," for a description of how this field has been used in existing implementations.

FSR_reserved (res)

Bits 21 and 20 are reserved. When read by an STFSR instruction, these bits deliver zeroes. For future compatibility, software should only issue LDFSR instructions with zero values in these bits.

FSR_version (*ver*)

Bits 19 through 17 identify one or more particular implementations of the FPU architecture. For each SPARC IU implementation (as identified by its PSR.*impl* and PSR.*vers* fields), there may be one or more FPU implementations, or none. This field identifies the particular FPU implementation present. Version number 7 is reserved to indicate that no hardware floating-point controller is present. See Appendix L, "Implementation Characteristics," for a description of how this field has been used in existing implementations.

FSR_floating-point_trap_type
(*ftt*)

Bits 16 through 14 identify floating-point exception trap types. After a floating-point exception occurs, the *ftt* field encodes the type of floating-point exception until an STFSR or another FPop is executed.

The *ftt* field can be read by the STFSR instruction. An LDFSR instruction does not affect *ftt*.

Supervisor-mode software which handles floating-point traps must execute an STFSR to determine the floating-point trap type. Whether STFSR explicitly zeroes *ftt* is implementation-dependent; if STFSR does not zero *ftt*, then the trap software must ensure that a subsequent STFSR from user mode shows a value of zero for *ftt*.

Programming Note    LDFSR cannot be used for this purpose since it leaves *ftt* unchanged, although executing a non-trapping FPop such as "fmovs %f0,%f0" prior to returning to user mode will zero *ftt*. *ftt* remains valid until the next FPop instruction completes execution.

This field encodes the exception type according to Table 4-4. Note that value 7 is reserved for future expansion.

Table 4-4    *Floating-point Trap Type (ftt) Field of FSR*

| *ftt* | Trap Type |
|---|---|
| 0 | None |
| 1 | IEEE_754_exception |
| 2 | unfinished_FPop |
| 3 | unimplemented_FPop |
| 4 | sequence_error |
| 5 | hardware_error |
| 6 | invalid_fp_register |
| 7 | *reserved* |

The sequence_error and hardware_error trap types are not expected to arise in the normal course of computation. They are essentially unrecoverable, from the point of view of user applications.

In contrast, IEEE_754_exception, unfinished_FPop, and unimplemented_FPop are expected to arise occasionally in the normal course of computation and must be recoverable by supervisor software. When a floating-point trap occurs (as observed by a user signal (trap) handler):

1)  The value of *aexc* is unchanged.

2)  The value of *cexc* is unchanged, except that on an IEEE_754_exception exactly one bit corresponding to the trapping exception will be set. Unfinished_FPop, unimplemented_FPop, and sequence_error floating point exceptions do not affect *cexc*.

3)  The source *f* registers are unchanged (usually implemented by leaving the destination *f* register unchanged).

4)  The value of *fcc* is unchanged.

The foregoing describes the result seen by a user signal handler if an IEEE exception is signaled, either immediately from an IEEE_754_exception or after recovery from an unfinished_FPop or unimplemented_FPop. In either case, *cexc* as seen by the trap handler will reflect the exception causing the trap.

In the cases of unfinished_FPop and unimplemented_FPop traps that don't subsequently generate IEEE exceptions, the recovery software is expected to define *cexc*, *aexc*, and either the destination *f* register or *fcc*, as appropriate.

*ftt* = IEEE_754_exception

An IEEE_754_exception floating-point trap type indicates that a floating-point exception occurred that conforms to the ANSI/IEEE Standard 754-1985. The exception type is encoded in the *cexc* field. Note that *aexc*, *fcc*, and the destination *f* register are not affected by an IEEE_754_exception trap.

*ftt* = unfinished_FPop

An unfinished_FPop indicates that an implementation's FPU was unable to generate correct results or exceptions as defined by ANSI/IEEE Standard 754-1985. In this case, the *cexc* field is unchanged.

*ftt* = unimplemented_FPop

An unimplemented_FPop indicates that an implementation's FPU decoded an FPop that it does not implement. In this case, the *cexc* field is unchanged.

Programming Note

In the case of an unfinished_FPop or unimplemented_FPop floating-point trap type, software should emulate or re-execute the exception-causing instruction, and update the FSR, destination *f* register(s), and *fcc*.

*ftt* = sequence_error

A sequence_error indicates one of three abnormal error conditions in the FPU, all caused by erroneous supervisor software:

— An attempt was made to execute a STDFQ instruction on an implementation without a floating-point deferred-trap queue (FQ).

— An attempt was made to execute a floating-point instruction when the FPU was not able to accept one. This type of sequence_error arises from a logic error in supervisor software that has caused a previous floating-point trap to be incompletely serviced (for example, the floating-point queue was not emptied after a previous floating-point exception).

— An attempt was made to execute a STDFQ instruction when the floating-point deferred-trap queue (FQ) was empty, that is, when FSR.*qne* = 0. (Note that generation of sequence_error is recommended, but not required in this case)

Programming Note

If a sequence_error fp_exception occurs during execution of user code (due to either of the above conditions), it may not be possible to recover sufficient state to continue execution of the user application.

*ftt* = hardware_error

A hardware_error indicates that the FPU detected a catastrophic internal error, such as an illegal state or a parity error on an *f* register access.

If a hardware_error occurs during execution of user code, it may not be possible to recover sufficient state to continue execution of the user application.

*ftt* = invalid_fp_register

An invalid_fp_register trap type indicates that one (or more) operands of an FPop are misaligned, that is, a double-precision register number is not 0 mod 2, or a quadruple-precision register number is not 0 mod 4. It is recommended that implementations generate an fp_exception trap with FSR.*ftt* = invalid_fp_register in this case, but an implementation may choose not to generate a trap.

SPARC International, Inc.

FSR_FQ_not_empty (*qne*)

Bit 13 indicates whether the optional floating-point deferred-trap queue (FQ) is empty after a deferred fp_exception trap or after a store double floating-point queue (STDFQ) instruction has been executed. If *qne* = 0, the queue is empty; if *qne* = 1, the queue is not empty.

The *qne* bit can be read by the STFSR instruction. The LDFSR instruction does not affect *qne*. However, executing successive STDFQ instructions will (eventually) cause the FQ to become empty (*qne* = 0). If an implementation does not provide an FQ, this bit reads as zero. Supervisor software must arrange for this bit to always read as zero to user mode software.

FSR_fp_condition_codes (*fcc*)

Bits 11 and 10 contain the FPU condition codes. These bits are updated by floating-point compare instructions (FCMP and FCMPE). They are read and written by the STFSR and LDFSR instructions, respectively. FBfcc bases its control transfer on this field.

In the following table, $f_{rs1}$ and $f_{rs2}$ correspond to the single, double, or quad values in the *f* registers specified by an instruction's *rs1* and *rs2* fields. The question mark (?) indicates an unordered relation, which is true if either $f_{rs1}$ or $f_{rs2}$ is a signaling NaN or quiet NaN. Note that *fcc* is unchanged if FCMP or FCMPE generates an IEEE_754_exception trap.

Table 4-5    *Floating-point Condition Codes (fcc) Field of FSR*

| *fcc* | Relation |
|---|---|
| 0 | $f_{rs1} = f_{rs2}$ |
| 1 | $f_{rs1} < f_{rs2}$ |
| 2 | $f_{rs1} > f_{rs2}$ |
| 3 | $f_{rs1} ? f_{rs2}$ (unordered) |

FSR_accrued_exception (*aexc*)

Bits 9 through 5 accumulate IEEE_754 floating-point exceptions while fp_exception traps are disabled using the TEM field. See Figure 4-10. After an FPop completes, the TEM and *cexc* fields are logically *and*'d together. If the result is nonzero, an fp_exception trap is generated; otherwise, the new *cexc* field is *or*'d into the *aexc* field. Thus, while traps are masked, exceptions are accumulated in the *aexc* field.

FSR_current_exception (*cexc*)

Bits 4 through 0 indicate that one or more IEEE_754 floating-point exceptions were generated by the most recently executed FPop instruction. The absence of an exception causes the corresponding bit to be cleared. See Figure 4-11.

The *cexc* bits are set as described in section 4.4.2 by the execution of an FPop that either does not cause a trap or causes an fp_exception trap with FSR.*ftt* = IEEE_754_exception. It is recommended that an IEEE_754_exception which traps should cause exactly one bit in FSR.*cexc* to be set, corresponding to the detected IEEE 754 exception. If the execution of an FPop causes a trap other than an fp_exception due to an IEEE 754 exception, FSR.*cexc* is left unchanged.

SPARC International, Inc.

**Floating-Point Exception Fields**

The current and accrued exception fields and the trap enable mask assume the following definitions of the floating-point exception conditions (per ANSI/IEEE Standard 754-1985):

Figure 4-9    *Trap Enable Mask (TEM) Fields of FSR*

| NVM | OFM | UFM | DZM | NXM |
|-----|-----|-----|-----|-----|
| 27  | 26  | 25  | 24  | 23  |

Figure 4-10    *Accrued Exception Bits (aexc) Fields of FSR*

| nva | ofa | ufa | dza | nxa |
|-----|-----|-----|-----|-----|
| 9   | 8   | 7   | 6   | 5   |

Figure 4-11    *Current Exception Bits (cexc) Fields of FSR*

| nvc | ofc | ufc | dzc | nxc |
|-----|-----|-----|-----|-----|
| 4   | 3   | 2   | 1   | 0   |

FSR_invalid (*nvc, nva*)

An operand is improper for the operation to be performed. For example, $0 \div 0$, and $\infty - \infty$ are invalid. 1 = invalid operand, 0 = valid operand(s).

FSR_overflow (*ofc, ofa*)

The rounded result would be larger in magnitude than the largest normalized number in the specified format. 1 = overflow, 0 = no overflow.

FSR_underflow (*ufc, ufa*)

The rounded result is inexact and would be smaller in magnitude than the smallest normalized number in the indicated format. 1 = underflow, 0 = no underflow.

Underflow is never indicated when the correct unrounded result is zero. Otherwise,

if UFM=0:  The *ufc* and *ufa* bits will be set if the correct unrounded result of an operation is less in magnitude than the smallest normalized number and the correctly-rounded result is inexact. These bits will be set if the correct unrounded result is less than the smallest normalized number, but the correct rounded result is the smallest normalized number. *nxc* and *nxa* are always set as well.

if UFM=1:  An IEEE-754_exception trap will occur if the correct unrounded result of an operation would be smaller than the smallest normalized number. A trap will occur if the correct unrounded result would be smaller than the smallest normalized number, but the correct rounded result would be the smallest normalized number.

FSR_division-by-zero (*dzc, dza*)  $X \div 0$, where X is subnormal or normalized.  Note that $0 \div 0$ does **not** set the *dzc* bit.  1 = division-by-zero, 0 = no division-by-zero.

FSR_inexact (*nxc, nxa*)  The rounded result of an operation differs from the infinitely precise correct result.  1 = inexact result, 0 = exact result.

## FSR Conformance

An implementation may choose to implement the TEM, *cexc*, and *aexc* fields in hardware in either of two ways:

(1)  Implement all three fields conformant to ANSI/IEEE Standard 754-1985.

(2)  Implement the NXM, *nxa*, and *nxc* bits of these fields conformant to ANSI/IEEE Standard 754-1985.  Implement each of the remaining bits in the three fields either

(a)  Conformant to the ANSI/IEEE Standard, or

(b)  As a state bit that may be set by software which calculates the ANSI/IEEE value of the bit.  For any bit implemented as a state bit:

- The IEEE exception corresponding to the state bit must **always** cause an exception (specifically, an unfinished_FPop exception).  During exception processing in the trap handler, the bit in the state field can be written to the appropriate value by an LDFSR instruction, and

- The state bit must be implemented in such a way that if it is written to a particular value by an LDFSR instruction, it will be read back as the same value in a subsequent STFSR.

*Programming Note*  The software must be capable of simulating the entire FPU to properly handle the unimplemented_FPop, unfinished_FPop, and IEEE_754_exception floating-point traps.  Thus, a user application program always "sees" an FSR that is fully compliant with ANSI/IEEE Standard 754-1985.

## Floating-Point Deferred-Trap Queue (FQ)

The floating-point deferred-trap queue (FQ), if present in an implementation, contains sufficient state information to implement resumable, deferred floating-point traps.

If floating-point instructions are to execute concurrently with (asynchronously from) integer instructions in a given implementation, the implementation must provide a floating-point queue.  If floating-point instructions execute synchronously with integer instructions, provision of a floating-point queue is optional.

The FQ can be read with the privileged store double floating-point queue instruction (STDFQ).  In a given implementation, it may also be readable or writable via privileged load/store double alternate (LDDA, STDA) instructions, or by read/write Ancillary State Register instructions (RDASR, WRASR).

The contents of and operations upon the FQ are implementation-dependent. However, if an FQ is present, supervisor software must be able to deduce the exception-causing instruction's opcode (*opf*), operands, and address from its FQ entry. This must also be true of any other pending floating-point operations in the queue. See Appendix L, "Implementation Characteristics," for a discussion of the formats and operation of implemented floating-point queues.

In an implementation without an FQ, the *qne* bit in the FSR is always 0, and an STDFQ instruction causes an fp_exception trap with FSR.*ftt* = 4 (sequence_error).

## 4.5. CP Registers

All of the coprocessor data and control/status registers are optional and implementation-dependent.

The coprocessor working registers are accessed via load/store coprocessor and CPop1/CPop2 format instructions.

The architecture also provides instruction support for reading and writing a Coprocessor State Register (CSR) and a coprocessor deferred-trap queue (CQ).

If that a higher priority trap is not pending, and the CP is not present or PSR.EC = 0, execution of a load or store to a coprocessor register or of a coprocessor operate instruction generates a cp_disabled trap.

# 5

Instructions

Instructions are accessed by the processor from memory and are executed, annulled, or trapped. Instructions are encoded in three 32-bit formats and can be partitioned into six general categories. There are 72 basic instruction operations.

## 5.1. Instruction Execution

Architecturally, an instruction is read from memory at the address given by the program counter (PC). It is then executed or not, depending on whether the previous instruction was an annulling branch (see below). An instruction may also generate a trap due to the detection of an exceptional condition, caused by the instruction itself (precise trap), a previous instruction (deferred trap), an external interrupt (interrupting trap), or an external reset request. If an instruction is executed, it may change program-visible processor and/or memory state.

If the instruction traps, control is vectored into a trap table at the address given by the Trap Base Register (TBR). If an instruction does not trap, the next program counter (nPC) is copied into the PC and the nPC is incremented by 4 (ignoring overflow, if any). If the instruction is a control-transfer instruction, the processor writes the target address to nPC. Thus, the two program counters provide for a delayed-branch execution model.

For each instruction access and each normal data access, the IU appends to the 32-bit memory address an 8-bit address space identifier, or **ASI**. The ASI encodes whether the processor is in supervisor or user mode, and whether the access is an instruction or data access. There are also privileged load/store alternate instructions (see below) that can provide an arbitrary ASI with their data addresses.

Implementation Note    The time required to execute an instruction is implementation-dependent, as is the degree of execution concurrency. The relationship between PC and nPC and the hardware that fetches and decodes instructions is also implementation-dependent. In the absence of traps, an implementation should cause the same program-visible register and memory state changes as if a program had executed according to the sequential model implied in this document. See Chapter 7, "Traps," for a definition of architectural compliance in the presence of traps.

## 5.2. Instruction Formats

Instructions are encoded in three major 32-bit formats. See Figure 5-1. There are also several minor formats that are illustrated in Appendix B, "Instruction Definitions."

SPARC International, Inc.

Figure 5-1    *Summary of Instruction Formats*

Format 1 (*op* = 1):  CALL

| op | disp30 | |
|----|--------|--|
| 31  29 | | 0 |

Format 2 (*op* = 0):  SETHI & Branches (Bicc, FBfcc, CBccc)

| op | | rd | op2 | imm22 | | | |
|----|--|----|-----|-------|--|--|--|
| op | a | cond | op2 | disp22 | | | |
| 31 | 29 | 28 | 24 | 21 | | | 0 |

Format 3 (*op* = 2 or 3):  Remaining instructions

| op | rd | op3 | rs1 | i=0 | asi | rs2 |
|----|----|-----|-----|-----|-----|-----|
| op | rd | op3 | rs1 | i=1 | simm13 | |
| op | rd | op3 | rs1 | | opf | rs2 |
| 31 | 29 | 24 | 18 | 13  12 | | 4    0 |

**Instruction Fields**    The instruction fields are interpreted as follows:

*op* and *op2*

These 2- and 3-bit fields encode the 3 major formats and the format 2 instructions according to Tables 5-1 and 5-2.

Table 5-1    *op Encoding (All Formats)*

| Format | *op* | Instructions |
|--------|------|--------------|
| 1 | 1 | CALL |
| 2 | 0 | Bicc, FBfcc, CBccc, SETHI |
| 3 | 3 | memory instructions |
| 3 | 2 | arithmetic, logical, shift, and remaining |

Table 5-2    *op2 Encoding (Format 2)*

| op2 | Instructions |
|-----|--------------|
| 0 | UNIMP |
| 1 | unimplemented |
| 2 | Bicc |
| 3 | unimplemented |
| 4 | SETHI |
| 5 | unimplemented |
| 6 | FBfcc |
| 7 | CBccc |

*rd*

This 5-bit field is the address of the destination (or source) *r* or *f* or coprocessor register(s) for a load/arithmetic (or store) instruction. For an instruction that read/writes a double (or quad), the least significant one (or two) bits are unused and should be supplied as zero by software.

*a*

The *a* bit in a branch instruction annuls the execution of the following instruction if the branch is conditional and untaken or if it is unconditional and taken.

*cond*

This 4-bit field selects the condition code(s) to test for a branch instruction. See Appendix F, "Opcodes and Condition Codes," for descriptions of its values.

*imm22*

This 22-bit field is a constant that SETHI places in the upper end of a destination register.

*disp22* and *disp30*

These 30-bit and 22-bit fields are word-aligned, sign-extended, PC-relative displacements for a call or branch, respectively.

*op3*

This 6-bit field (together with 1 bit from *op*) encodes the format 3 instructions. See Appendix F, "Opcodes and Condition Codes," for descriptions of its values.

*i*

The *i* bit selects the second ALU operand for (integer) arithmetic and load/store instructions. If *i* = 0, the operand is r[rs2]. If *i* = 1, the operand is *simm13*, sign-extended from 13 to 32 bits.

*asi*

This 8-bit field is the address space identifier supplied by a load/store alternate instruction.

*rs1*

This 5-bit field is the address of the first *r* or *f* or coprocessor register(s) source operand. For an instruction that reads a double (or quad), the least

SPARC International, Inc.

significant bit (or 2 bits) are unused and should be supplied as zero by software.

*rs2*

This 5-bit field is the address of the second *r* or *f* or coprocessor register(s) source operand when *i* = 0. For an instruction that reads a double-length (or quad-length) register sequence, the least significant bit (or 2 bits) are unused and should be supplied as zero by software.

*simm13*

This 13-bit field is a sign-extended 13-bit immediate value used as the second ALU operand for an (integer) arithmetic or load/store instruction when *i* = 1.

*opf*

This 9-bit field encodes a floating-point operate (FPop) instruction or a coprocessor operate (CPop) instruction. See Appendix F, "Opcodes and Condition Codes," for possible values and their meanings.

## 5.3. Instruction Categories

SPARC instructions can be grouped into six categories: load/store, integer arithmetic, control transfer (CTI), read/write control register, floating-point operate, and coprocessor operate.

### Load/Store Instructions

Load/store instructions are the only instructions that access memory. See Chapter 6, "Memory Model," which specifies their semantics and the order in which they appear to be executed by memory. Load and store instructions use two *r* registers or an *r* register and *simm13* to calculate a 32-bit, byte-aligned memory address. To this address, the IU appends an ASI that encodes whether the processor is in supervisor or user mode, and whether the access is an instruction or data access.

The destination field of the load/store instruction specifies either an *r* register, *f* register, or coprocessor register that supplies the data for a store, or receives the data from a load.

Integer load and store instructions support byte (8-bit), halfword (16-bit), word (32-bit), and doubleword (64-bit) accesses. Floating-point and coprocessor load and store instructions support word and doubleword memory accesses.

Programming Note

When *i* = 1 and *rs1* = 0, any location in the lowest or highest 4K bytes of an address space can be accessed without using a register to hold an address.

### Alignment Restrictions

Halfword accesses must be **aligned** on a 2-byte boundary, word accesses (which include instruction fetches) must be aligned on a 4-byte boundary, and doubleword accesses must be aligned on an 8-byte boundary. An improperly aligned address causes a load or store instruction to generate a mem_address_not_aligned trap.

Addressing Conventions

SPARC is a **big-endian** architecture: the address of a doubleword, word, or half-word is the address of its most significant byte.  Increasing the address generally means decreasing the significance of the unit being accessed.  The addressing conventions are illustrated in Figure 5-2 and defined as follows:

Byte
>   For a load/store byte instruction, the most significant byte of a word (bits 31 to 24) is accessed when address bits <1:0> = 0 and the least significant byte (bits 7 to 0) is accessed when address bits <1:0> = 3.

Halfwords
>   For a load/store halfword instruction, the more significant halfword of a word (bits 31 to 16) is accessed when address bits <1:0> = 0, and the less significant halfword is accessed when address bits <1:0> = 2.

Doublewords
>   For a load/store double instruction, the more significant word (bits 63 to 32) is accessed when address bits <2:0> = 0, and the less significant word (bits 31 to 0) is accessed when address bits <2:0> = 4.

SPARC International, Inc.

Figure 5-2    *Addressing Conventions*

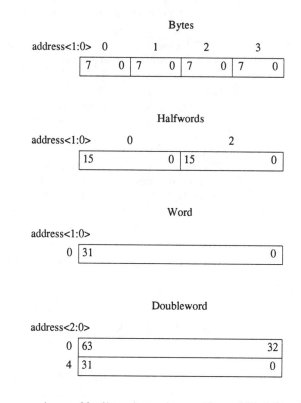

Address Space Identifiers
(ASIs)

A normal load/store instruction provides an ASI of either 0x0A or 0x0B for the data access, depending on whether the processor is in user or supervisor mode. However, privileged load from alternate space instructions and privileged store into alternate space instructions supply explicit address space identifiers, from the *asi* field in the instructions.

The ASI assignments are shown in Table 5-3.

Implementation Note    The definitions of the alternate spaces are implementation-dependent. Whether an implementation decodes all eight ASI bits is also implementation-dependent. See Appendix I, "Suggested ASI Assignments for SPARC Systems," for a set of recommended assignments.

Table 5-3    *Address Space Identifiers*

| ASI | Address Space |
|-----|---------------|
| 0x00 – 0x07 | implementation-dependent |
| 0x08 | User Instruction |
| 0x09 | Supervisor Instruction |
| 0x0A | User Data |
| 0x0B | Supervisor Data |
| 0x0C – 0xFF | implementation-dependent |

**Separate Instruction Memory**

The SPARC architecture is defined in this manual as if store instructions access the same memory from which instructions are fetched. However, an implementation may explicitly partition instructions and data into independent instruction and data memories (caches), commonly referred to as a "Harvard" architecture or "split I & D caches".

If a program includes self-modifying code, it must issue a FLUSH instruction for each modified instruction word [1], which ensures that the modified instruction will be flushed to memory. In general, a store of an instruction must be followed by a FLUSH[1] before the new instruction can be reliably fetched from the instruction stream. See Chapter 6, "Memory Model," and Appendix B, "Instruction Definitions."

**Input/Output**

SPARC assumes that input/output registers are accessed via load/store alternate instructions, normal load/store instructions, coprocessor instructions, or read/write Ancillary State Register instructions (RDASR, WRASR). In the first case, the I/O registers can only be accessed by the supervisor. In the last case, whether the I/O registers can be accessed from user code or not is implementation-dependent.

The addresses and contents of I/O registers are implementation-dependent.

**Integer Arithmetic Instructions**

The integer arithmetic instructions are generally triadic-register-address instructions which compute a result that is a function of two source operands, and either write the result into the destination register r[*rd*] or discard it. One of the source operands is always r[*rs1*]. The other source operand depends on the *i* bit in the instruction: if *i* = 0, the operand is r[*rs2*], but if *i* = 1, the operand is the constant *simm13* sign-extended to a width of 32 bits.

Reading r[0] produces the value zero. If the destination field indicates a write into r[0], no *r* register is modified and the result is discarded.

---

[1] Or, issue supervisor calls (traps) having that effect.

SPARC International, Inc.

Set Condition Codes

Most of these instructions are available in dual versions; one version sets the integer condition codes (*icc*) as a side effect; the other version does not affect the condition codes. A special comparison instruction for integer values is not needed, as it is easily synthesized from the "subtract and set condition codes" (SUBcc) instruction.

Shift Instructions

Shift instructions shift an *r* register left or right by a constant or variable amount. None of the shift instructions changes the condition codes.

Set High 22 Bits

The "set high 22 bits of an *r* register" instruction (SETHI) writes a 22-bit constant from the instruction into the high-order bits of the destination register. It clears the low-order 10 bits, and does not affect the condition codes. Its primary use is in construction of a 32-bit constant in a register.

Integer Multiply/Divide

The integer multiply instructions perform $32 \times 32 \rightarrow 64$-bit operations, and the integer divide instructions perform $64 \div 32 \rightarrow 32$-bit operations. There are versions of these instructions that set the condition codes, and others that do not. Division by zero causes a division-by-zero trap.

Tagged Add/Subtract

The tagged add/subtract instructions assume tagged-format data, where the tag is the two low-order bits of each operand. "Tag overflow" occurs if either of the two operands has a nonzero tag, or if 32-bit arithmetic overflow occurs. If tag overflow occurs, TADDcc and TSUBcc set the PSR's overflow bit, and TADDccTV and TSUBccTV cause a tag_overflow trap (but do not affect PSR.*icc*.V).

**Control-Transfer Instructions (CTIs)**

A control-transfer instruction changes the value of the next program counter (nPC). There are five basic control-transfer instruction (**CTI**) types:

- Conditional branch (Bicc, FBfcc, CBccc)

- Call and Link (CALL)

- Jump and Link (JMPL)

- Return from trap (RETT)

- Trap (Ticc)

CTI Categories

The control-transfer instructions can be categorized (Table 5-4) according to how the target address is calculated (PC-relative vs. register-indirect), and the time at which the control transfer takes place relative to the CTI (non-delayed vs. delayed vs. conditional-delayed).

Table 5-4    *CTI Categories*

| Control-Transfer Instruction | Target Address Calculation | Transfer Time Relative to CTI |
|---|---|---|
| Bicc, FBfcc, CBccc | PC-relative | conditional-delayed |
| CALL | PC-relative | delayed |
| JMPL, RETT | register-indirect | delayed |
| Ticc | register-indirect-vectored | non-delayed |

PC-relative CTI

A PC-relative CTI computes its target address by sign-extending its immediate field to 32 bits, left-shifting that word displacement by two bits to create a byte displacement, and adding the resulting byte displacement to the contents of the PC.

register-indirect CTI

A register-indirect CTI computes its target address as either "r[$rs1$] + r[$rs2$]" if $i = 0$, or "r[$rs1$] + sign_ext($simm13$)" if $i = 1$.

register-indirect-vectored CTI

A register-indirect-vectored CTI computes its target address in stages. First, a trap type is calculated as "127 + r[rs1] + r[rs2]" if $i = 0$, or as "127 + r[rs1] + sign_ext($simm13$)" if $i = 1$. This trap type is stored in the *tt* field of the TBR register. The resulting contents of the TBR register is the target address of the CTI.

delayed CTI (DCTI)

A delayed control transfer changes control to the instruction at the target address after a 1-instruction delay. The **delay instruction** executed after the CTI is executed before the target of the CTI is executed.

non-delayed CTI

A non-delayed control transfer changes control to the instruction at the target address immediately after the CTI is executed.

conditional delayed CTI (conditional DCTI)

A conditional delayed control transfer causes either a delayed or a non-delayed control transfer, depending on the value of the instruction's annul *a* bit and whether the transfer is conditional or not.

Note that both a delayed and a conditional delayed control-transfer instruction are classified as delayed CTIs, or **DCTIs**.

Delay Instruction

The instruction pointed to by the nPC when a delayed control-transfer instruction is encountered is the **delay instruction**. Normally, this is the next sequential instruction in the instruction space (that is, at location PC + 4). However, if the instruction that immediately precedes a particular DCTI is itself a DCTI, the address of the delay instruction is actually the target of the preceding DCTI (since that is where the nPC will point when the DCTI in question is executed). This is explained further in the section *Delayed Control-Transfer Couples* below.

SPARC International, Inc.

Delayed Transfer

Table 5-5 demonstrates the order of execution for a generic delayed control transfer. The order of execution by address is 8, 12, 16, and 40. If the delayed control-transfer instruction is not taken, the order of execution by address is 8, 12, 16, and 20.

Table 5-5    *Delayed Control Transfer*

| PC before execution | nPC before execution | Instruction |
|---|---|---|
| 8 | 12 | not-a-CTI |
| 12 | 16 | delayed CTI to 40 |
| 16 | 40 | not-a-CTI |
| : | : | |
| 40 | 44 | ... |

Conditional Delayed Transfer

A conditional delayed transfer instruction changes control depending on the value of the instruction's annul (*a*) bit and whether the specified condition is true or not. Note that the *a* bit is only specifiable in the branch instructions (Bicc, FBfcc, and CBccc).

When the annul bit is 0 in a conditional delayed transfer instruction, its delay instruction is **always** executed. When the annul bit is 1 in a conditional delayed transfer instruction, the delay instruction is **not** executed, **except** when the control-transfer instruction is a taken conditional branch. Table 5-6 summarizes the conditions under which a delay instruction is or is not executed.

An annulled delay instruction has the same effect as would a NOP instruction.

Table 5-6    *Conditions for Execution of Delay Instruction*

| *a* bit | Type of branch | Delay instruction executed? |
|---|---|---|
| *a* = 0 | conditional, taken | Yes |
| | conditional, not taken | Yes |
| | unconditional, taken (BA, etc) | Yes |
| | unconditional, not taken (BN, etc) | Yes |
| *a* = 1 | conditional, taken | Yes |
| | conditional, not taken | No (annulled) |
| | unconditional, taken (BA, etc) | No (annulled) |
| | unconditional, not taken (BN, etc) | No (annulled) |

Conditional with *a* = 1

If *a* = 1 in a conditional branch (not including branch always) and the branch is **not taken**, the delay instruction is **annulled** (not executed). If the branch is taken, the delay instruction is executed.

Table 5-7  *Untaken Branch with a = 1*

| PC | nPC | Instruction | Action |
|----|-----|-------------|--------|
| 8  | 12  | not-a-CTI | executed |
| 12 | 16  | conditional branch (a=1) to 40 | not taken |
| 16 | 20  | not-a-CTI | not executed (annulled) |
| 20 | 24  | ... | executed |

Conditional with $a = 0$

If $a = 0$ in a conditional branch (including branch always), the delay instruction is executed regardless of whether the branch is taken.

Table 5-8  *Untaken Branch with a = 0*

| PC | nPC | Instruction | Action |
|----|-----|-------------|--------|
| 8  | 12  | not-a-CTI | executed |
| 12 | 16  | conditional branch (a=0) to 40 | not taken |
| 16 | 20  | not-a-CTI | executed |
| 20 | 24  | ... | executed |

Unconditional Delayed Transfer

If $a = 0$ in an unconditional ("branch-always" or "branch-never") branch instruction (that is, BA, FBA, CBA, BN, FBN, and CBN), the delay instruction is always executed. If $a = 1$ in an unconditional branch instruction, the delay instruction is **not** executed.

Programming Note

A branch always with $a = 1$ can be used by the supervisor at program runtime to dynamically replace an unimplemented instruction with a branch to an associated emulation routine that it writes into the user address space. When re-executed, the overhead for emulating the unimplemented instruction is significantly reduced. The first few instructions of the emulation routine can be tailored at runtime to make available the operands of the replaced instruction.

Programming Note

The annul bit increases the likelihood that a compiler can find a useful instruction to fill the delay slot after a branch, thereby reducing the number of instructions executed by a program. Here are two examples:

The annul bit can be used to move an instruction from within a loop to fill the delay slot of the branch which closes the loop. If the Bicc in Table 5-9 has $a = 0$, a compiler can move a non-control-transfer instruction from within the loop into location D. If the Bicc has $a = 1$, the compiler can copy the non-control-transfer instruction at location L into location D and change the branch to Bicc L'.

The annul bit can be used to move an instruction from either the "else" or the "then" arm of an "if-then-else" program block to the delay slot of the branch which selects between them. Since the conditional branch instructions provide both true and false tests for all the conditions, a compiler can arrange the code (possibly reversing the sense of the branch test conditions) so that a non-control-transfer instruction from either the "else" branch or the "then" branch can be moved into the delay position after the "if" branch instruction. See Table 5-10.

Table 5-9    *Example Loop Code*

| Address | Instruction |
|---------|-------------|
| L:      | not-a-CTI   |
| L':     | not-a-CTI   |
|         | ...         |
|         | Bicc to L   |
| D:      | not-a-CTI   |

Table 5-10    *If-Then-Else Optimization*

| Address | Instruction | Address | Instruction |
|---------|-------------|---------|-------------|
|         | Bicc(cond, a=1) THEN |         | Bicc(cond, a=1) ELSE |
| DELAY:  | then-phrase-instr-1 | DELAY:  | else-phrase-instr-1 |
| ELSE:   | else-phrase-instr-1 | THEN:   | then-phrase-instr-1 |
|         | goto ...            |         | goto ...            |
| THEN:   | then-phrase-instr-2 | ELSE:   | else-phrase-instr-2 |

## CALL and JMPL Instructions

The CALL instruction writes the contents of the PC (which point to the CALL instruction itself) into r[15] (*out* register 7). CALL causes a delayed transfer of control to an arbitrary PC-relative target address.

JMPL writes the contents of the PC (which point to the JMPL instruction) into the *r* register specified by the *rd* field. JMPL causes a delayed transfer of control to an arbitrary target address.

## SAVE Instruction

The SAVE instruction is identical to an ADD instruction, except that it also decrements the CWP by 1. This causes the CWP−1 window to become the new current window, thereby "saving" the caller's window. Also, the source registers for the addition are from the CWP window, while the result is written into a register in the CWP−1 window.

## RESTORE Instruction

The RESTORE instruction is also identical to an ADD instruction, except that it increments the CWP by 1. This causes the CWP+1 window to become the current window, thereby "restoring" the caller's window. Also, the source registers for the addition are from the CWP window, while the result is written into a register in the CWP+1 window.

Both SAVE and RESTORE compare the new CWP against the Window Invalid Mask (WIM) to check for window overflow or underflow.

**Programming Note**    A procedure is invoked by executing a CALL (or a JMPL) instruction. If the procedure requires a register window, it executes a SAVE instruction. A routine that has not allocated a register window of its own (possibly a "leaf" procedure) should not write on any windowed registers except *out* registers 0...6.

A procedure that uses a register window returns by executing both a RESTORE and a JMPL instruction. A procedure that was not allocated a register window returns by executing a JMPL only. The JMPL instruction typically returns to the instruction following the CALL's or JMPL's delay instruction; in other words, the typical return address is 8 plus the address saved by the CALL or JMPL.

SPARC International, Inc.

The SAVE and RESTORE instructions can be used to atomically establish a new memory stack pointer in an *r* register and update the CWP. See Appendix D, "Software Considerations."

**Trap (Ticc) Instruction**

The Ticc instruction evaluates the condition codes specified by its *cond* field and, if the result is true, causes a trap. That is, it modifies the *tt* field of the Trap Base Register (TBR), and causes a non-delayed control transfer to the address in the TBR. If the selected condition codes evaluate to false, it executes as a NOP.

A Ticc instruction can specify one of 128 software trap types to be used in the *tt* field of the TBR. After a taken Ticc, the processor disables traps, enters supervisor mode, decrements the CWP, saves PC and nPC into r[17] and r[18] (*local* registers 1 and 2) of the new window, places 128 + its source operand into the *tt* field of the TBR, and transfers control to the address given in the TBR. See Chapter 7, "Traps," for more information.

**Programming Note**   Ticc can be used to implement breakpointing, tracing, and calls to supervisor software. Ticc can also be used for runtime checks, such as out-of-range array indices, integer overflow, etc.

**Delayed Control-Transfer Couples (DCTI)**

When a delay instruction is itself a control-transfer instruction, the pair of instructions are referred to as a delayed control-transfer instruction couple (DCTI couple). The order of execution for DCTI couples is summarized in Table 5-12 based on the code sequence in Table 5-11.

**Table 5-11**   *Example DCTI Couple Code*

| address: | instruction | target |
|---|---|---|
| 8: | not-a-CTI | |
| 12: | CTI | 40 |
| 16: | CTI | 60 |
| 20: | not-a-CTI | |
| 24: | ... | |
| | | |
| 40: | not-a-CTI | |
| 44: | ... | |
| | | |
| 60: | not-a-CTI | |
| 64: | ... | |

**First-Taken Case**

In the first five cases of Table 5-12, the first instruction of a DCTI couple is a CTI that causes a transfer of control. These cases are representative of the DCTI couples that can occur during a return from a trap handler to user code, which can happen via a "JMPL, RETT" instruction couple. Both the "JMPL, RETT" couple and an "RETT, user-CTI" couple can occur during returns from trap handlers.

**First-Untaken Case**

In the sixth case in Table 5-12, the first instruction of a DCTI couple is a (possibly untaken) conditional branch, the targets of the DCTI couple are within the same address space as the DCTI couple, but are otherwise unpredictable.

Table 5-12    *Order of Execution by Address for DCTI Couples*

| Case | 12:  CTI 40 | 16:  CTI 60 | Order of Execution by Address |
|------|-------------|-------------|-------------------------------|
| 1 | DCTI unconditional | DCTI taken | 12, 16, 40, 60, 64, ... |
| 2 | DCTI unconditional | B*cc(a=0) untaken | 12, 16, 40, 44, ... |
| 3 | DCTI unconditional | B*cc(a=1) untaken | 12, 16, 44, 48, ... (40 annulled) |
| 4 | DCTI unconditional | B*A(a=1) | 12, 16, 60, 64, ... (40 annulled) |
| 5 | B*A(a=1) | any CTI | 12, 40, 44, ... (16 annulled) |
| 6 | B*cc | DCTI | 12, *unpredictable* |

Note:    Where the *a* bit is not indicated above, it may be either 0 or 1. See next table for abbreviations.

Table 5-13    *Abbreviations used in Previous Table*

| Abbreviation | Refers to Instructions |
|--------------|------------------------|
| B*A | BA, FBA or CBA |
| B*cc | Bicc, FBfcc, or CBccc |
|  | (including BN, FBN, CBN, but excluding B*A) |
| DCTI unconditional | CALL, JMPL, RETT, or B*A(with a=0) |
| DCTI taken | CALL, JMPL, RETT, B*A(with a=0), or B*cc taken |

**Read/Write State Registers**

The read/write state register instructions access the program-visible state and status registers. These instructions read/write the state registers into/from *r* registers. A read/write Ancillary State Register instruction is privileged if the accessed register is privileged.

**Floating-Point Operate (FPop) Instructions**

Floating-point operate instructions (FPop's) are generally triadic-register-address instructions. They compute a result that is a function of one or two source operands and place the result in a destination *f* register. The exceptions are floating-point convert operations (which use one source and one destination operands) and floating-point compare operations (which do not write to an *f* register but update the *fcc* field of the FSR). If there is no attached floating-point unit or if PSR.EF = 0, an FPop instruction generates an fp_disabled trap.

The term "FPop" refers to those instructions encoded by the FPop1 and FPop2 opcodes and does **not** include branches based on the floating-point condition codes (FBfcc) or the load/store floating-point instructions.

All FPop instructions clear the *ftt* field and set the *cexc* field, unless they trap. Some FPop instructions also write the *fcc* field. All FPop instructions that can generate IEEE exceptions set the *cexc* and *aexc* fields, unless they trap. FABSs, FMOVs,and FNEGs can't generate IEEE exceptions, so clear *cexc* and leave *aexc* unchanged.

**Coprocessor Operate (CPop) Instructions**

The coprocessor operate instructions are executed by the attached coprocessor. If there is no attached coprocessor or PSR.EC = 0, a CPop instruction generates a cp_disabled trap.

The instruction fields of a CPop instruction, except for *op* and *op3*, are interpreted only by the coprocessor.

The term "CPop" refers to those instructions encoded by the CPop1 and CPop2 opcodes and does **not** include branches based on the coprocessor condition codes (CBccc) or the load/store coprocessor instructions.

SPARC International, Inc.

# 6

Memory Model

The SPARC **memory model** defines the semantics of memory operations such as load and store, and specifies how the order in which these operations are issued by a processor is related to the order in which they are executed by memory. It also specifies how instruction fetches are synchronized with memory operations.

The model applies both to uniprocessors and to shared-memory multiprocessors.

In the case of multiprocessor systems, the non-deterministic aspect of the memory model (see below) requires that the result of executing a program on a given implementation must be a possible result of executing the same program on the model machine defined by the architecture. This allows for unspecified (and unpredictable) timing-dependent effects of inter-processor interaction. Note that other events, such as interrupts and I/O, can also cause non-deterministic behavior.

As mentioned in Chapter 1, "Introduction", the SPARC architecture is a **model** which specifies the behavior observed by **software** on SPARC systems. Therefore, access to memory can be implemented in any manner in hardware, as long as the model described here is the one observed by software.

The standard memory model is called **Total Store Ordering (TSO)**. All SPARC implementations must provide at least the TSO model. An additional model called **Partial Store Ordering (PSO)** is defined, which allows higher-performance memory systems to be built. If present, this model is enabled via a system mode bit; if a SPARC Reference MMU is used, this bit is the PSO mode bit in the MMU control register. See Appendix H, "SPARC Reference MMU Architecture."

Machines that implement Strong Consistency (also called Strong Ordering) automatically support both TSO and PSO because the requirements of Strong Consistency are more stringent than either. In Strong Consistency, the loads, stores, and atomic load-stores of all processors are executed by memory serially in an order that conforms to the order in which these instructions were issued by individual processors. However, a machine that implements Strong Consistency may deliver lower performance than an equivalent machine that implements TSO or PSO. Although particular SPARC implementations may support Strong Consistency, software must not rely on having this model available on all machines. Strong Consistency is not the standard SPARC memory model.

SPARC International, Inc.

Programs written using single-writer-multiple-readers locks are portable across PSO, TSO, and Strong Consistency. Programs that use write-locks but read without locking are portable across PSO,TSO, and Strong Consistency only if writes to shared data are separated by STBAR instructions. If these STBAR instructions are omitted, then the code is portable only across TSO and Strong Consistency. The guidelines for other programs are as follows: Programs written for PSO work automatically on a machine running in TSO mode or on a machine that implements Strong Consistency; programs written for TSO work automatically on a machine that implements Strong Consistency; programs written for Strong Consistency may not work on a TSO or PSO machine; programs written for TSO may not work on a PSO machine.

Multithreaded programs in which all threads are restricted to run on a single processor behave the same on PSO and TSO as they would on a Strongly Consistent machine.

## 6.1. Basic Definitions

Memory is the collection of locations accessed by the load/store instructions (described in Appendix B, Sections B.1 through B.8). These locations include traditional memory, as well as I/O registers, and registers accessible via address space identifiers.

### Real Memory

**Real** (or **main**) memory is defined to be those memory locations accessed when either:

- the ASI field is 8, 9, 0xA, or 0xB, or

- the ASI field, together with a field in a corresponding MMU entry, implies a reference to real memory. (For example, when the Reference MMU is used, physical address pass-through ASIs 0x20-2F refer to real memory.)

Real memory should not be accessed by any other ASI, be in a coprocessor register, or be in an ancillary state register. The exact ASI assignments and MMU implementation details that define a real memory access are implementation-dependent.

A defining characteristic of real memory is that operations defined on it are free of side-effects; that is, a load, store, or atomic load-store to a location in real memory has no observable effect except on that location. All of the semantics of operations defined on real memory are captured by the memory model.

### Input/Output Locations

I/O registers are locations that are not real memory. In contrast to operations on real memory, load, store and atomic load-store operations on these locations may have observable side-effects. The semantics of operations on I/O locations are **not** defined by the memory model, since these semantics are typically implementation-dependent. All of the axioms of the memory model that constrain the ordering of operations apply equally to operations on real memory and I/O locations. In addition, the order in which operations to I/O locations by a given processor are executed by memory must conform to the "program order" of these operations for that processor. In other words, references to I/O locations are "strongly ordered" among themselves, but behave like TSO or PSO (whichever is applicable) when compared with references to real memory. I/O locations include the following:

(1)    Those memory locations accessed when the ASI field is **not** 8, 9, 0xA, 0xB, or 0x20-2F

(2)    Those memory locations accessed when the ASI field is 8, 9, 0xA, or 0xB and a field in a corresponding MMU entry (such as the cacheable bit in the Reference MMU described in Appendix H) identifies the access as an I/O access

(3)    Possibly coprocessor registers

(4)    Possibly ancillary state registers

SPARC assumes that input/output registers are accessed via load/store alternate instructions, normal load/store instructions, coprocessor instructions, or read/write ancillary state register instructions (RDASR, WRASR). In the load/store alternate instructions case, the I/O registers can only be accessed by the supervisor. If coprocessor instructions are used, whether the I/O registers can be accessed outside of supervisor code or not is implementation-dependent.

The contents and addresses of I/O registers are implementation-dependent.

**Overview of Model**

Memory is byte-addressed, with halfword accesses aligned on 2-byte boundaries, word accesses aligned on 4-byte boundaries, and doubleword accesses aligned on 8-byte boundaries. The largest datum that is atomically read or written by memory hardware is a doubleword. Also, memory references to different bytes, halfwords, and words in a given doubleword are treated for ordering purposes as references to the same location. Thus the unit of ordering for memory is a doubleword.

Memory is modeled as an $N$-port device (refer to Figure 6-1), where $N$ is the number of processors. A processor initiates memory operations via its port in what is called the **issuing order**. Each port contains a Store Buffer used to hold stores, FLUSHes, and atomic load-stores. A switch connects a single-port memory to one of the ports at a time, for the duration of each memory operation. The order in which this switch is thrown from one port to another is nondeterministic and defines the **memory order** of operations.

Figure 6-1    *Model of Memory*

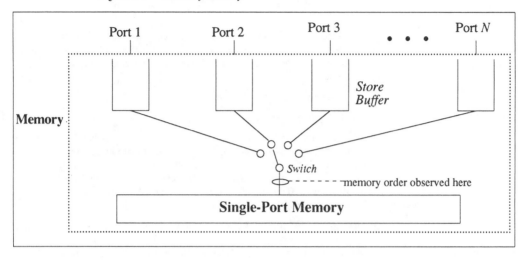

For purposes of the memory model, a processor consists of an Idealized Processor IP and an instruction buffer IBuf (refer to Figure 6-2). IP executes instructions one at a time as specified by the ISP, without overlap, in what is called **program order**. For each instruction, IP fetches the instruction from IBuf and then executes it, issuing any data loads and stores directly to the processor's memory port. For such a given **instruction fetch**, IBuf issues an **instruction load** via the processor's memory port if the instruction is not already in IBuf. The distinction between instruction fetches and instruction loads is important; confusing the two will lead to incorrect conclusions about the memory model. IBuf may also prefetch instructions via the memory port. Thus IBuf models the effects of instruction pipelining, FIFO instruction buffering, and/or a **non-consistent** instruction cache in a processor implementation. Note that the issuing order of data loads and stores conforms to the order of the corresponding instructions in program order. However, the issuing order of instruction loads in general **does not** conform to the order of instruction fetches, which defines program order. Also, the interleaving of instruction loads relative to data loads and stores is in general not known. The FLUSH instruction synchronizes instruction fetches with data loads and stores: when a processor executes FLUSH *A*, the data corresponding to location *A* is removed from the IBufs of **all** processors in the system some time after the execution of the FLUSH. An implementation may choose to flush any portion of IBuf as long as location *A* is included.

Figure 6-2     *Model of a Processor*

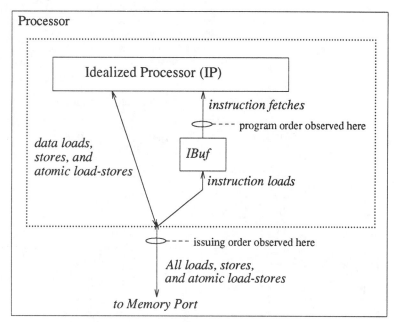

## 6.2. Total Store Ordering (TSO)

**Total Store Ordering** guarantees that the store, FLUSH, and atomic load-store instructions of all processors appear to be executed by memory serially in a single order called the memory order. Furthermore, the sequence of store, FLUSH, and atomic load-store instructions in the memory order for a given processor is identical to the sequence in which they were issued by the processor. Figure 6-3 shows the ordering constraints for this model graphically. A complete formal specification appears in Appendix K, "Formal Specification of the Memory Model."

Figure 6-3    *Total Store Ordering Model of Memory*

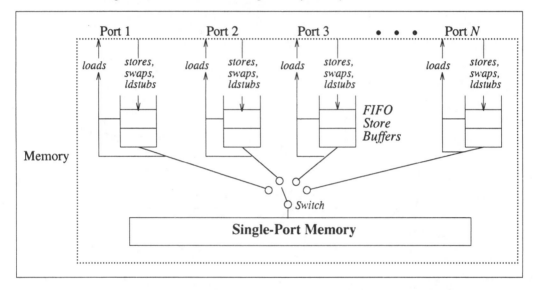

Stores, FLUSHes, and atomic load-stores issued by a processor are placed in its dedicated Store Buffer, which is FIFO. Thus the order in which memory executes these operations for a given processor is the same as the order in which the processor issued them. The memory order of these operations corresponds to the order in which the switch is thrown from one port to another.

A load by a processor first checks its Store Buffer to see if it contains a store to the same location (atomic load-stores do not need to be checked for because they block the processor). If it does, then the load returns the value of the most recent such store; otherwise the load goes directly to memory. Since not all loads go to memory, loads in general **do not** appear in the memory order. A processor is blocked from issuing further memory operations until the load returns a value.

An atomic load-store (SWAP or LDSTUB) behaves like both a load and a store. It is placed in the Store Buffer like a store, and it blocks the processor like a load. In other words, the atomic load-store blocks until the store buffer is empty and then proceeds to memory. A load therefore does not need to check for atomic load-stores in the Store Buffer because this situation cannot arise. When memory services an atomic load-store, it does so atomically: no other operation may intervene between the load and store parts of the load-store.

Programming Note    In the definition of TSO, the term "processor" may be replaced everywhere by the term "process" or "thread" as long as the process or thread switch sequence is written properly. See Appendix J, "Programming with the Memory Model," for the correct process switch sequence.

## 6.3. Partial Store Ordering (PSO)

**Partial Store Ordering** guarantees that the store, FLUSH, and atomic load-store instructions of all processors appear to be executed by memory serially in a single order called the memory order. However, the memory order of store, FLUSH, and atomic load-store instructions for a given processor is, in general, **not** the same as the order in which they were issued by that processor. Conformance between issuing order and memory order is provided by use of the STBAR instruction: if two of the above instructions are separated by an STBAR in the issuing order of a processor, or if they reference the same location, then the memory order of the two instructions is the same as the issuing order. Figure 6-4 shows the ordering constraints for this model graphically. A complete formal specification appears in Appendix K, "Formal Specification of the Memory Model."

Figure 6-4    *Partial Store Ordering Model of Memory*

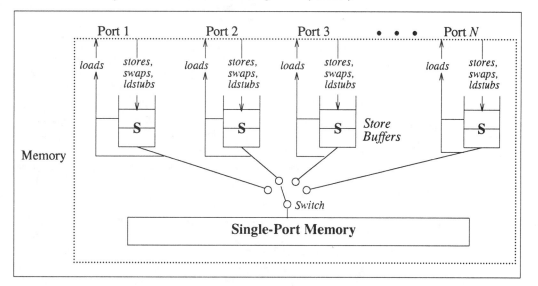

Stores, FLUSHes, and atomic load-stores issued by a processor are placed in its dedicated Store Buffer. This buffer is not guaranteed to be FIFO as it was in TSO; it does maintain the order of stores and atomic load-stores to the same location, but otherwise it is partitioned only by the occurrence of STBAR instructions. These instructions are shown in the figure as $S$ s. Thus the order in which memory executes two stores or atomic load-stores separated by an STBAR for a given processor is the same as the order in which the processor issued them. The memory order of these operations corresponds to the order in which the switch is thrown from one port to another.

Loads first check the Store Buffer for the processor to see if it contains a store to the same location (atomic load-stores don't need to be checked for because they block the processor). If it does, then the load returns the value of the most recent such store; otherwise the load goes directly to memory. Since not all loads go to memory, loads in general **do not** appear in the memory order. A processor is blocked from issuing further memory operations until the load returns a value.

An atomic load-store (SWAP or LDSTUB) behaves both like a load and a store. It is placed in the Store Buffer like a store, and it blocks the processor like a load. A load therefore does not need to check for atomic load-stores because this situation cannot arise. When memory services an atomic load-store, it does so atomically: no other operation may intervene between the load and store parts of an atomic load-store.

Implementation Note    The advantage of PSO over TSO is that it allows an implementation to have a higher-performance memory system. PSO therefore should be thought of as a performance optimization over TSO.

Implementation Note    See Appendix L, "Implementation Characteristics," for information on which of the various SPARC implementations support the PSO mode.

Programming Note    In the definition of PSO, the term "processor" may be replaced everywhere by the term "process" or "thread" as long as the process or thread switch sequence is written properly. See Figure J-4-2 in Appendix J, for the correct process switch sequence.

## 6.4. Mode Control

The memory model seen by a processor is controlled by the PSO bit in the MMU control register for that processor, if the processor has a SPARC Reference MMU. PSO = 0 specifies Total Store Ordering, while PSO = 1 specifies Partial Store Ordering. See Appendix H, "SPARC Reference MMU Architecture," for the location of this bit.

The STBAR instruction must execute as a NOP on machines that implement strong consistency, machines that implement only TSO, and machines that implement PSO but are running with PSO mode disabled.

Implementation Note    A given SPARC implementation must provide TSO, but it may or may not provide PSO. In implementations that do not provide PSO, setting the PSO mode bit has no effect.

Programming Note    Programs written for PSO will work automatically on a processor that is running in TSO mode. However, programs written for TSO will not in general work on a processor that is running in PSO mode. See Appendix J, "Programming with the Memory Model," for a more detailed discussion of portability.

## 6.5. FLUSH: Synchronizing Instruction Fetches with Memory Operations

The FLUSH instruction ensures that subsequent instruction fetches to the target of the FLUSH by the processor executing the FLUSH appear to execute after any loads, stores and atomic load-stores issued by that processor prior to the FLUSH. In a multiprocessor, FLUSH also ensures that stores and atomic load-stores to the target of the FLUSH issued by the processor executing the FLUSH prior to the FLUSH become visible to the instruction fetches of **all** other processors some time after the execution of the FLUSH. When a processor executes a sequence of store or atomic load-stores interspersed with appropriate FLUSH and STBAR instructions (the latter are needed only for PSO), the changes appear to the instruction fetches of all processors to occur in the order in which they were made. Figure 6-5 shows the operation of FLUSH graphically, assuming Processor 1 is the one executing the FLUSH. A complete formal specification of FLUSH appears in Appendix K, "Formal Specification of the Memory Model."

Figure 6-5    *Operation of a FLUSH Instruction, by Processor 1*

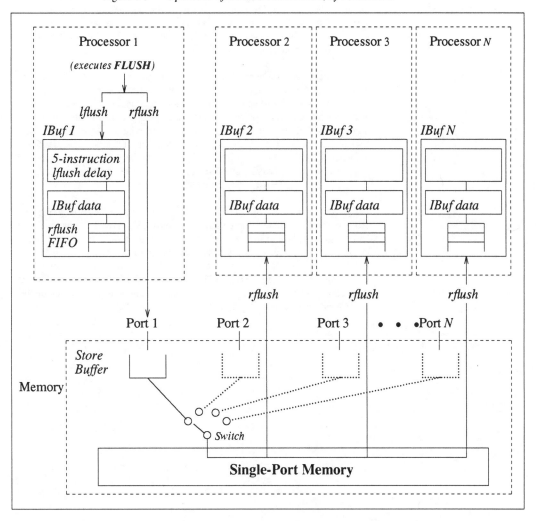

The IBuf of each processor consists of three elements: a 5-instruction local flush (*lflush*) delay that delays the execution of locally generated FLUSHes by at most 5 instructions; the IBuf data; and a remote flush (*rflush*) FIFO that contains flushes generated by remote processors. Processor 1 executes a FLUSH *A* by issuing a local flush (*lflush*) command to its IBuf and placing a remote flush

SPARC International, Inc.

(*rflush*) command in its store buffer and then proceeds to execute the next instruction. Processor 1's IBuf executes the *lflush* after at most a 5-instruction delay by invalidating the contents of address *A* in IBuf1. The *rflush* placed in the Store Buffer is treated exactly like a store for ordering purposes: it appears in the global memory order by going through the single port to memory and is then placed in the *rflush* FIFOs of processors other than the one executing the FLUSH. The *rflush* **does not** have any effect on the contents of Memory. A remote processor's IBuf invalidates the contents of address *A* when the *rflush* comes to the head of that processor's *rflush* FIFO.

The *lflush* guarantees that an instruction fetch to address *A* issued 5 instructions or more after the FLUSH *A* by Processor 1 will miss the IBuf and turn into an instruction load that will appear in the issuing order defined at Processor 1's memory port. Given the guarantees provided by the memory model, the instruction fetch will observe the value of a store done to *A* before the FLUSH. Note also, that the order of *lflush*es is preserved, so that if a processor executes the sequence ST *A*, FLUSH *A*, STBAR, ST *B*, FLUSH *B*, the instruction fetches of this processor will observe the two stores in the order in which they were issued. In TSO mode the STBAR is superfluous.

The guarantee provided by *rflush* is weaker: copies of *A* in the IBufs of remote processors are invalidated some time after the FLUSH is executed by Processor 1. In particular, Processor 1 **may not** assume that the remote IBufs have been invalidated at the time when it starts the execution of the instruction just after the FLUSH. Also note that since *rflush*es are ordered just like stores, the two stores in the sequence ST *A*, FLUSH *A*, STBAR, ST *B*, FLUSH *B* are observed by the instruction fetches of remote processors in the issuing order. In TSO mode the STBAR is superfluous, of course.

# 7

# Traps

A **trap** is a vectored transfer of control to the supervisor through a special trap table that contains the first 4 instructions of each trap handler. The base address of the table is established by the supervisor, by writing the Trap Base Address (TBA) field of an IU state register called the Trap Base Register (TBR). The displacement within the table is determined by the type of trap. Half of the table is reserved for hardware traps, and the other half is reserved for software traps as generated by software trap (Ticc) instructions.

A trap is like an unexpected procedure call. It decrements the current window pointer to the next register window and causes the hardware to write the trapped program counters into two *local* registers of the new window. In general, the trap handler saves the value of the PSR in another *local* register, and is free to use the other 5 *local* registers in the new window.

A trap may be caused by an instruction-induced **exception** or an external **interrupt request** not directly related to a particular instruction. Before it begins executing each instruction, the IU selects the highest-priority exception or interrupt request, and if there are any, causes a trap.

A **"non-resumable machine-check error"** exception is due to the detection of a hardware malfunction from which, due to its nature, the state of the processor at the time of the exception cannot be restored. Since the processor state cannot be restored, execution after such an exception is not resumable. Non-resumable machine-check errors are implementation-dependent. A possible example of such an error is a bus parity error.

## 7.1. Trap Categories

An exception or interrupt request can cause any of three categories of traps:

— A precise trap

— A deferred trap

— An interrupting trap

**Precise Trap**

A **precise trap** is induced by a particular instruction and occurs before any program-visible state has been changed by the trap-inducing instruction. When a precise trap occurs, several conditions must hold:

(1) The PC saved in r[17] (*local* register 1) points to the instruction which induced the trap, and the nPC saved in r[18] (*local* register 2) points at the

SPARC International, Inc.

instruction which was to be executed next.

(2)  The instructions before the one which induced the trap have completed execution.

(3)  The instructions after the one which induced the trap remain unexecuted.

**Deferred Trap**

A **deferred trap** is also induced by a particular instruction, but unlike a precise trap, a deferred trap may occur after program-visible state is changed. Such state may have been changed by the execution of either the trap-inducing instruction itself, or by one or more instructions that follow it.

A deferred trap may occur one or more instructions after the trap-inducing instruction is executed. However, a deferred trap must occur before the execution of any instruction that depends on the trap-inducing instruction. That is, a deferred trap may not be deferred past the execution of an instruction that specifies source registers, destination registers, condition codes, or any software-visible machine state that could be modified by the trap-inducing instruction.

A deferred trap may not be deferred past a precise trap, except for a floating-point exception or coprocessor exception, which may be deferred past a precise trap.

Associated with a particular deferred trap implementation there must exist:

(1)  An instruction that provokes a potentially outstanding deferred-trap exception to be taken as a trap.

(2)  The ability to resume execution of the trapped instruction stream.

(3)  Privileged instructions that access the state required for the supervisor to emulate a deferred-trap-inducing instruction, and resume execution of the trapped instruction stream. (This state is referred to as **deferred-trap queue(s)** in Chapter 4, "Registers.")

Note that resumable execution may involve emulation of instructions that did not complete execution by the time of the deferred trap (that is, those instructions in the deferred-trap queue).

Whether any deferred traps (and associated deferred-trap queues) are present is implementation-dependent. Note that to avoid deferred traps entirely, an implementation would need to execute all floating-point (and coprocessor, if any) instructions and take any exceptions they generate synchronously with the execution of integer instructions. A deferred-trap queue (e.g. FQ or CQ) would be superfluous in such an implementation.

**Interrupting Trap**

An **interrupting trap** is neither a precise trap nor a deferred trap. Interrupting traps are controlled by a combination of the Processor Interrupt Level (PIL) field of the PSR and the Trap Enable (ET) field of the PSR.

An interrupting trap may be due to:

(1)  An external interrupt request not directly related to a previously-executed instruction,

(2)  An exception not directly related to a previously-executed instruction, or

(3)  An exception caused by a previously-executed instruction.

The meaning of these causes is as follows:

Cause (1):  An external interrupt request can be induced by the assertion of an external signal not directly related to any particular processor or memory state. An example of this is the assertion of an "I/O done" signal.

Cause (2):  An interrupting trap due to an exception not directly related to a previously-executed instruction can be caused by the detection of arbitrary implementation-dependent processor or system state. An example of this is an exception generated by breakpoint logic that depends on fetched but unexecuted instructions, or on processor execution history.

Cause (3):  An interrupting trap due to an earlier instruction causing an exception, is similar to a deferred trap in that it occurs after instructions following the trap-inducing instruction have modified the processor or memory state. The difference is that an instruction that induces such an interrupting trap cannot necessarily be emulated, since the implementation does not preserve the necessary state. An example of this is an ECC data access error reported after the corresponding load instruction has completed.

## 7.2. Trap Models

Since user application programs do not "see" traps unless they install user trap handlers via supervisor software, and the treatment of implementation-dependent "non-resumable machine-check" error exceptions can vary across systems, SPARC allows an implementation to provide alternative trap models for a particular exception type.

Specifically, a particular exception may result in either a precise trap, a deferred trap, or an interrupting trap, depending on the implementation. (Note that external interrupt requests by definition always cause interrupting traps.)

However, in order to support user trap handlers and virtualizable instructions, SPARC defines a **default trap model that must be available in all implementations**.

### Default Trap Model

The SPARC **default trap model** predicates that all traps must be **precise**, with four exceptions:

(1)  Floating-point and coprocessor exceptions (fp_exception, cp_exception) may be deferred.

(2)  Implementation-dependent "non-resumable machine-check" exceptions may be deferred or interrupting.

(3)  An exception caused after the primary access of a multiple-access load/store instruction (load/store double, atomic load/store, and SWAP) may be interrupting if it is due to a "non-resumable machine-check" exception. Thus, a

trap due to the second memory access can occur after the processor or memory state has been modified by the first access.

(4)  An exception caused by an event unrelated to the instruction stream is an interrupting trap, therefore is not precise.

These four cases are implementation-dependent.

If another floating-point exception is currently deferred, an attempt to execute a floating-point instruction (FPop, FBfcc, or floating-point load/store) invokes or causes the outstanding fp_exception trap. Likewise, if a coprocessor exception is currently deferred, an attempt to execute another coprocessor instruction (CPop, CBccc, or coprocessor load/store) invokes the outstanding cp_exception trap.

Implementation Note    To provide the capability to terminate a user process on the occurrence of a "mnon-resumable machine-check" exception that can cause a deferred or interrupting trap, an implementation should provide one or more instructions that provoke an outstanding condition to be taken as a trap. For example, an outstanding floating-point exception is provoked into causing an fp_exception trap by execution of any FPop, load or store floating-point including STFSR), or FBfcc instruction.

## Enhanced Trap Model

User-application programs do not "see" traps unless they explicitly request to handle them. Thus, SPARC provides an implementation-dependent performance enhancement to the default model and allows for implementations with an **enhanced trap model,** wherein certain traps may be deferred or interrupting instead of precise.

Specifically, whether a particular trap must be precise or not depends on whether a user application program requests of the supervisor the capability to handle the particular exception that generates the trap. A user trap-handler registration request implies that when a particular trap occurs, the supervisor will return control to the user application program at a predetermined address specified by the program.

The SPARC enhanced trap model predicates that a particular trap **must adhere to the default model if a user application program installs a user trap handler for that trap with the supervisor.** Thus, an exception must be able to trap in hardware as:

(1)  A precise trap,  or

(2)  A deferred trap for floating-point or coprocessor exceptions, or

(3)  A deferred or interrupting trap for an implementation-dependent "non-resumable machine-check" exception.

If a user application program does not install a trap handler (via supervisor software) for a given trap, that trap can be a deferred or an interrupting trap. The type (precise, deferred, or interrupting) of a particular trap must remain constant for all occurrences of the associated exception for a particular program or process. Therefore, if a user program is to install its own trap handler for a given trap, it must do so before the first occurrence of that trap in the program.

An instruction that accesses hardware state that controls whether a particular trap is precise or not must be a privileged instruction (for example, load/store alternate, privileged read/write ASR, read/write PSR *ver* field).

Whether a particular trap is implemented according to the enhanced trap model is supervisor- and implementation-dependent.

Programming Note    A request to the supervisor to register a user trap handler can specify that the associated exception will be handled by the user program in a non-resumable manner. In this case, the supervisor can elect not to cause the associated trap to be precise.

Programming Note    After a precise trap, the supervisor can:

(1) Return to the instruction that caused the trap and re-execute it (PC ← old PC, nPC ← old nPC), or

(2) Emulate the instruction that caused the trap and return to the instruction (temporally) following that instruction (PC ← old nPC, nPC ← old nPC + 4), or

(3) Terminate the program or process associated with the trap.

After a deferred trap, the supervisor can:

(1) Emulate the instruction that caused the exception, emulate or cause to execute any other execution-deferred instructions that were in an associated deferred-trap state queue, and return control to the instruction at which the deferred trap was invoked, or

(2) Terminate the program or process associated with the trap.

After an interrupting trap, the supervisor can:

(1) Return to the instruction at which the trap was invoked (PC ← old PC, nPC ← old nPC), or

(2) Terminate the program or process associated with the trap.

In the presence of user trap handlers, the supervisor can pass a record to the user trap handler containing the address of the trap-inducing instruction, the trapped PC and nPC addresses, and any associated state required to emulate the instruction. The user trap handler can resume execution at an alternate address or can return control to the supervisor. The supervisor can process any remaining entries in an associated deferred-trap state queue and can eventually return to the instructions at the trap PC and nPC.

## 7.3. Trap Control

Traps are controlled by several registers: exception and interrupt requests via the enable traps (ET) field in the PSR, interrupt requests via the processor interrupt level (PIL) field in the PSR, and floating-point exceptions via the trap enable mask (TEM) in the FSR.

### ET and PIL Control

The ET bit in the PSR must be 1 for traps to occur normally. While ET = 1, the IU — between the execution of instructions — prioritizes the outstanding exceptions and interrupt requests according to Table 7-1. At a given time, only the highest priority exception or interrupt request is taken as a trap. (When there are multiple outstanding exceptions or interrupt requests, SPARC assumes that lower priority interrupt requests will persist and lower priority exceptions will recur if an exception-causing instruction is re-executed.)

For interrupt requests, the IU compares the interrupt request level (bp_IRL) against the processor interrupt level (PIL) field of the PSR. If bp_IRL is greater than PIL, or if bp_IRL = 15 (unmaskable), then the processor takes the interrupt request trap — assuming that there are no higher priority exceptions outstanding. How quickly a processor responds to an interrupt request, and the method by which an interrupt request is removed, is implementation-dependent.

While ET = 0:

- Interrupting traps cannot occur, and all interrupt requests are ignored, even if bp_IRL = 15.

- If a precise trap occurs, or if there is an attempt to execute an instruction that can invoke a deferred trap and there is a pending deferred-trap exception, the processor halts execution and enters the error_mode state.

- If a deferred trap occurs which was caused by an instruction that began execution while ET = 0, the deferred trap causes the processor to halt execution and enter the error_mode state.

- Any deferred-trap exception that was caused by an instruction that began execution while ET = 1 is ignored.

**TEM Control**

The occurrence of floating-point IEEE_754_exceptions can be controlled via the user-accessible trap enable mask (TEM) field of the FSR. If a particular bit of TEM is 1, the associated IEEE_754_exception can cause an fp_exception trap.

If a particular bit of TEM is 0, the associated IEEE_754_exception does not cause an fp_exception trap. Instead, the occurrence of the IEEE_754_exception is recorded in the FSR's accrued exception field (*aexc*).

If a floating-point exception of type IEEE_754_exception results in an fp_exception trap, then the destination *f* register, *fcc*, and *aexc* fields remain unchanged. However, if an IEEE_754_exception does not result in a trap, then the *f* register, *fcc*, and *aexc* fields are updated to their new values.

## 7.4. Trap Identification

The supervisor initializes the trap base address (TBA) field of the trap base register (TBR) to the upper 20 bits of the trap table address.

**Trap Type (*tt*)**

When a trap occurs (except for an external reset request), a value that uniquely identifies the trap is written into the 8-bit *tt* field of the TBR by the hardware. Control is then transferred into the supervisor trap table to the address contained in the 32-bit TBR. Since the low 4 bits of the TBR are zero, each entry in the trap table contains the first 16 bytes (4 words) of the corresponding trap handler.

The *tt* field allows for 256 distinct types of traps — half for hardware traps and half for software traps. Values 0 to 0x7F are reserved for hardware traps. Values 0x80 to 0xFF are reserved for software traps (traps caused by execution of a Ticc instruction). The assignment of *tt* values to traps is shown in Table 7-1. Note that the *tt* field remains valid until another trap occurs.

Since the assignment of exceptions and interrupt requests to particular trap vector addresses and the priority levels are not visible to a user application program, implementations are allowed to define additional hardware traps.

Specifically, *tt* values 0x60 to 0x7F are reserved for implementation-dependent exceptions. See Appendix L, "Implementation Characteristics."

Values in the range 0 to 0x5F that are not assigned in Table 7-1 are reserved for future versions of the architecture.

**Error Mode**

The processor enters error_mode state when a trap occurs while ET = 0. An implementation should preserve as much processor state as possible when this happens. Standard trap actions (such as decrementing CWP and saving state information in *locals*) should not occur when entering error_mode. In particular, the *tt* field of the TBR is only written during a transition into error_mode state in the singular case of a RETT instruction that traps while ET = 0. In this case, *tt* is written to indicate the type of exception that was induced by the RETT instruction.

What occurs after error_mode is entered is implementation-dependent; typically the processor triggers an external reset, causing a reset trap (see below).

**Reset Trap**

A reset trap is triggered by an external reset request, and causes a transfer of control to address 0.

Supervisor software may not assume that any particular processor or memory state, except for the PSR's ET and S bits, has been initialized after a reset trap.

When a reset trap occurs, the *tt* field is not written and reflects its value from the last previous trap. In the case of an external reset request caused by power-up, the value of the *tt* field is undefined.

**Trap Priorities**

The following table shows the assignment of exceptions to *tt* values and the relative priority of exceptions and interrupt requests. Priority 1 is highest and priority 31 is lowest; that is, if X < Y, a pending exception or interrupt request of priority X is taken instead of a pending exception or interrupt request of priority Y.

Note that particular trap priorities are implementation-dependent, because a future version of the architecture may define new traps, and implementations can define implementation-dependent traps. However, the *tt* values for the exceptions and interrupt requests shown in Table 7-1 must remain the **same** for every implementation.

Table 7-1    *Exception and Interrupt Request Priority and tt Values*

| Exception or Interrupt Request | Priority | tt |
|---|---|---|
| reset | 1 | (see text) |
| data_store_error | 2 | 0x2B |
| instruction_access_MMU_miss | 2 | 0x3C |
| instruction_access_error | 3 | 0x21 |
| r_register_access_error | 4 | 0x20 |
| instruction_access_exception | 5 | 0x01 |
| privileged_instruction | 6 | 0x03 |
| illegal_instruction | 7 | 0x02 |
| fp_disabled | 8 | 0x04 |
| cp_disabled | 8 | 0x24 |
| unimplemented_FLUSH | 8 | 0x25 |
| watchpoint_detected | 8 | 0x0B |
| window_overflow | 9 | 0x05 |
| window_underflow | 9 | 0x06 |
| mem_address_not_aligned | 10 | 0x07 |
| fp_exception | 11 | 0x08 |
| cp_exception | 11 | 0x28 |
| data_access_error | 12 | 0x29 |
| data_access_MMU_miss | 12 | 0x2C |
| data_access_exception | 13 | 0x09 |
| tag_overflow | 14 | 0x0A |
| division_by_zero | 15 | 0x2A |
| trap_instruction | 16 | 0x80 – 0xFF |
| interrupt_level_15 | 17 | 0x1F |
| interrupt_level_14 | 18 | 0x1E |
| interrupt_level_13 | 19 | 0x1D |
| interrupt_level_12 | 20 | 0x1C |
| interrupt_level_11 | 21 | 0x1B |
| interrupt_level_10 | 22 | 0x1A |
| interrupt_level_9 | 23 | 0x19 |
| interrupt_level_8 | 24 | 0x18 |
| interrupt_level_7 | 25 | 0x17 |
| interrupt_level_6 | 26 | 0x16 |
| interrupt_level_5 | 27 | 0x15 |
| interrupt_level_4 | 28 | 0x14 |
| interrupt_level_3 | 29 | 0x13 |
| interrupt_level_2 | 30 | 0x12 |
| interrupt_level_1 | 31 | 0x11 |
| impl.-dependent exception | impl.-dep. | 0x60 – 0x7F |

SPARC International, Inc.

**7.5. Trap Definition**

A trap causes the following to occur, if ET = 1:

□   Traps are disabled: ET ← 0.

□   The existing user/supervisor mode is preserved: PS ← S.

□   The user/supervisor mode is changed to supervisor: S ← 1.

□   The register window is advanced to a new window:
    CWP ← ((CWP − 1) modulo NWINDOWS)
    [note: *without* test for window overflow].

□   The trapped program counters are saved in *local* registers 1 and 2 of the new window: r[17] ← PC, r[18] ← nPC.

□   The *tt* field is written to the particular value that identifies the exception or interrupt request, except as defined for "Reset Trap" and "Error Mode" above.

□   If the trap is a reset trap, control is transferred to address 0:
    PC ← 0, nPC ← 4.
    If the trap is not a reset trap, control is transferred into the trap table:
    PC ← TBR, nPC ← TBR + 4.

If ET=0 and a precise trap occurs, the processor enters the error_mode state and halts execution. If ET=0 and an interrupt request or an interrupting or deferred exception occurs, it is ignored.

Implementation Note    When error_mode is entered, a minimum amount of processor state should be altered. From error_mode, the processor can be restarted via an external reset request, which results in a reset trap.

Programming Note    A trap handler should alter the PSR fields in a reversible way (ET, CWP), or should not change them until the PSR has been saved.

**7.6. Exception/Interrupt Descriptions**

The following paragraphs describe the various exceptions and interrupt requests and the conditions that cause them. Appendix B, "Instruction Definitions," and Appendix C, "ISP Descriptions," also summarize which traps can be generated by each instruction.

Since the precise conditions for some of these exceptions are implementation-dependent, several of these definitions cannot be precise. In particular, the definition of the terms "peremptory error exception" and "blocking error exception" are implementation-dependent. Further, whether a SPARC processor generates an exception of either of these types is implementation-dependent. Example exception conditions are included for these cases.

reset
    A reset trap is caused by an external reset request. It causes the processor to begin executing at virtual address 0. Supervisor software cannot assume that particular processor or memory state, except for the PSR's ET and S bits, has been initialized after a reset trap.

SPARC International, Inc.

data_store_error
> A peremptory error exception occurred on a data store to memory (for example, a bus parity error on a store from a store buffer).

instruction_access_MMU_miss
> A miss in an MMU occurred on an instruction access from memory. For example, a PDC or TLB did not contain a translation for the virtual adddress.

instruction_access_error
> A peremptory error exception occurred on an instruction access (for example, a parity error on an instruction cache access).

r_register_access_error
> A peremptory error exception occurred on an *r* register access (for example, a parity error on an *r* register read).

instruction_access_exception
> A blocking error exception occurred on an instruction access (for example, an MMU indicated that the page was invalid or read-protected).

privileged_instruction
> An attempt was made to execute a privileged instruction while S = 0.

illegal_instruction
> An attempt was made to execute an instruction with an unimplemented opcode, or an UNIMP instruction, or an instruction that would result in illegal processor state (for example, writing an illegal CWP into the PSR). Note that unimplemented FPop and unimplemented CPop instructions generate fp_exception and cp_exception traps, and that an implementor may cause an unimplemented FLUSH instruction to generate an unimplemented_FLUSH trap instead of an illegal_instruction trap.

unimplemented_FLUSH
> An attempt was made to execute a FLUSH instruction, the semantics of which are not fully implemented in hardware. Use of this trap is implementation-dependent. See the FLUSH Instruction page in Appendix B.

watchpoint_detected

>An instruction fetch memory address or load/store data memory address matched the contents of a pre-loaded implementation-dependent "watchpoint" register. Whether a SPARC processor generates watchpoint_detected exceptions is implementation-dependent.

fp_disabled

>An attempt was made to execute an FPop, FBfcc, or a floating-point load/store instruction while EF = 0 or an FPU was not present.

cp_disabled

>An attempt was made to execute an CPop, CBccc, or a coprocessor load/store instruction while EC = 0 or a coprocessor was not present.

window_overflow

>A SAVE instruction attempted to cause the CWP to point to a window marked invalid in the WIM.

window_underflow

>A RESTORE or RETT instruction attempted to cause the CWP to point to a window marked invalid in the WIM.

mem_address_not_aligned

>A load/store instruction would have generated a memory address that was not properly aligned according to the instruction, or a JMPL or RETT instruction would have generated a non-word-aligned address.

fp_exception

>An FPop instruction generated an IEEE_754_exception and its corresponding trap enable mask (TEM) bit was 1, or the FPop was unimplemented, or the FPop did not complete, or there was a sequence or hardware error in the FPU. The type of floating-point exception is encoded in the FSR's *ftt* field.

cp_exception

>A coprocessor instruction generated an exception.

data_access_error

>A peremptory error exception occurred on a load/store data access from/to memory (for example, a parity error on a data cache access, or an uncorrectable ECC memory error).

SPARC International, Inc.

data_access_MMU_miss

> A miss in an MMU occurred on a load/store access from/to memory. For example, a PDC or TLB did not contain a translation for the virtual adddress.

data_access_exception

> A blocking error exception occurred on a load/store data access. (for example, an MMU indicated that the page was invalid or write-protected).

tag_overflow

> A TADDccTV or TSUBccTV instruction was executed, and either arithmetic overflow occurred or at least one of the tag bits of the operands was nonzero.

division_by_zero

> An integer divide instruction attempted to divide by zero.

trap_instruction

> A Ticc instruction was executed and the trap condition evaluated to true.

interrupt_level_$n$

> An external interrupt request level (bp_IRL) of value $n$ was presented to the IU, while ET = 1 **and** ( (bp_IRL = 15) **or** (bp_IRL > PIL) ).

# A

# Suggested Assembly Language Syntax

This appendix supports Appendix B, "Instruction Definitions." Each instruction description in Appendix B includes a table that describes the suggested assembly language format for that instruction. This appendix describes the notation used in those assembly language syntax descriptions and lists some synthetic instructions that may be provided by a SPARC assembler for the convenience of assembly language programmers.

**A.1. Notation Used**

**Understanding the use of type fonts is crucial to understanding the syntax descriptions in Appendix B.** Items in `typewriter font` are literals to be written exactly as they appear. Items in *italic font* are metasymbols which are to be replaced by numeric or symbolic values when actual SPARC assembly language code is written. For example, *"asi"* would be replaced by a number in the range 0 to 255 (the value of the asi bits in the binary instruction), or by a symbol bound to such a number.

Subscripts on metasymbols further identify the placement of the operand in the generated binary instruction. For example, $reg_{rs2}$ is a *reg* (register name) whose binary value will be placed in the *rs2* field of the resulting instruction.

Register Names

*reg*   A *reg* is an integer register name. It can have one of the following values † :

```
%r0 ... %r31
%g0 ... %g7    (global registers; same as %r0  ... %r7 )
%o0 ... %o7    (out   registers; same as %r8  ... %r15)
%l0 ... %l7    (local  registers; same as %r16 ... %r23)
%i0 ... %i7    (in    registers; same as %r24 ... %r31)
%fp            (frame pointer; conventionally same as %i6)
%sp            (stack pointer; conventionally same as %o6)
```

Subscripts further identify the placement of the operand in the binary instruction as one of the following:

| | |
|---|---|
| $reg_{rs1}$ | (*rs1* field) |
| $reg_{rs2}$ | (*rs2* field) |
| $reg_{rd}$ | (*rd* field) |

---

† In actual usage, the `%sp`, `%fp`, `%g`n, `%o`n, `%l`n, and `%i`n forms are preferred over `%r`n.

SPARC International, Inc.

*freg*    An *freg* is a floating-point register name. It can have one of the
following values:

    `%f0 ... %f31`

Subscripts further identify the placement of the operand in the
binary instruction as one of the following:

| | |
|---|---|
| $freg_{rs1}$ | (*rs1* field) |
| $freg_{rs2}$ | (*rs2* field) |
| $freg_{rd}$ | (*rd* field) |

*creg*    A *creg* is a coprocessor register name. It can have one of the following values:

    `%c0 ... %c31`

Subscripts further identify the placement of the operand in the
binary instruction as one of the following:

| | |
|---|---|
| $creg_{rs1}$ | (*rs1* field) |
| $creg_{rs2}$ | (*rs2* field) |
| $creg_{rd}$ | (*rd* field) |

*asr_reg*

An *asr_reg* is an Ancillary State Register name. It can have one
of the following values:
    `%asr1 ... %asr31`

Subscripts further identify the placement of the operand in the
binary instruction as one of the following:

| | |
|---|---|
| $asr\_reg_{rs1}$ | (*rs1* field) |
| $asr\_reg_{rd}$ | (*rd* field) |

## Special Symbol Names

Certain special symbols appear in the syntax table in `typewriter`
`font`. They need to be written exactly as they are shown, including the
leading percent sign (`%`). The percent sign is part of the symbol name and
must appear literally.

The symbol names and the registers or operators to which they refer are
as follows:

| | |
|---|---|
| `%psr` | Processor State Register |
| `%wim` | Window Invalid Mask register |
| `%tbr` | Trap Base Register |
| `%y` | Y register |
| `%fsr` | Floating-Point State Register |
| `%csr` | Coprocessor State Register |
| `%fq` | Floating-Point Queue |
| `%cq` | Coprocessor Queue |
| `%hi` | Unary operator which extracts high 22 bits of its operand |
| `%lo` | Unary operator which extracts low 10 bits of its operand |

Immediate Values

| | |
|---|---|
| *imm7* | An immediate constant in the range -64..127 (representable in 7 bits, signed or unsigned) |
| *uimm7* | An immediate constant in the range 0..127 (representable in 7 bits, unsigned) |
| *simm13* | An immediate constant in the range -4096..4095 (representable in 13 bits, signed) |
| *const22* | A constant that can be represented in 22 bits |
| *asi* | An address space identifier; an immediate constant in the range 0..255 (representable in 8 bits, unsigned) |

Labels

A label is a sequence of characters comprised of alphabetic letters (a–z, A–Z [upper and lower case distinct]), underscores (_), dollar signs ($), periods (.), and decimal digits (0-9). A label may contain decimal digits, but cannot begin with one.

Other Operand Syntax

Some instructions use a variety of operand syntax. This syntax are defined as follows:

*address* may be any of the following:
$reg_{rs1}$       (equivalent to: $reg_{rs1}$ + %g0)
$reg_{rs1}$ + $reg_{rs2}$
$reg_{rs1}$ + $simm13$
$reg_{rs1}$ − $simm13$
$simm13$       (equivalent to: %g0 + $simm13$)
$simm13$ + $reg_{rs1}$     (equivalent to: $reg_{rs1}$ + $simm13$)

*regaddr* ("register-only address") may be any of the following:
$reg_{rs1}$       (equivalent to: $reg_{rs1}$ + %g0)
$reg_{rs1}$ + $reg_{rs2}$

*reg_or_imm* ("register or immediate value") may be either of:
$reg_{rs2}$
$simm13$

*software_trap#* may be any of the following:
$reg_{rs1}$       (equivalent to: $reg_{rs1}$ + %g0)
$reg_{rs1}$ + $reg_{rs2}$
$reg_{rs1}$ + $imm7$
$reg_{rs1}$ − $imm7$
$uimm7$       (equivalent to: %g0 + $uimm7$)
$imm7$ + $reg_{rs1}$     (equivalent to: $reg_{rs1}$ + $imm7$)

The resulting operand value (software trap number) must be in the range 0 ... 127, inclusive.

SPARC International, Inc.

Other Operand Syntax

Some instructions use a variety of operand syntax. This syntax are defined as follows:

*address* may be any of the following:

| | |
|---|---|
| $reg_{rs1}$ | (equivalent to: $reg_{rs1}$ + %g0) |
| $reg_{rs1}$ + $reg_{rs2}$ | |
| $reg_{rs1}$ + $simm13$ | |
| $reg_{rs1}$ − $simm13$ | |
| $simm13$ | (equivalent to: %g0 + $simm13$) |
| $simm13$ + $reg_{rs1}$ | (equivalent to: $reg_{rs1}$ + $simm13$) |

*regaddr* ("register-only address") may be any of the following:

| | |
|---|---|
| $reg_{rs1}$ | (equivalent to: $reg_{rs1}$ + %g0) |
| $reg_{rs1}$ + $reg_{rs2}$ | |

*reg_or_imm* ("register or immediate value") may be either of:

$reg_{rs2}$
$simm13$

*software_trap#* may be any of the following:

| | |
|---|---|
| $reg_{rs1}$ | (equivalent to: $reg_{rs1}$ + %g0) |
| $reg_{rs1}$ + $reg_{rs2}$ | |
| $reg_{rs1}$ + $simm13$ | |
| $reg_{rs1}$ − $simm13$ | |
| $simm13$ | (equivalent to: %g0 + $simm13$) |
| $simm13$ + $reg_{rs1}$ | (equivalent to: $reg_{rs1}$ + $simm13$) |

The resulting operand value (software trap number) must be in the range 0 ... 127, inclusive.

Comments

Two types of comments are accepted by most SPARC assemblers: C-style "/ * . . . * /" comments (which may span multiple lines), and " ! . . ." comments, which extend from the " ! " to the end of the line.

## A.2. Syntax Design

The suggested SPARC assembly language syntax is designed so that:

- The destination operand (if any) is consistently specified as the last (right-most) operand in an assembly language statement.

- A reference to the **contents** of a memory location (in a Load, Store, or SWAP instruction) is always indicated by square brackets ( [ ] ). A reference to the **address** of a memory location (such as in a JMPL, CALL, or SETHI) is specified directly, without square brackets.

## A.3. Synthetic Instructions

The table shown below describes the mapping of a set of synthetic (or "pseudo") instructions to actual SPARC instructions. These synthetic instructions may be provided in a SPARC assembler for the convenience of assembly language programmers.

Note that synthetic instructions should not be confused with "pseudo-ops", which typically provide information to the assembler but do not generate instructions. Synthetic instructions always generate instructions; they provide more mnemonic syntax for standard SPARC instructions.

Table A-1     *Mapping of Synthetic Instructions to SPARC Instructions*

| Synthetic Instruction | SPARC Instruction(s) | Comment |
|---|---|---|
| cmp      $reg_{rs1}$, $reg\_or\_imm$ | subcc     $reg_{rs1}$, $reg\_or\_imm$, %g0 | *compare* |
| jmp      *address* | jmpl     *address*, %g0 | |
| call     *address* | jmpl     *address*, %o7 | |
| tst      $reg_{rs2}$ | orcc     %g0, $reg_{rs2}$, %g0 | *test* |
| ret | jmpl     %i7+8, %g0 | *return from subroutine* |
| retl | jmpl     %o7+8, %g0 | *return from leaf subroutine* |
| restore | restore %g0, %g0, %g0 | *trivial* restore |
| save | save     %g0, %g0, %g0 | *trivial* save<br>*(Warning: trivial* save *should only be used in kernel code!)* |
| set      *value*, $reg_{rd}$ | sethi     %hi(*value*), $reg_{rd}$<br>**or**<br>or     %g0, *value*, $reg_{rd}$<br>**or**<br>sethi     %hi(*value*), $reg_{rd}$;<br>or     $reg_{rd}$, %lo(*value*), $reg_{rd}$ | *(when ((value&0x1fff) == 0))*<br><br>*(when -4096 ≤ value ≤ 4095)*<br><br>*(otherwise)*<br><br>*Warning: do not use* set *in the delay slot of a DCTI.* |
| not      $reg_{rs1}$, $reg_{rd}$<br>not      $reg_{rd}$ | xnor     $reg_{rs1}$, %g0, $reg_{rd}$<br>xnor     $reg_{rd}$, %g0, $reg_{rd}$ | *one's complement*<br>*one's complement* |
| neg      $reg_{rs2}$, $reg_{rd}$<br>neg      $reg_{rd}$ | sub     %g0, $reg_{rs2}$, $reg_{rd}$<br>sub     %g0, $reg_{rd}$, $reg_{rd}$ | *two's complement*<br>*two's complement* |

Table A-1    *Mapping of Synthetic Instructions to SPARC Instructions— Continued*

| Synthetic Instruction | | SPARC Instruction(s) | | Comment |
|---|---|---|---|---|
| inc | $reg_{rd}$ | add | $reg_{rd}, 1, reg_{rd}$ | *increment by 1* |
| inc | $const13, reg_{rd}$ | add | $reg_{rd}, const13, reg_{rd}$ | *increment by const13* |
| inccc | $reg_{rd}$ | addcc | $reg_{rd}, 1, reg_{rd}$ | *increment by 1 and set icc* |
| inccc | $const13, reg_{rd}$ | addcc | $reg_{rd}, const13, reg_{rd}$ | *increment by const13 and set icc* |
| dec | $reg_{rd}$ | sub | $reg_{rd}, 1, reg_{rd}$ | *decrement by 1* |
| dec | $const13, reg_{rd}$ | sub | $reg_{rd}, const13, reg_{rd}$ | *decrement by const13* |
| deccc | $reg_{rd}$ | subcc | $reg_{rd}, 1, reg_{rd}$ | *decrement by 1 and set icc* |
| deccc | $const13, reg_{rd}$ | subcc | $reg_{rd}, const13, reg_{rd}$ | *decrement by const13 and set icc* |
| btst | $reg\_or\_imm, reg_{rs1}$ | andcc | $reg_{rs1}, reg\_or\_imm, \%g0$ | *bit test* |
| bset | $reg\_or\_imm, reg_{rd}$ | or | $reg_{rd}, reg\_or\_imm, reg_{rd}$ | *bit set* |
| bclr | $reg\_or\_imm, reg_{rd}$ | andn | $reg_{rd}, reg\_or\_imm, reg_{rd}$ | *bit clear* |
| btog | $reg\_or\_imm, reg_{rd}$ | xor | $reg_{rd}, reg\_or\_imm, reg_{rd}$ | *bit toggle* |
| clr | $reg_{rd}$ | or | $\%g0, \%g0, reg_{rd}$ | *clear(zero) register* |
| clrb | $[address]$ | stb | $\%g0, [address]$ | *clear byte* |
| clrh | $[address]$ | sth | $\%g0, [address]$ | *clear halfword* |
| clr | $[address]$ | st | $\%g0, [address]$ | *clear word* |
| mov | $reg\_or\_imm, reg_{rd}$ | or | $\%g0, reg\_or\_imm, reg_{rd}$ | |
| mov | $\%y, reg_{rd}$ | rd | $\%y, reg_{rd}$ | |
| mov | $\%asrn, reg_{rd}$ | rd | $\%asrn, reg_{rd}$ | |
| mov | $\%psr, reg_{rd}$ | rd | $\%psr, reg_{rd}$ | |
| mov | $\%wim, reg_{rd}$ | rd | $\%wim, reg_{rd}$ | |
| mov | $\%tbr, reg_{rd}$ | rd | $\%tbr, reg_{rd}$ | |
| mov | $reg\_or\_imm, \%y$ | wr | $\%g0, reg\_or\_imm, \%y$ | |
| mov | $reg\_or\_imm, \%asrn$ | wr | $\%g0, reg\_or\_imm, \%asrn$ | |
| mov | $reg\_or\_imm, \%psr$ | wr | $\%g0, reg\_or\_imm, \%psr$ | |
| mov | $reg\_or\_imm, \%wim$ | wr | $\%g0, reg\_or\_imm, \%wim$ | |
| mov | $reg\_or\_imm, \%tbr$ | wr | $\%g0, reg\_or\_imm, \%tbr$ | |

# B

![decorative band]

# Instruction Definitions

This Appendix includes a description of each SPARC instruction. More detailed algorithmic definitions appear in Appendix C, "ISP Descriptions."

Related instructions are grouped into subsections. Each subsection consists of five parts:

(1) A table of the opcodes defined in the subsection with the values of the field(s) which uniquely identify the instruction(s).

(2) An illustration of the applicable instruction format(s).

(3) A list of the suggested assembly language syntax. (The syntax notation is described in Appendix A.)

(4) A description of the salient features, restrictions, and trap conditions. Note that in these descriptions, the symbol ⬜ designates concatenation of bit vectors. A comma ',' on the left side of an assignment separates quantities that are concatenated for the purpose of assignment. For example, if X, Y, and Z are 1-bit vectors, and the 2-bit vector T equals $11_2$, then:

$$(X, \ Y, \ Z) \ \leftarrow \ 0\,\square\,T$$

results in X=0, Y=1, and Z=1.

(5) A list of the traps that can occur as a consequence of attempting to execute the instruction(s). Traps due to an instruction_access_error, instruction_access_exception, or r_register_access_error, and interrupt requests are not listed since they can occur on any instruction. Also, any instruction may generate an illegal_instruction trap if it is not implemented in hardware.

This Appendix does not include any timing information (in either cycles or clock time) since timing is strictly implementation-dependent.

The following table summarizes the instruction set; the instruction definitions follow the table.

SPARC International, Inc.

Table B-1    *Instruction Set*

| Opcode | Name |
|---|---|
| LDSB (LDSBA†) | Load Signed Byte (from Alternate space) |
| LDSH (LDSHA†) | Load Signed Halfword (from Alternate space) |
| LDUB (LDUBA†) | Load Unsigned Byte (from Alternate space) |
| LDUH (LDUHA†) | Load Unsigned Halfword (from Alternate space) |
| LD (LDA†) | Load Word (from Alternate space) |
| LDD (LDDA†) | Load Doubleword (from Alternate space) |
| LDF | Load Floating-point |
| LDDF | Load Double Floating-point |
| LDFSR | Load Floating-point State Register |
| LDC | Load Coprocessor |
| LDDC | Load Double Coprocessor |
| LDCSR | Load Coprocessor State Register |
| STB (STBA†) | Store Byte (into Alternate space) |
| STH (STHA†) | Store Halfword (into Alternate space) |
| ST (STA†) | Store Word (into Alternate space) |
| STD (STDA†) | Store Doubleword (into Alternate space) |
| STF | Store Floating-point |
| STDF | Store Double Floating-point |
| STFSR | Store Floating-point State Register |
| STDFQ† | Store Double Floating-point deferred-trap Queue |
| STC | Store Coprocessor |
| STDC | Store Double Coprocessor |
| STCSR | Store Coprocessor State Register |
| STDCQ† | Store Double Coprocessor deferred-trap Queue |
| LDSTUB (LDSTUBA†) | Atomic Load-Store Unsigned Byte (in Alternate space) |
| SWAP (SWAPA†) | Swap r Register with Memory (in Alternate space) |
| SETHI | Set High 22 bits of *r* Register |
| NOP | No Operation |
| AND (ANDcc) | And (and modify icc) |
| ANDN (ANDNcc) | And Not (and modify icc) |
| OR (ORcc) | Inclusive-Or (and modify icc) |
| ORN (ORNcc) | Inclusive-Or Not (and modify icc) |
| XOR (XORcc) | Exclusive-Or (and modify icc) |
| XNOR (XNORcc) | Exclusive-Nor (and modify icc) |
| SLL | Shift Left Logical |
| SRL | Shift Right Logical |
| SRA | Shift Right Arithmetic |
| ADD (ADDcc) | Add (and modify icc) |
| ADDX (ADDXcc) | Add with Carry (and modify icc) |
| TADDcc (TADDccTV) | Tagged Add and modify icc (and Trap on overflow) |
| SUB (SUBcc) | Subtract (and modify icc) |
| SUBX (SUBXcc) | Subtract with Carry (and modify icc) |
| TSUBcc (TSUBccTV) | Tagged Subtract and modify icc (and Trap on overflow) |

SPARC International, Inc.

Table B-1    *Instruction Set— Continued*

| Opcode | Name |
|---|---|
| MULScc | Multiply Step (and modify icc) |
| UMUL (UMULcc)<br>SMUL (SMULcc) | Unsigned Integer Multiply (and modify icc)<br>Signed Integer Multiply (and modify icc) |
| UDIV (UDIVcc)<br>SDIV (SDIVcc) | Unsigned Integer Divide (and modify icc)<br>Signed Integer Divide (and modify icc) |
| SAVE<br>RESTORE | Save caller's window<br>Restore caller's window |
| Bicc<br>FBfcc<br>CBccc | Branch on integer condition codes<br>Branch on floating-point condition codes<br>Branch on coprocessor condition codes |
| CALL<br>JMPL<br>RETT† | Call and Link<br>Jump and Link<br>Return from Trap |
| Ticc | Trap on integer condition codes |
| RDASR‡<br>RDY<br>RDPSR†<br>RDWIM†<br>RDTBR† | Read Ancillary State Register<br>Read Y Register<br>Read Processor State Register<br>Read Window Invalid Mask Register<br>Read Trap Base Register |
| WRASR‡<br>WRY<br>WRPSR†<br>WRWIM†<br>WRTBR† | Write Ancillary State Register<br>Write Y Register<br>Write Processor State Register<br>Write Window Invalid Mask Register<br>Write Trap Base Register |
| STBAR | Store Barrier |
| UNIMP | Unimplemented |
| FLUSH | Flush Instruction Memory |
| FPop | Floating-point Operate:  FiTO(s,d,q), F(s,d,q)TOi,<br>  FsTOd, FsTOq, FdTOs, FdTOq, FqTOs, FqTOd,<br>  FMOVs, FNEGs, FABSs,<br>  FSQRT(s,d,q), FADD(s,d,q), FSUB(s,d,q), FMUL(s,d,q), FDIV(s,d,q),<br>  FsMULd, FdMULq,<br>  FCMP(s,d,q), FCMPE(s,d,q) |
| CPop | Coprocessor Operate:  implementation-dependent |

† privileged instruction
‡ privileged instruction if the referenced ASR register is privileged

SPARC International, Inc.

## B.1. Load Integer Instructions

| opcode | op3 | operation |
|--------|-----|-----------|
| LDSB   | 001001 | Load Signed Byte |
| LDSH   | 001010 | Load Signed Halfword |
| LDUB   | 000001 | Load Unsigned Byte |
| LDUH   | 000010 | Load Unsigned Halfword |
| LD     | 000000 | Load Word |
| LDD    | 000011 | Load Doubleword |
| LDSBA† | 011001 | Load Signed Byte from Alternate space |
| LDSHA† | 011010 | Load Signed Halfword from Alternate space |
| LDUBA† | 010001 | Load Unsigned Byte from Alternate space |
| LDUHA† | 010010 | Load Unsigned Halfword from Alternate space |
| LDA†   | 010000 | Load Word from Alternate space |
| LDDA†  | 010011 | Load Doubleword from Alternate space |

† privileged instruction

Format (3):

| 11 | rd | op3 | rs1 | i=0 | asi | rs2 |
|----|----|-----|-----|-----|-----|-----|
| 31 | 29 | 24 | 18 | 13 | 12 | 4    0 |

| 11 | rd | op3 | rs1 | i=1 | simm13 |
|----|----|-----|-----|-----|--------|
| 31 | 29 | 24 | 18 | 13 | 12            0 |

| Suggested Assembly Language Syntax |
|-------------------------------------|
| ldsb   [*address*], *reg$_{rd}$* |
| ldsh   [*address*], *reg$_{rd}$* |
| ldub   [*address*], *reg$_{rd}$* |
| lduh   [*address*], *reg$_{rd}$* |
| ld     [*address*], *reg$_{rd}$* |
| ldd    [*address*], *reg$_{rd}$* |
| ldsba   [*regaddr*]*asi* , *reg$_{rd}$* |
| ldsha   [*regaddr*]*asi* , *reg$_{rd}$* |
| lduba   [*regaddr*]*asi* , *reg$_{rd}$* |
| lduha   [*regaddr*]*asi* , *reg$_{rd}$* |
| lda    [*regaddr*]*asi* , *reg$_{rd}$* |
| ldda   [*regaddr*]*asi* , *reg$_{rd}$* |

Description:

The load integer instructions copy a byte, a halfword, or a word from memory into r[*rd*]. A fetched byte or halfword is right-justified in destination register r[*rd*]; it is either sign-extended or zero-filled on the left, depending on whether or not the opcode specifies a signed or unsigned operation, respectively.

The load doubleword integer instructions (LDD, LDDA) move a doubleword from memory into an *r* register pair. The more significant word at the effective memory address is moved into the even *r* register. The less significant word (at the effective memory address + 4) is moved into the following odd *r* register. (Note that a load doubleword with *rd* = 0 modifies only r[1].) The least significant bit of the *rd* field is unused and should be set to zero by software. An attempt to execute a load doubleword instruction that refers to a mis-aligned (odd) destination register number may cause an illegal_instruction trap.

The effective address for a load instruction is "r[*rs1*] + r[*rs2*]" if the *i* field is zero, or "r[*rs1*] + sign_ext(*simm13*)" if the *i* field is one. Instructions that load from an alternate address space contain the address space identifier to be used for the load in the *asi* field, and must contain zero in the *i* field or an illegal_instruction trap will occur. Load instructions that do not load from an alternate address space access either a user data space or system data space, according to the S bit of the PSR.

A successful load (notably, load doubleword) instruction operates atomically.

LD and LDA cause a mem_address_not_aligned trap if the effective address is not word-aligned; LDUH, LDSH, LDUHA, and LDSHA trap if the address is not halfword-aligned; and LDD and LDDA trap if the address is not doubleword-aligned.

See Appendix L, "Implementation Characteristics," for information on the timing of the integer load instructions.

Implementation Note    During execution of a load doubleword instruction, if an exception is generated during the memory cycle in which the second word is being loaded, the destination register(s) may be modified before the trap is taken. See Chapter 7, "Traps."

Traps:

illegal_instruction (load alternate with *i* = 1; LDD, LDDA with odd *rd*)
privileged_instruction (load alternate space only)
mem_address_not_aligned (excluding LDSB, LDSBA, LDUB, LDUBA)
data_access_exception
data_access_error

## B.2. Load Floating-point Instructions

| opcode | op3 | operation |
|--------|--------|-----------|
| LDF | 100000 | Load Floating-point Register |
| LDDF | 100011 | Load Double Floating-point Register |
| LDFSR | 100001 | Load Floating-point State Register |

Format (3):

| 11 | rd | op3 | rs1 | i=0 | unused(zero) | rs2 |
|----|----|-----|-----|-----|--------------|-----|
| 31 | 29 | 24 | 18 | 13 | 12 | 4 | 0 |

| 11 | rd | op3 | rs1 | i=1 | simm13 |
|----|----|-----|-----|-----|--------|
| 31 | 29 | 24 | 18 | 13 | 12 | 0 |

| Suggested Assembly Language Syntax |
|------------------------------------|
| ld     [address], freg$_{rd}$ |
| ldd    [address], freg$_{rd}$ |
| ld     [address], %fsr |

Description:

The load single floating-point instruction (LDF) moves a word from memory into f[rd].

The load doubleword floating-point instruction (LDDF) moves a doubleword from memory into an f register pair. The most significant word at the effective memory address is moved into the even f register. The least significant word at the effective memory address + 4 is moved into the following odd f register. The least significant bit of the rd field is unused and should always be set to zero by software. If this bit is non-zero, it is recommended that LDDF cause an fp_exception trap with FSR.ftt = invalid_fp_register.

The load floating-point state register instruction (LDFSR) waits for all FPop instructions that have not finished execution to complete, and then loads a word from memory into the FSR. If any of the three instructions that follow (in time) a LDFSR is an FBfcc, the value of the fcc field of the FSR which is seen by the FBfcc is undefined.

The effective address for the load instruction is "r[rs1] + r[rs2]" if the i field is zero, or "r[rs1] + sign_ext(simm13)" if the i field is one.

LDF and LDFSR cause a mem_address_not_aligned trap if the effective address is not word-aligned; LDDF traps if the address is not doubleword-aligned. If the EF field of the PSR is 0, or if no FPU is present, a load floating-point instruction causes an fp_disabled trap.

Implementation Note

If a load floating-point instruction traps with a data access exception, the destination f register(s) either remain unchanged or are set to an implementation-dependent predetermined constant value. See Chapter 7, "Traps," and Appendix L, "Implementation Characteristics."

Traps:

fp_disabled
fp_exception (sequence_error, invalid_fp_register(LDDF))
data_access_exception

data_access_error
mem_address_not_aligned

## B.3. Load Coprocessor Instructions

| opcode | op3 | operation |
|--------|--------|--------------------------------------|
| LDC | 110000 | Load Coprocessor Register |
| LDDC | 110011 | Load Double Coprocessor Register |
| LDCSR | 110001 | Load Coprocessor State Register |

Format (3):

| 11 | rd | op3 | rs1 | i=0 | unused(zero) | rs2 |
|----|----|-----|-----|-----|--------------|-----|
| 31 | 29 | 24 | 18 | 13 | 12 | 4   0 |

| 11 | rd | op3 | rs1 | i=1 | simm13 |
|----|----|-----|-----|-----|--------|
| 31 | 29 | 24 | 18 | 13 | 12   0 |

| Suggested Assembly Language Syntax |
|---|
| ld    [address], creg$_{rd}$ |
| ldd   [address], creg$_{rd}$ |
| ld    [address], %csr |

Description:

The load single coprocessor instruction (LDC) moves a word from memory into a coprocessor register. The load double coprocessor instruction (LDDC) moves a doubleword from memory into a coprocessor register pair. The load coprocessor state register instruction (LDCSR) moves a word from memory into the Coprocessor State Register. The semantics of these instructions depend on the implementation of the attached coprocessor.

The effective address for the load instruction is "r[$rs1$] + r[$rs2$]" if the $i$ field is zero, or "r[$rs1$] + sign_ext($simm13$)" if the $i$ field is one.

LDC and LDCSR cause a mem_address_not_aligned trap if the effective address is not word-aligned; LDDC traps if the address is not doubleword-aligned. If the EC field of the PSR is 0, or if no coprocessor is present, a load coprocessor instruction causes a cp_disabled trap.

Implementation Note     An implementation might cause a data_access_exception trap due to a "non-resumable machine-check" error during an "effective address + 4" memory access, even though the corresponding "effective address" access did not cause an error. Thus, the *even* destination CP register may be changed in this case. (Note that this cannot happen across a page boundary because of the doubleword-alignment restriction.) See Chapter 7, "Traps."

Traps:

cp_disabled
cp_exception
mem_address_not_aligned
data_access_exception
data_access_error

**B.4. Store Integer Instructions**

| opcode | op3 | operation |
|--------|--------|-----------|
| STB | 000101 | Store Byte |
| STH | 000110 | Store Halfword |
| ST | 000100 | Store Word |
| STD | 000111 | Store Doubleword |
| STBA† | 010101 | Store Byte into Alternate space |
| STHA† | 010110 | Store Halfword into Alternate space |
| STA† | 010100 | Store Word into Alternate space |
| STDA† | 010111 | Store Doubleword into Alternate space |

† privileged instruction

Format (3):

| 11 | rd | op3 | rs1 | i=0 | asi | rs2 |
|----|----|-----|-----|-----|-----|-----|
| 31 | 29 | 24 | 18 | 13 | 12 | 4    0 |

| 11 | rd | op3 | rs1 | i=1 | simm13 |
|----|----|-----|-----|-----|--------|
| 31 | 29 | 24 | 18 | 13 | 12    0 |

| Suggested Assembly Language Syntax | | |
|---|---|---|
| stb | $reg_{rd}$ , [address] | (synonyms: stub, stsb) |
| sth | $reg_{rd}$ , [address] | (synonyms: stuh, stsh) |
| st | $reg_{rd}$ , [address] | |
| std | $reg_{rd}$ , [address] | |
| stba | $reg_{rd}$ , [regaddr] asi | (synonyms: stuba, stsba) |
| stha | $reg_{rd}$ , [regaddr] asi | (synonyms: stuha, stsha) |
| sta | $reg_{rd}$ , [regaddr] asi | |
| stda | $reg_{rd}$ , [regaddr] asi | |

Description:

The store integer instructions copy the word, the less significant halfword, or the least significant byte from r[$rd$] into memory.

The store doubleword integer instructions (STD, STDA) copy a doubleword from an $r$ register pair into memory. The more significant word (in the even-numbered $r$ register) is written into memory at the effective address, and the less significant word (in the following odd-numbered $r$ register) is written into memory at the "effective address + 4". The least significant bit of the $rd$ field of a store doubleword instruction is unused and should always be set to zero by software. An attempt to execute a store doubleword instruction that refers to a mis-aligned (odd) $rd$ may cause an illegal_instruction trap.

The effective address for a store instruction is "r[$rs1$] + r[$rs2$]" if the $i$ field is zero, or "r[$rs1$] + sign_ext($simm13$)" if the $i$ field is one. Instructions that store to an alternate address space contain the address space identifier to be

SPARC International, Inc.

used for the store in the *asi* field, and must contain zero in the *i* field or an illegal_instruction trap will occur. Store instructions that do not store to an alternate address space access either a user data space or system data space, according to the S bit of the PSR.

A successful store (notably, store doubleword) instruction operates atomically.

ST and STA cause a mem_address_not_aligned trap if the effective address is not word-aligned. STH and STHA trap if the effective address is not halfword-aligned. STD and STDA trap if the effective address is not doubleword-aligned.

See Chapter 6, "Memory Model," for the definition of how stores by different processors are ordered relative to one another in a multiprocessor environment.

Implementation Note  An implementation might cause a data_access_exception trap due to a "non-resumable machine-check" error during an "effective address + 4" memory access, even though the corresponding "effective address" access did not cause an error. Thus, memory data at the effective memory address may be changed in this case. Note that this cannot happen across a page boundary because of the doubleword-alignment restriction. See Chapter 7, "Traps."

Traps:

illegal_instruction (store alternate with $i = 1$; STD, STDA with odd *rd*)
privileged_instruction (store alternate only)
mem_address_not_aligned (excluding STB and STBA)
data_access_exception
data_access_error
data_store_error

## B.5. Store Floating-point Instructions

| opcode | op3 | operation |
|--------|-----|-----------|
| STF | 100100 | Store Floating-point |
| STDF | 100111 | Store Double Floating-point |
| STFSR | 100101 | Store Floating-point State Register |
| STDFQ† | 100110 | Store Double Floating-point deferred-trap Queue |

† privileged instruction

Format (3):

| 11 | rd | op3 | rs1 | i=0 | unused(zero) | rs2 |
|----|----|----|----|----|----|----|
| 31 | 29 | 24 | 18 | 13 | 12 | 4  0 |

| 11 | rd | op3 | rs1 | i=1 | simm13 |
|----|----|----|----|----|----|
| 31 | 29 | 24 | 18 | 13 | 12      0 |

| Suggested Assembly Language Syntax |
|-----------------------------------|
| st    $freg_{rd}$ , [address ] |
| std   $freg_{rd}$ , [address ] |
| st    %fsr, [address ] |
| std   %fq,  [address ] |

Description:

The store single floating-point instruction (STF) copies f[$rd$] into memory.

The store double floating-point instruction (STDF) copies a doubleword from an $f$ register pair into memory. The more significant word (in the even-numbered $f$ register) is written into memory at the effective address, and the less significant word (in the odd-numbered $f$ register) is written into memory at "effective address + 4". The least significant bit of the $rd$ field is unused and should always be set to zero by software. If this bit is non-zero, it is recommended that STDF cause an fp_exception trap with FSR.$ftt$ = invalid_fp_register.

The store floating-point deferred-trap queue instruction (STDFQ) stores the front doubleword of the Floating-point Queue (FQ) into memory. An attempt to execute STDFQ on an implementation without a floating-point queue causes an fp_exception trap with FSR.$ftt$ set to 4 (sequence_error). On an implementation with a floating-point queue, an attempt to execute STDFQ when the FQ is empty (FSR.$qne$ = 0) should cause an fp_exception trap with FSR.$ftt$ set to 4 (sequence_error). Any additional semantics of this instruction are implementation-dependent. See Appendix L, "Implementation Characteristics," for information on the formats of the deferred-trap queues.

The store floating-point state register instruction (STFSR) waits for any concurrently executing FPop instructions that have not completed to complete, and then writes the FSR into memory. STFSR may zero FSR.$ftt$ after

SPARC International, Inc.

writing the FSR to memory.

The effective address for a store instruction is "r[*rs1*] + r[*rs2*]" if the *i* field is zero, or "r[*rs1*] + sign_ext(*simm13*)" if the *i* field is one.

STF and STFSR cause a mem_address_not_aligned trap if the address is not word-aligned and STDF and STDFQ trap if the address is not doubleword-aligned. If the EF field of the PSR is 0, or if the FPU is not present, a store floating-point instruction causes an fp_disabled trap.

See Chapter 6, "Memory Model," for the definition of how stores by different processors are ordered relative to one another in a multiprocessor environment.

Implementation Note    An implementation might cause a data_access_exception trap due to a "non-resumable machine-check" error during an "effective address + 4" memory access, even though the corresponding "effective address" access did not cause an error. Thus, memory data at the effective memory address may be changed in this case. (Note that this cannot happen across a page boundary because of the doubleword-alignment restriction.) See Appendix L, "Implementation Characteristics."

Traps:

fp_disabled
fp_exception (sequence_error(STDFQ),
                           invalid_fp_register(STDF, STDFQ))
privileged_instruction (STDFQ only)
mem_address_not_aligned
data_access_exception
data_access_error
data_store_error

## B.6. Store Coprocessor Instructions

| opcode | op3 | operation |
|--------|--------|-----------|
| STC | 110100 | Store Coprocessor |
| STDC | 110111 | Store Double Coprocessor |
| STCSR | 110101 | Store Coprocessor State Register |
| STDCQ† | 110110 | Store Double Coprocessor Queue |

† privileged instruction

Format (3):

| 11 | rd | op3 | rs1 | i=0 | unused(zero) | rs2 |
|----|----|-----|-----|-----|--------------|-----|
| 31 | 29 | 24 | 18 | 13 | 12 | 4 0 |

| 11 | rd | op3 | rs1 | i=1 | simm13 |
|----|----|-----|-----|-----|--------|
| 31 | 29 | 24 | 18 | 13 | 12 0 |

| *Suggested Assembly Language Syntax* |
|---|
| st      $creg_{rd}$ , [ *address* ] |
| std     $creg_{rd}$ , [ *address* ] |
| st      %csr, [ *address* ] |
| std     %cq,  [ *address* ] |

Description:

The store single coprocessor instruction (STC) copies the contents of a coprocessor register into memory.

The store double coprocessor instruction (STDC) copies the contents of a coprocessor register pair into memory.

The store coprocessor state register instruction (STCSR) copies the contents of the coprocessor state register into memory. The store doubleword coprocessor queue instruction (STDCQ) moves the front entry of the coprocessor queue into memory. On an implementation without a coprocessor queue, STDCQ may cause a cp_exception trap. The semantics of these instructions depend on the implementation of the attached coprocessor, if any.

The effective address for a store instruction is "r[*rs1*] + r[*rs2*]" if the *i* field is zero, or "r[*rs1*] + sign_ext(*simm13*)" if the *i* field is one.

STC and STCSR cause a mem_address_not_aligned trap if the address is not word-aligned. STDC and STDCQ trap if the address is not doubleword-aligned. A store coprocessor instruction causes a cp_disabled trap if the EC field of the PSR is 0 or if no coprocessor is present.

See Chapter 6, "Memory Model," for the definition of how stores by different processors are ordered relative to one another in a multiprocessor environment.

SPARC International, Inc.

Traps:

cp_disabled
cp_exception
privileged_instruction (STDCQ only)
mem_address_not_aligned
data_access_exception
illegal_instruction (STDCQ only; implementation-dependent)
data_access_error
data_store_error

SPARC International, Inc.

**B.7. Atomic Load-Store Unsigned Byte Instructions**

| opcode | op3 | operation |
|--------|-----|-----------|
| LDSTUB | 001101 | Atomic Load-Store Unsigned Byte |
| LDSTUBA† | 011101 | Atomic Load-Store Unsigned Byte into Alternate space |

† privileged instruction

Format (3):

| 11 | rd | op3 | rs1 | i=0 | asi | rs2 |
|----|----|----|----|----|----|----|
| 31 | 29 | 24 | 18 | 13 | 12 | 4 | 0 |

| 11 | rd | op3 | rs1 | i=1 | simm13 |
|----|----|----|----|----|----|
| 31 | 29 | 24 | 18 | 13 | 12 | 0 |

| Suggested Assembly Language Syntax |
|---|
| ldstub    [*address*] , *reg_rd* |
| ldstuba   [*regaddr*] *asi* , *reg_rd* |

Description:

The atomic load-store instructions copy a byte from memory into r[*rd*], then rewrite the addressed byte in memory to all ones. The operation is performed atomically, that is, without allowing intervening interrupts or deferred traps. In a multiprocessor system, two or more processors executing atomic load-store unsigned byte, SWAP, or SWAPA instructions addressing the same byte or word simultaneously are guaranteed to execute them in an undefined, but serial order.

The effective address of an atomic load-store is "r[*rs1*] + r[*rs2*]" if the *i* field is zero, or "r[*rs1*] + sign_ext(*simm13*)" if the *i* field is one. LDSTUBA must contain zero in the *i* field, or an illegal_instruction trap will occur. The address space identifier used for the memory accesses is taken from the *asi* field. For LDSTUB, the address space is either a user or a system data space access, according to the S bit in the PSR.

See Chapter 6, "Memory Model," for the definition of how stores by different processors are ordered relative to one another in a multiprocessor environment.

Implementation Note    An implementation might cause a data_access_exception trap due to a "non-resumable machine-check" error during the store memory access, even though there was no error during the corresponding load access. In this case, the destination register may be changed. See Chapter 7, "Traps."

Traps:
illegal_instruction (LDSTUBA with *i* = 1 only)
privileged_instruction (LDSTUBA only)
data_access_exception
data_access_error
data_store_error

SPARC International, Inc.

## B.8. SWAP Register with Memory Instruction

| opcode | op3 | operation |
|--------|--------|-----------|
| SWAP | 001111 | SWAP register with memory |
| SWAPA† | 011111 | SWAP register with Alternate space memory |

† privileged instruction

Format (3):

| 11 | rd | op3 | rs1 | i=0 | asi | rs2 |
|----|----|-----|-----|-----|-----|-----|
| 31 | 29 | 24 | 18 | 13 12 | 4 | 0 |

| 11 | rd | op3 | rs1 | i=1 | simm13 |
|----|----|-----|-----|-----|--------|
| 31 | 29 | 24 | 18 | 13 12 | 0 |

| Suggested Assembly Language Syntax |
|------------------------------------|
| swap    [ address ] , reg$_{rd}$ |
| swapa   [ regaddr ] asi , reg$_{rd}$ |

Description:

The SWAP and SWAPA instructions exchange r[rd] with the contents of the word at the addressed memory location. The operation is performed atomically, that is, without allowing intervening interrupts or deferred traps. In a multiprocessor system, two or more processors executing SWAP, SWAPA, or atomic load-store unsigned byte instructions addressing the same word or byte simultaneously are guaranteed to execute them in an undefined, but serial order.

The effective address of a SWAP instruction is "r[rs1] + r[rs2]" if the i field is zero, or "r[rs1] + sign_ext(simm13)" if the i field is one. SWAPA must contain zero in the i field, or an illegal_instruction trap will occur. The address space identifier used for the memory accesses is taken from the asi field. For SWAP, the address space is either a user or a system data space, according to the S bit in the PSR.

These instructions cause a mem_address_not_aligned trap if the effective address is not word-aligned.

See Chapter 6, "Memory Model," for the definition of how stores by different processors are ordered relative to one another in a multiprocessor environment.

Programming Note    See Appendix G, "SPARC ABI Software Considerations," regarding use of SWAP instructions in SPARC ABI software.

Implementation Note    An implementation might cause a data_access_exception trap due to a "non-resumable machine-check" error during the store memory access, but not during the load access. In this case, the destination register can be changed. See Chapter 7, "Traps."

Implementation Note    See Appendix L, "Implementation Characteristics," for information on the presence of hardware support for these instructions in the various SPARC implementations.

SPARC International, Inc.

Traps:

illegal instruction (when $i = 1$, SWAPA only)
privileged_instruction (SWAPA only)
mem_address_not_aligned
data_access_exception
data_access_error
data_store_error

SPARC International, Inc.

## B.9.  SETHI Instruction

| opcode | op | op2 | operation |
|--------|----|----|-----------|
| SETHI | 00 | 100 | Set High-Order 22 bits |

Format (2):

| 00 | rd | 100 | imm22 |
|----|----|-----|-------|

31    29    24    21                                                    0

| Suggested Assembly Language Syntax |
|-----------------------------------|
| sethi    const22 , reg_{rd} |
| sethi    %hi(value) , reg_{rd} |

Description:

SETHI zeroes the least significant 10 bits of "r[$rd$]", and replaces its high-order 22 bits with the value from its *imm22* field.

SETHI does not affect the condition codes.

A SETHI instruction with $rd = 0$ and $imm22 = 0$ is defined to be a NOP instruction. See the NOP instruction page in Section B.10.

Traps:

(none)

## B.10. NOP Instruction

| opcode | op | op2 | operation |
|--------|-----|-----|--------------|
| NOP | 00 | 100 | No Operation |

Format (2):

| 00 | 00000 | 100 | — 0 — |
|----|-------|-----|-------|
| 31 | 29 | 24 | 21                                    0 |

| Suggested Assembly Language Syntax |
|------------------------------------|
| nop |

Description:

The NOP instruction changes no program-visible state (except the PC and nPC).

Note that NOP is a special case of the SETHI instruction, with $imm22 = 0$ and $rd = 0$.

Traps:

(none)

SPARC International, Inc.

## B.11. Logical Instructions

| opcode | op3 | operation |
|--------|--------|-----------|
| AND | 000001 | And |
| ANDcc | 010001 | And and modify icc |
| ANDN | 000101 | And Not |
| ANDNcc | 010101 | And Not and modify icc |
| OR | 000010 | Inclusive Or |
| ORcc | 010010 | Inclusive Or and modify icc |
| ORN | 000110 | Inclusive Or Not |
| ORNcc | 010110 | Inclusive Or Not and modify icc |
| XOR | 000011 | Exclusive Or |
| XORcc | 010011 | Exclusive Or and modify icc |
| XNOR | 000111 | Exclusive Nor |
| XNORcc | 010111 | Exclusive Nor and modify icc |

Format (3):

| 10 | rd | op3 | rs1 | i=0 | unused(zero) | rs2 |
|----|----|-----|-----|-----|--------------|-----|
| 31 | 29 | 24 | 18 | 13 | 12 | 4    0 |

| 10 | rd | op3 | rs1 | i=1 | simm13 |
|----|----|-----|-----|-----|--------|
| 31 | 29 | 24 | 18 | 13 | 12              0 |

| Suggested Assembly Language Syntax | |
|-----|-----|
| and | $reg_{rs1}$ , reg_or_imm , $reg_{rd}$ |
| andcc | $reg_{rs1}$ , reg_or_imm , $reg_{rd}$ |
| andn | $reg_{rs1}$ , reg_or_imm , $reg_{rd}$ |
| andncc | $reg_{rs1}$ , reg_or_imm , $reg_{rd}$ |
| or | $reg_{rs1}$ , reg_or_imm , $reg_{rd}$ |
| orcc | $reg_{rs1}$ , reg_or_imm , $reg_{rd}$ |
| orn | $reg_{rs1}$ , reg_or_imm , $reg_{rd}$ |
| orncc | $reg_{rs1}$ , reg_or_imm , $reg_{rd}$ |
| xor | $reg_{rs1}$ , reg_or_imm , $reg_{rd}$ |
| xorcc | $reg_{rs1}$ , reg_or_imm , $reg_{rd}$ |
| xnor | $reg_{rs1}$ , reg_or_imm , $reg_{rd}$ |
| xnorcc | $reg_{rs1}$ , reg_or_imm , $reg_{rd}$ |

Description:

These instructions implement the bitwise logical operations. They compute "r[$rs1$] **operation** r[$rs2$]" if the $i$ field is zero, or "r[$rs1$] **operation** sign_ext($simm13$)" if the $i$ field is one, and write the result into r[$rd$].

ANDcc, ANDNcc, ORcc, ORNcc, XORcc, and XNORcc modify the integer condition codes (icc).

ANDN, ANDNcc, ORN, and ORNcc logically negate their second operand before applying the main (AND or OR) operation.

Programming Note:    XNOR and XNORcc logically implement XOR-Not and XOR-Not-cc, respectively.

Traps: (none)

## B.12.  Shift Instructions

| opcode | op3 | operation |
|--------|-----|-----------|
| SLL | 100101 | Shift Left Logical |
| SRL | 100110 | Shift Right Logical |
| SRA | 100111 | Shift Right Arithmetic |

Format (3):

| 10 | rd | op3 | rs1 | i=0 | unused(zero) | rs2 |
|----|----|----|-----|-----|--------------|-----|
| 31 | 29 | 24 | 18 | 13 | 12 | 4    0 |

| 10 | rd | op3 | rs1 | i=1 | unused(zero) | shcnt |
|----|----|----|-----|-----|--------------|-------|
| 31 | 29 | 24 | 18 | 13 | 12 | 4    0 |

| Suggested Assembly Language Syntax |
|------------------------------------|
| sll    $reg_{rs1}$ , reg_or_imm , $reg_{rd}$ |
| srl    $reg_{rs1}$ , reg_or_imm , $reg_{rd}$ |
| sra    $reg_{rs1}$ , reg_or_imm , $reg_{rd}$ |

Description:

The shift count for these instructions is the least significant five bits of r[$rs2$] if the $i$ field is zero, or the least significant five bits of $simm13$ if the $i$ field is one.

The least significant five bits of $simm13$ is called $shcnt$ in the above format. The most significant 8 bits of $simm13$ are reserved and should be supplied as zero by software. The most significant 27 bits of r[$rs2$] are ignored.

SLL shifts the value of r[$rs1$] left by the number of bits given by the shift count.

SRL and SRA shift the value of r[$rs1$] right by the number of bits implied by the shift count.

SLL and SRL replace vacated positions with zeroes, whereas SRA fills vacated positions with the most significant bit of r[$rs1$].  No shift occurs when the shift count is zero.

All of these instructions write the shifted result into r[$rd$].

These instructions do **not** modify the condition codes.

Programming Note    "Arithmetic left shift by 1 (and calculate overflow)" can be effected with an ADDcc instruction.

Traps:

(none)

SPARC International, Inc.

## B.13. Add Instructions

| opcode | op3 | operation |
|--------|--------|---------------------------------|
| ADD | 000000 | Add |
| ADDcc | 010000 | Add and modify icc |
| ADDX | 001000 | Add with Carry |
| ADDXcc | 011000 | Add with Carry and modify icc |

Format (3):

| 10 | rd | op3 | rs1 | i=0 | unused(zero) | rs2 |
|----|----|-----|-----|-----|--------------|-----|
| 31 | 29 | 24  | 18  | 13  | 12         4 | 0   |

| 10 | rd | op3 | rs1 | i=1 | simm13 |
|----|----|-----|-----|-----|--------|
| 31 | 29 | 24  | 18  | 13  | 12   0 |

| Suggested Assembly Language Syntax | |
|-------|-----------------------------------------|
| add | $reg_{rs1}$ , reg_or_imm , $reg_{rd}$ |
| addcc | $reg_{rs1}$ , reg_or_imm , $reg_{rd}$ |
| addx | $reg_{rs1}$ , reg_or_imm , $reg_{rd}$ |
| addxcc | $reg_{rs1}$ , reg_or_imm , $reg_{rd}$ |

Description:

ADD and ADDcc compute "r[$rs1$] + r[$rs2$]" if the $i$ field is zero, or "r[$rs1$] + sign_ext($simm13$)" if the $i$ field is one, and write the sum into r[$rd$].

ADDX and ADDXcc ("ADD eXtended") also add the PSR's carry ($c$) bit; that is, they compute "r[$rs1$] + r[$rs2$] + $c$" or "r[$rs1$] + sign_ext($simm13$) + $c$" and write the sum into r[$rd$].

ADDcc and ADDXcc modify the integer condition codes ($icc$). Overflow occurs on addition if both operands have the same sign and the sign of the sum is different.

Traps:

(none)

## B.14. Tagged Add Instructions

| opcode | op3 | operation |
|--------|-----|-----------|
| TADDcc | 100000 | Tagged Add and modify icc |
| TADDccTV | 100010 | Tagged Add, modify icc and Trap on Overflow |

Format (3):

| 10 | rd | op3 | rs1 | i=0 | unused(zero) | rs2 |
|----|----|-----|-----|-----|--------------|-----|
| 31 | 29 | 24 | 18 | 13 | 12 | 4 |

| 10 | rd | op3 | rs1 | i=1 | simm13 |
|----|----|-----|-----|-----|--------|
| 31 | 29 | 24 | 18 | 13 | 12 |

| Suggested Assembly Language Syntax | |
|---|---|
| taddcc | $reg_{rs1}$ , reg_or_imm , $reg_{rd}$ |
| taddcctv | $reg_{rs1}$ , reg_or_imm , $reg_{rd}$ |

Description:

These instructions compute a sum that is "r[$rs1$] + r[$rs2$]" if the $i$ field is zero, or "r[$rs1$] + sign_ext($simm13$)" if the $i$ field is one.

TADDcc modifies the integer condition codes (*icc*), and TADDccTV does so also if it does not trap.

A tag_overflow occurs if bit 1 or bit 0 of either operand is nonzero, or if the addition generates an arithmetic overflow (both operands have the same sign and the sign of the sum is different).

If a TADDccTV causes a tag_overflow, a tag_overflow trap is generated and r[$rd$] and the condition codes remain unchanged. If a TADDccTV does not cause a tag_overflow, the integer condition codes are updated (in particular, the overflow bit ($v$) is set to 0) and the sum is written into r[$rd$].

If a TADDcc causes a tag_overflow, the overflow bit ($v$) of the PSR is set; if it does not cause a tag_overflow, the overflow bit is cleared. In either case, the remaining integer condition codes are also updated and the sum is written into r[$rd$].

See Appendix D, "Software Considerations," for a suggested tagging scheme.

Traps:

tag_overflow (TADDccTV only)

SPARC International, Inc.

## B.15. Subtract Instructions

| opcode | op3 | operation |
|--------|--------|-----------|
| SUB | 000100 | Subtract |
| SUBcc | 010100 | Subtract and modify icc |
| SUBX | 001100 | Subtract with Carry |
| SUBXcc | 011100 | Subtract with Carry and modify icc |

Format (3):

| 10 | rd | op3 | rs1 | i=0 | unused(zero) | rs2 |
|----|----|-----|-----|-----|--------------|-----|
| 31 | 29 | 24 | 18 | 13 12 | | 4   0 |

| 10 | rd | op3 | rs1 | i=1 | simm13 |
|----|----|-----|-----|-----|--------|
| 31 | 29 | 24 | 18 | 13 12 | 0 |

| Suggested Assembly Language Syntax | |
|---|---|
| sub | $reg_{rs1}$ , reg_or_imm , $reg_{rd}$ |
| subcc | $reg_{rs1}$ , reg_or_imm , $reg_{rd}$ |
| subx | $reg_{rs1}$ , reg_or_imm , $reg_{rd}$ |
| subxcc | $reg_{rs1}$ , reg_or_imm , $reg_{rd}$ |

Description:

These instructions compute "r[$rs1$] – r[$rs2$]" if the $i$ field is zero, or "r[$rs1$] – sign_ext($simm13$)" if the $i$ field is one, and write the difference into r[$rd$].

SUBX and SUBXcc ("SUBtract eXtended") also subtract the PSR's carry ($c$) bit; that is, they compute "r[$rs1$] – r[$rs2$] – $c$" or "r[$rs1$] – sign_ext($simm13$) – $c$", and write the difference into r[$rd$].

SUBcc and SUBXcc modify the integer condition codes ($icc$). Overflow occurs on subtraction if the operands have different signs and the sign of the difference differs from the sign of r[$rs1$].

Programming Note    A SUBcc with $rd = 0$ can be used to effect a signed or unsigned integer comparison. See the cmp synthetic instruction in Appendix A.

Traps:

(none)

## B.16. Tagged Subtract Instructions

| opcode | op3 | operation |
|--------|-----|-----------|
| TSUBcc | 100001 | Tagged Subtract and modify icc |
| TSUBccTV | 100011 | Tagged Subtract, modify icc and Trap on Overflow |

Format (3):

| 10 | rd | op3 | rs1 | i=0 | unused(zero) | rs2 |
|----|----|----|----|----|----|----|
| 31 | 29 | 24 | 18 | 13 | 12 | 4    0 |

| 10 | rd | op3 | rs1 | i=1 | simm13 |
|----|----|----|----|----|----|
| 31 | 29 | 24 | 18 | 13 | 12           0 |

| Suggested Assembly Language Syntax |
|-----------------------------------|
| tsubcc      $reg_{rs1}$ , $reg\_or\_imm$ , $reg_{rd}$ |
| tsubcctv    $reg_{rs1}$ , $reg\_or\_imm$ , $reg_{rd}$ |

Description:

These instructions compute "r[*rs1*] − r[*rs2*]" if the *i* field is zero, or "r[*rs1*] − sign_ext(*simm13*)" if the *i* field is one.

TSUBcc modifies the integer condition codes (*icc*) and TSUBccTV does so also if it does not trap.

A tag_overflow occurs if bit 1 or bit 0 of either operand is nonzero, or if the subtraction generates an arithmetic overflow (the operands have different signs and the sign of the difference differs from the sign of r[*rs1*]).

If a TSUBccTV causes a tag_overflow, a tag_overflow trap is generated and the destination register and condition codes remain unchanged. If a TSUBccTV does not cause a tag_overflow condition, the integer condition codes are updated (in particular, the overflow bit (*v*) is set to 0) and the difference is written into r[*rd*].

If a TSUBcc causes a tag_overflow, the overflow bit (*v*) of the PSR is set; if it does not cause a tag_overflow, the overflow bit is cleared. In either case, the remaining integer condition codes are also updated and the difference is written into r[*rd*].

See Appendix D, "Software Considerations." for a suggested tagging scheme.

Traps:

tag_overflow (TSUBccTV only)

SPARC International, Inc.

## B.17. Multiply Step Instruction

| opcode | op3 | operation |
|--------|--------|---------------------------|
| MULScc | 100100 | Multiply Step and modify icc |

Format (3):

| 10 | rd | op3 | rs1 | i=0 | reserved | rs2 |
|----|----|-----|-----|-----|----------|-----|
| 31 | 29 | 24 | 18 | 13 | 12 | 4 0 |

| 10 | rd | op3 | rs1 | i=1 | simm13 |
|----|----|-----|-----|-----|--------|
| 31 | 29 | 24 | 18 | 13 | 12 0 |

| Suggested Assembly Language Syntax |
|-------------------------------------|
| mulscc    $reg_{rs1}$ , $reg\_or\_imm$ , $reg_{rd}$ |

Description:

MULScc treats r[*rs1*] and the Y register as a single 64-bit, right-shiftable doubleword register. The least significant bit of r[*rs1*] is treated as if it were adjacent to the most significant bit of the Y register. The MULScc instruction conditionally adds, based on the least significant bit of Y.

Multiplication assumes that the Y register initially contains the multiplier, r[*rs1*] contains the most significant bits of the product, and r[*rs2*] contains the multiplicand. Upon completion of the multiplication, the Y register contains the least significant bits of the product.

Note that a standard MULScc instruction has *rs1* = *rd*. See Appendix E, "Example Integer Multiplication and Division Routines," for a $32 \times 32 \rightarrow 64$ signed multiplication example program based on MULScc.

MULScc operates as follows:

(1)  The multiplier is established as r[*rs2*] if the *i* field is zero, or sign_ext(*simm13*) if the *i* field is one.

(2)  A 32-bit value is computed by shifting r[*rs1*] right by one bit with "N **xor** V" from the PSR replacing the high-order bit. (This is the proper sign for the previous partial product.)

(3)  If the least significant bit of the Y register = 1, the shifted value from step (2) is added to the multiplier.
If the LSB of the Y register = 0, then 0 is added to the shifted value from step (2).

(4)  The sum from step (3) is written into r[*rd*].

(5)  The integer condition codes, *icc*, are updated according to the addition performed in step (3).

(6)  The Y register is shifted right by one bit, with the LSB of the unshifted r[*rs1*] replacing the MSB of Y.

Traps:

(none)

SPARC International, Inc.

## B.18. Multiply Instructions

| opcode | op3 | operation |
|--------|--------|-----------|
| UMUL | 001010 | Unsigned Integer Multiply |
| SMUL | 001011 | Signed Integer Multiply |
| UMULcc | 011010 | Unsigned Integer Multiply and modify icc |
| SMULcc | 011011 | Signed Integer Multiply and modify icc |

Format (3):

| 10 | rd | op3 | rs1 | i=0 | unused(zero) | rs2 |
|----|----|-----|-----|-----|--------------|-----|
| 31 | 29 | 24 | 18 | 13 | 12 | 4    0 |

| 10 | rd | op3 | rs1 | i=1 | simm13 |
|----|----|-----|-----|-----|--------|
| 31 | 29 | 24 | 18 | 13 | 12                0 |

| Suggested Assembly Language Syntax | |
|---|---|
| umul | $reg_{rs1}$ , reg_or_imm , $reg_{rd}$ |
| smul | $reg_{rs1}$ , reg_or_imm , $reg_{rd}$ |
| umulcc | $reg_{rs1}$ , reg_or_imm , $reg_{rd}$ |
| smulcc | $reg_{rs1}$ , reg_or_imm , $reg_{rd}$ |

Description:

The multiply instructions perform 32-bit by 32-bit multiplications, producing 64-bit results. They compute "r[$rs1$] × r[$rs2$]" if the $i$ field is zero, or "r[$rs1$] × sign_ext($simm13$)" if the $i$ field is one. They write the 32 most significant bits of the product into the Y register and the 32 least significant bits into r[$rd$].

An unsigned multiply (UMUL, UMULcc) assumes unsigned integer word operands and computes an unsigned integer doubleword product. A signed multiply (SMUL, SMULcc) assumes signed integer word operands and computes a signed integer doubleword product.

UMUL and SMUL do not affect the condition code bits. UMULcc and SMULcc write the integer condition code bits, $icc$, as follows. Note that negative (N) and zero (Z) are set according to the **less** significant word of the product.

| $icc$ bit | UMULcc | SMULcc |
|-----------|--------|--------|
| N | Set if product[31] = 1 | Set if product[31] = 1 |
| Z | Set if product[31:0] = 0 | Set if product[31:0] = 0 |
| V | Zero † | Zero † |
| C | Zero † | Zero † |

† Specification of this condition code may change in a future revision to the architecture. Software should not test this condition code.

SPARC International, Inc.

| | |
|---|---|
| Programming Note | 32-bit overflow after UMUL/UMULcc is indicated by    Y != 0.<br>32-bit overflow after SMUL/SMULcc is indicated by    Y != ( r[*rd*] >> 31 ). |
| Programming Note | See Appendix G, "SPARC ABI Software Considerations," regarding use of multiply instructions in SPARC ABI software. |
| Implementation Note | An implementation may assume that the smaller operand will typically be in r[*rs2*] or *simm13*. |
| Implementation Note | See Appendix L, "Implementation Characteristics," for information on whether these instructions are executed in hardware or software in the various SPARC implementations. |

Traps:

(none)

## B.19. Divide Instructions

| opcode | op3 | operation |
|--------|--------|-----------|
| UDIV | 001110 | Unsigned Integer Divide |
| SDIV | 001111 | Signed Integer Divide |
| UDIVcc | 011110 | Unsigned Integer Divide and modify icc |
| SDIVcc | 011111 | Signed Integer Divide and modify icc |

Format (3):

| 10 | rd | op3 | rs1 | i=0 | unused(zero) | rs2 |
|----|----|-----|-----|-----|--------------|-----|
| 31 | 29 | 24 | 18 | 13 | 12        4 | 0 |

| 10 | rd | op3 | rs1 | i=1 | simm13 |
|----|----|-----|-----|-----|--------|
| 31 | 29 | 24 | 18 | 13 | 12                0 |

| Suggested Assembly Language Syntax | |
|---|---|
| udiv | $reg_{rs1}$ , reg_or_imm , $reg_{rd}$ |
| sdiv | $reg_{rs1}$ , reg_or_imm , $reg_{rd}$ |
| udivcc | $reg_{rs1}$ , reg_or_imm , $reg_{rd}$ |
| sdivcc | $reg_{rs1}$ , reg_or_imm , $reg_{rd}$ |

Description:

The divide instructions perform 64-bit by 32-bit division, producing a 32-bit result. If the $i$ field is zero, they compute "$(Y \square r[rs1]) \div r[rs2]$". Otherwise (the $i$ field is one), the divide instructions compute "$(Y \square r[rs1]) \div$ sign_ext($simm13$)". In either case, the 32 bits of the integer quotient are written into r[$rd$]. The remainder (if generated) is discarded.

An unsigned divide (UDIV, UDIVcc) assumes an unsigned integer double-word dividend ($Y \square r[rs1]$) and an unsigned integer word divisor (r[$rs2$]) and computes an unsigned integer word quotient (r[$rd$]). A signed divide (SDIV, SDIVcc) assumes a signed integer doubleword dividend ($Y \square r[rs1]$) and a signed integer word divisor (r[$rs2$] or sign_ext($simm13$)) and computes a signed integer word quotient (r[$rd$]).

Signed division rounds an inexact quotient toward zero if there is a nonzero remainder; for example, $-3 \div 2$ equals $-1$ with a remainder of $-1$ (not $-2$ with a remainder of 1). An implementation may choose to strictly adhere to this rounding, in which case overflow for a negative result must be detected using method [A] below. Or, it may choose to make an exception for rounding with the maximum negative quotient, in which case overflow for a negative result must be detected using method [B].

The result of a divide instruction can overflow the 32-bit destination register r[rd] under certain conditions. When overflow occurs (whether or not the instruction sets the condition codes in *icc*), the largest appropriate integer is returned as the quotient in r[rd]. The conditions under which overflow occurs and the value returned in r[rd] under those conditions are specified in

SPARC International, Inc.

the following table.

| Divide Overflow Detection and Value Returned | | |
|---|---|---|
| Instruction | Condition under which overflow occurs ("result" refers to quotient + remainder) | Value returned in r[rd] |
| UDIV, UDIVcc | result > $(2^{32}-1$ with a remainder of divisor$-1)$ | $2^{32}-1$ (0xffffffff) |
| SDIV, SDIVcc (positive result) | result > $(2^{31}-1$ with a remainder of $\|$divisor$\|-1)$ | $2^{31}-1$ (0x7fffffff) |
| SDIV, SDIVcc (negative result) | **either** † [A] result < $(-2^{31}$ with a remainder of $-(\|$divisor$\|-1))$ **or** † [B] result < $(-2^{31}$ with a remainder of 0) | $-2^{31}$ (0x80000000) |

† which of these two overflow-detection conditions is used is implementation-dependent, but must be consistent within an implementation.

UDIV and SDIV do not affect condition code bits. UDIVcc and SDIVcc write the integer condition code bits as follows. Note that negative(N) and zero(Z) are set according to the value of the quotient (after it has been set to reflect overflow, if any), and that UDIVcc and SDIVcc set overflow(V) differently.

| *icc* bit | UDIVcc | SDIVcc |
|---|---|---|
| N | Set if quotient[31] = 1 | Set if quotient[31] = 1 |
| Z | Set if quotient[31:0] = 0 | Set if quotient[31:0] = 0 |
| V | Set if overflow (*per above table*) | Set if overflow (*per above table*) |
| C | Zero | Zero |

For future compatibility, software should assume that the contents of the Y register are **not** preserved by the divide instructions.

Programming Note    See Appendix G, "SPARC ABI Software Considerations," regarding use of divide instructions in SPARC ABI software.

Implementation Note    The integer division instructions may generate a remainder. If they do, it is recommended that the remainder be stored in the Y register.

Implementation Note    See Appendix L, "Implementation Characteristics," for information on whether these instructions are executed in hardware or software, and the condition which triggers signed overflow for negative quotients in the various SPARC implementations.

Traps:

division_by_zero

**B.20. SAVE and RESTORE Instructions**

| opcode | op3 | operation |
|--------|-----|-----------|
| SAVE | 111100 | Save caller's window |
| RESTORE | 111101 | Restore caller's window |

Format (3):

| 10 | rd | op3 | rs1 | i=0 | unused(zero) | rs2 |
|----|----|----|----|----|----|----|
| 31 | 29 | 24 | 18 | 13 | 12 | 4    0 |

| 10 | rd | op3 | rs1 | i=1 | simm13 |
|----|----|----|----|----|----|
| 31 | 29 | 24 | 18 | 13 | 12    0 |

| *Suggested Assembly Language Syntax* |
|--------|
| save     $reg_{rs1}$ , $reg\_or\_imm$ , $reg_{rd}$ |
| restore  $reg_{rs1}$ , $reg\_or\_imm$ , $reg_{rd}$ |

Description:

The SAVE instruction subtracts one from the CWP (modulo NWINDOWS) and compares this value (new_CWP) against the Window Invalid Mask (WIM) register. If the WIM bit corresponding to the new_CWP is 1, that is, (WIM and $2^{new\_CWP}$) = 1, then a window_overflow trap is generated. If the WIM bit corresponding to the new_CWP is 0, then no window_overflow trap is generated and new_CWP is written into CWP. This causes the current window to become the CWP−1 window, thereby saving the caller's window.

The RESTORE instruction adds one to the CWP (modulo NWINDOWS) and compares this value (new_CWP) against the Window Invalid Mask (WIM) register. If the WIM bit corresponding to the new_CWP is 1, that is, (WIM and $2^{new\_CWP}$) = 1, then a window_underflow trap is generated. If the WIM bit corresponding to the new_CWP = 0, then no window_underflow trap is generated and new_CWP is written into CWP. This causes the CWP+1 window to become the current window, thereby restoring the caller's window.

Furthermore, if and only if an overflow or underflow trap is not generated, SAVE and RESTORE behave like normal ADD instructions, except that the source operands r[*rs1*] and/or r[*rs2*] are read from the **old** window (that is, the window addressed by the original CWP) and the sum is written into r[*rd*] of the **new** window (that is, the window addressed by new_CWP).

Note that CWP arithmetic is performed modulo the number of implemented windows, NWINDOWS.

Programming Note    The SAVE instruction can be useed to atomically allocate a new window in the register file and a new software stack frame in main memory. See Appendix D, "Software Considerations," for details.

Programming Note    Typically, if a SAVE (RESTORE) instruction traps, the overflow (underflow) trap handler returns to the trapped instruction to reexecute it. So, although the ADD operation is not performed the first time (when the instruction traps), it is performed the second time.

SPARC International, Inc.

Traps:
    window_overflow (SAVE only)
    window_underflow (RESTORE only)

## B.21. Branch on Integer Condition Codes Instructions

| opcode | cond | operation | icc test |
|--------|------|-----------|----------|
| BA | 1000 | Branch Always | 1 |
| BN | 0000 | Branch Never | 0 |
| BNE | 1001 | Branch on Not Equal | not Z |
| BE | 0001 | Branch on Equal | Z |
| BG | 1010 | Branch on Greater | not (Z or (N xor V)) |
| BLE | 0010 | Branch on Less or Equal | Z or (N xor V) |
| BGE | 1011 | Branch on Greater or Equal | not (N xor V) |
| BL | 0011 | Branch on Less | N xor V |
| BGU | 1100 | Branch on Greater Unsigned | not (C or Z) |
| BLEU | 0100 | Branch on Less or Equal Unsigned | (C or Z) |
| BCC | 1101 | Branch on Carry Clear (Greater than or Equal, Unsigned) | not C |
| BCS | 0101 | Branch on Carry Set (Less than, Unsigned) | C |
| BPOS | 1110 | Branch on Positive | not N |
| BNEG | 0110 | Branch on Negative | N |
| BVC | 1111 | Branch on Overflow Clear | not V |
| BVS | 0111 | Branch on Overflow Set | V |

Format (2):

| 00 | a | cond | 010 | disp22 |
|----|---|------|-----|--------|
| 31 | 29 | 28 | 24  21 | 0 |

| Suggested Assembly Language Syntax | | |
|---|---|---|
| ba{,a} | label | |
| bn{,a} | label | |
| bne{,a} | label | (synonym: bnz) |
| be{,a} | label | (synonym: bz) |
| bg{,a} | label | |
| ble{,a} | label | |
| bge{,a} | label | |
| bl{,a} | label | |
| bgu{,a} | label | |
| bleu{,a} | label | |
| bcc{,a} | label | (synonym: bgeu) |
| bcs{,a} | label | (synonym: blu) |
| bpos{,a} | label | |
| bneg{,a} | label | |
| bvc{,a} | label | |
| bvs{,a} | label | |

Note    To set the "annul" bit for Bicc instructions, append ",a" to the opcode mnemonic. For example, use "bgu,a label". The preceding table indicates that the ",a" is optional by enclosing it in braces ({}).

Description:

Unconditional Branches (BA, BN)

If its annul field is 0, a BN (Branch Never) instruction acts like a "NOP". If its annul field is 1, the following (delay) instruction is annulled (not executed). In neither case does a transfer of control take place.

BA (Branch Always) causes a PC-relative, delayed control transfer to the address "PC + (4 × sign_ext(*disp22*))", regardless of the values of the integer condition code bits. If the annul field of the branch instruction is 1, the delay instruction is annulled (not executed). If the annul field is 0, the delay instruction is executed.

*Icc*-Conditional Branches

Conditional Bicc instructions (all except BA and BN) evaluate the integer condition codes (*icc*), according to the *cond* field of the instruction. Such evaluation produces either a "true" or "false" result. If "true", the branch is taken, that is, the instruction causes a PC-relative, delayed control transfer to the address "PC + (4 × sign_ext(*disp22*))". If "false", the branch is not taken.

If a conditional branch is taken, the delay instruction is always executed regardless of the value of the annul field. If a conditional branch is not taken and the *a* (annul) field is 1, the delay instruction is annulled (not executed). (Note that the annul bit has a **different** effect on conditional branches than it does on unconditional branches.)

Annulment, delay instructions, and delayed control transfers are described further in Chapter 5, "Instructions." In particular, note that a Bicc should not be placed in the delay slot of a conditional branch instruction.

See Appendix L, "Implementation Characteristics," for information on the timing of the Bicc instructions.

Traps:

(none)

## B.22. Branch on Floating-point Condition Codes Instructions

| opcode | cond | operation | fcc test |
|--------|------|-----------|----------|
| FBA | 1000 | Branch Always | 1 |
| FBN | 0000 | Branch Never | 0 |
| FBU | 0111 | Branch on Unordered | U |
| FBG | 0110 | Branch on Greater | G |
| FBUG | 0101 | Branch on Unordered or Greater | G or U |
| FBL | 0100 | Branch on Less | L |
| FBUL | 0011 | Branch on Unordered or Less | L or U |
| FBLG | 0010 | Branch on Less or Greater | L or G |
| FBNE | 0001 | Branch on Not Equal | L or G or U |
| FBE | 1001 | Branch on Equal | E |
| FBUE | 1010 | Branch on Unordered or Equal | E or U |
| FBGE | 1011 | Branch on Greater or Equal | E or G |
| FBUGE | 1100 | Branch on Unordered or Greater or Equal | E or G or U |
| FBLE | 1101 | Branch on Less or Equal | E or L |
| FBULE | 1110 | Branch on Unordered or Less or Equal | E or L or U |
| FBO | 1111 | Branch on Ordered | E or L or G |

Format (2):

| 00 | a | cond | 110 | disp22 |
|----|---|------|-----|--------|
| 31 | 29 | 28 | 24  21 | 0 |

| Suggested Assembly Language Syntax | |
|---|---|
| fba{,a}    *label* | |
| fbn{,a}    *label* | |
| fbu{,a}    *label* | |
| fbg{,a}    *label* | |
| fbug{,a}   *label* | |
| fbl{,a}    *label* | |
| fbul{,a}   *label* | |
| fblg{,a}   *label* | |
| fbne{,a}   *label* | *(synonym:* fbnz*)* |
| fbe{,a}    *label* | *(synonym:* fbz*)* |
| fbue{,a}   *label* | |
| fbge{,a}   *label* | |
| fbuge{,a}  *label* | |
| fble{,a}   *label* | |
| fbule{,a}  *label* | |
| fbo{,a}    *label* | |

Note    To set the "annul" bit for FBfcc instructions, append " , a" to the opcode mnemonic. For example, use "fbl,a    label". The preceding table indicates that the " , a" is optional by enclosing it in braces ({}).

SPARC International, Inc.

Description:

Unconditional Branches (FBA, FBN)

If its annul field is 0, a FBN (Branch Never) instruction acts like a "NOP". If its annul field is 1, the following (delay) instruction is annulled (not executed). In neither case does a transfer of control take place.

FBA (Branch Always) causes a PC-relative, delayed control transfer to the address "PC + (4 × sign_ext(*disp22*))", regardless of the value of the floating-point condition code bits. If the annul field of the branch instruction is 1, the delay instruction is annulled (not executed). If the annul field is 0, the delay instruction is executed.

*Fcc*-Conditional Branches

Conditional FBfcc instructions (all except FBA and FBN) evaluate the floating-point condition codes (*fcc*), according to the *cond* field of the instruction. Such evaluation produces either a "true" or "false" result. If "true", the branch is taken, that is, the instruction causes a PC-relative, delayed control transfer to the address "PC + (4 × sign_ext(*disp22*))". If "false", the branch is not taken.

If a conditional branch is taken, the delay instruction is always executed regardless of the value of the annul field. If a conditional branch is not taken and the *a* (annul) field is 1, the delay instruction is annulled (not executed). (Note that the annul bit has a **different** effect on conditional branches than it does on unconditional branches.)

Annulment, delay instructions, and delayed control transfers are described further in Chapter 5, "Instructions." In particular, note that an FBfcc should not be placed in the delay slot of a conditional branch instruction.

If the PSR's EF bit is 0, or if an FPU is not present, an FBfcc instruction does not branch, does not annul the following instruction, and generates an fp_disabled trap.

If the instruction executed immediately before an FBfcc is an FPop2 instruction, the result of the FBfcc is undefined. Therefore, at least one non-FPop2 instruction should be executed between an FPop2 and a subsequent FBfcc.

If any of the three instructions that follow (in time) an LDFSR is an FBfcc, the value of the *fcc* field of the FSR that is seen by the FBfcc is undefined.

See Appendix L, "Implementation Characteristics," for information on the timing of the FBfcc instructions.

Traps:

fp_disabled
fp_exception

SPARC International, Inc.

**B.23. Branch on Coprocessor Condition Codes Instructions**

| opcode | cond | bp_CP_cc[1:0] test |
|--------|------|---------------------|
| CBA | 1000 | Always |
| CBN | 0000 | Never |
| CB3 | 0111 | 3 |
| CB2 | 0110 | 2 |
| CB23 | 0101 | 2 **or** 3 |
| CB1 | 0100 | 1 |
| CB13 | 0011 | 1 **or** 3 |
| CB12 | 0010 | 1 **or** 2 |
| CB123 | 0001 | 1 **or** 2 **or** 3 |
| CB0 | 1001 | 0 |
| CB03 | 1010 | 0 **or** 3 |
| CB02 | 1011 | 0 **or** 2 |
| CB023 | 1100 | 0 **or** 2 **or** 3 |
| CB01 | 1101 | 0 **or** 1 |
| CB013 | 1110 | 0 **or** 1 **or** 3 |
| CB012 | 1111 | 0 **or** 1 **or** 2 |

Format (2):

| 00 | a | cond | 111 | disp22 |
|----|---|------|-----|--------|
| 31 | 29 | 28 | 24  21 | 0 |

| Suggested Assembly Language Syntax | |
|---|---|
| cba{,a} | *label* |
| cbn{,a} | *label* |
| cb3{,a} | *label* |
| cb2{,a} | *label* |
| cb23{,a} | *label* |
| cb1{,a} | *label* |
| cb13{,a} | *label* |
| cb12{,a} | *label* |
| cb123{,a} | *label* |
| cb0{,a} | *label* |
| cb03{,a} | *label* |
| cb02{,a} | *label* |
| cb023{,a} | *label* |
| cb01{,a} | *label* |
| cb013{,a} | *label* |
| cb012{,a} | *label* |

Note    To set the "annul" bit for CBccc instructions, append ",a" to the opcode mnemonic. For example, use "cb12,a  label". The preceding table indicates that the ",a" is optional by enclosing it in braces ({}).

SPARC International, Inc.

Description:

Unconditional Branches (CBA, CBN)

If its annul field is 0, a CBN (Branch Never) instruction acts like "NOP". If its annul field is 1, the following (delay) instruction is annulled (not executed). In neither case does a transfer of control take place.

CBA (Branch Always) causes a PC-relative, delayed control transfer to the address "PC + ($4 \times$ sign_ext($disp22$))", regardless of the value of the condition code bits. If the annul field of the branch instruction is 1, the delay instruction is annulled (not executed). If the annul field is 0, the delay instruction is executed.

*Ccc*-Conditional Branches

Conditional CBccc instructions (all except CBA and CBN) evaluate the coprocessor condition codes (*ccc*), according to the *cond* field of the instruction. Such evaluation produces either a "true" or "false" result. If "true", the branch is taken; that is, the instruction causes a PC-relative, delayed control transfer to the address "PC + ($4 \times$ sign_ext($disp22$))". If "false", the branch is not taken.

If a conditional branch is taken, the delay instruction is always executed regardless of the value of the annul field. If a conditional branch is not taken and the *a* (annul) field is 1, the delay instruction is annulled (not executed). (Note that the annul bit has a **different** effect on conditional branches than it does on unconditional branches.)

Annulment, delay instructions, and delayed control transfers are described further in Chapter 5, "Instructions." In particular, note that a CBccc should not be placed in the delay slot of a conditional branch instruction.

If the PSR's EC bit is 0, or if a coprocessor is not present, a CBccc instruction does not branch, does not annul the following instruction, and generates a cp_disabled trap.

See Appendix L, "Implementation Characteristics," for information on the timing of the CBccc instructions.

Traps:

cp_disabled
cp_exception

**B.24. Call and Link Instruction**

| opcode | op | operation |
|--------|-----|-----------|
| CALL | 01 | Call and Link |

Format (1):

| 01 | disp30 |
|----|--------|

_31   29_                                                                                      _0_

| Suggested Assembly Language Syntax |
|-----------------------------------|
| call    _label_ |

Description:

The CALL instruction causes an unconditional, delayed, PC-relative control transfer to address "PC + $(4 \times disp30)$". Since the word displacement (_disp30_) field is 30 bits wide, the target address can be arbitrarily distant. The PC-relative displacement is formed by appending two low-order zeros to the instruction's 30-bit word displacement field.

The CALL instruction also writes the value of PC, which contains the address of the CALL, into r[15] (_out_ register 7).

Traps:

(none)

## B.25. Jump and Link Instruction

| opcode | op3 | operation |
|--------|--------|---------------|
| JMPL | 111000 | Jump and Link |

Format (3):

| 10 | rd | op3 | rs1 | i=0 | unused(zero) | rs2 |
|----|----|-----|-----|-----|--------------|-----|

31    29         24              18      13   12            4    0

| 10 | rd | op3 | rs1 | i=1 | simm13 |
|----|----|-----|-----|-----|--------|

31    29         24              18      13   12              0

| Suggested Assembly Language Syntax |
|------------------------------------|
| jmpl    address , reg$_{rd}$ |

Description:

The JMPL instruction causes a register-indirect delayed control transfer to the address given by "r[*rs1*] + r[*rs2*]" if the *i* field is zero, or "r[*rs1*] + sign_ext(*simm13*)" if the *i* field is one.

The JMPL instruction copies the PC, which contains the address of the JMPL instruction, into register r[*rd*].

If either of the low-order two bits of the jump address is nonzero, a mem_address_not_aligned trap occurs.

Programming Note
A JMPL instruction with *rd* = 15 functions as a register-indirect call using the standard link register. JMPL with *rd* = 0 can be used to return from a subroutine. The typical return address is "r[31]+8", if a non-leaf (uses SAVE instruction) subroutine is entered by a CALL instruction, or "r[15]+8" if a leaf (doesn't use SAVE instruction) subroutine is entered by a CALL instruction.

Implementation Note
When a RETT instruction appears in the delay slot of a JMPL, the target of the JMPL must be fetched from the address space implied by the **new** (i.e. post-RETT) value of the PSR's S bit. In particular, this applies to a return from trap to a user address space.

Traps:

mem_address_not_aligned

## B.26. Return from Trap Instruction

| opcode | op3 | operation |
|--------|-----|-----------|
| RETT† | 111001 | Return from Trap |

† privileged instruction

Format (3):

| 10 | unused (zero) | op3 | rs1 | i=0 | unused(zero) | rs2 |
|----|----|----|----|----|----|----|
| 31 | 29 | 24 | 18 | 13 | 12 | 4    0 |

| 10 | unused (zero) | op3 | rs1 | i=1 | simm13 |
|----|----|----|----|----|----|
| 31 | 29 | 24 | 18 | 13 | 12    0 |

| Suggested Assembly Language Syntax |
|------------------------------------|
| rett    address |

Description:

RETT is used to return from a trap handler. Under some circumstances, RETT may itself cause a trap. If a RETT instruction does not cause a trap, it (1) adds 1 to the CWP (modulo NWINDOWS), (2) causes a delayed control transfer to the target address, (3) restores the S field of the PSR from the PS field, and (4) sets the ET field of the PSR to 1. The target address is "r[$rs1$] + r[$rs2$]" if the $i$ field is zero, or "r[$rs1$] + sign_ext($simm13$)" if the $i$ field is one.

One of several traps may occur when an RETT is executed. These are described in priority order (highest priority first):

□ If traps are enabled (ET=1) and the processor is in user mode (S=0), a privileged_instruction trap occurs.

□ If traps are enabled (ET=1) and the processor is in supervisor mode (S=1), an illegal_instruction trap occurs.

□ If traps are disabled (ET=0), and (a) the processor is in user mode (S=0), or (b) a window_underflow condition is detected (WIM **and** $2^{new\_CWP}$) = 1, or (c) either of the low-order two bits of the target address is nonzero, then the processor indicates a trap condition of (a) privileged_instruction, (b) window_underflow, or (c) mem_address_not_aligned (respectively) in the $tt$ field of the TBR register, and enters the error_mode state.

The instruction executed immediately before an RETT must be a JMPL instruction. (If not, one or more instruction accesses following the RETT may be to an incorrect address space.)

Programming Note    To reexecute the trapped instruction when returning from a trap handler use the sequence:

```
jmpl    %r17,%r0    ! old PC
rett    %r18        ! old nPC
```

To return to the instruction after the trapped instruction (for example, after emulating an instruction) use the sequence:

```
jmpl    %r18,%r0    ! old nPC
```

SPARC International, Inc.

```
                    rett   %r18+4    ! old nPC + 4
```

Traps:

illegal_instruction
privileged_instruction
privileged_instruction (may cause processor to enter error_mode)
mem_address_not_aligned (may cause processor to enter error_mode)
window_underflow (may cause processor to enter error_mode)

SPARC International, Inc.

## B.27.  Trap on Integer Condition Codes Instruction

| opcode | cond | operation | icc test |
|--------|------|-----------|----------|
| TA | 1000 | Trap Always | 1 |
| TN | 0000 | Trap Never | 0 |
| TNE | 1001 | Trap on Not Equal | not Z |
| TE | 0001 | Trap on Equal | Z |
| TG | 1010 | Trap on Greater | not (Z or (N xor V)) |
| TLE | 0010 | Trap on Less or Equal | Z or (N xor V) |
| TGE | 1011 | Trap on Greater or Equal | not (N xor V) |
| TL | 0011 | Trap on Less | N xor V |
| TGU | 1100 | Trap on Greater Unsigned | not (C or Z) |
| TLEU | 0100 | Trap on Less or Equal Unsigned | (C or Z) |
| TCC | 1101 | Trap on Carry Clear (Greater than or Equal, Unsigned) | not C |
| TCS | 0101 | Trap on Carry Set (Less Than, Unsigned) | C |
| TPOS | 1110 | Trap on Positive | not N |
| TNEG | 0110 | Trap on Negative | N |
| TVC | 1111 | Trap on Overflow Clear | not V |
| TVS | 0111 | Trap on Overflow Set | V |

Format (3):

| 10 | reserved | cond | 111010 | rs1 | i=0 | reserved | rs2 |
|----|----------|------|--------|-----|-----|----------|-----|
| 31 | 29 | 28 | 24 | 18 | 13 | 12 | 4  0 |

| 10 | reserved | cond | 111010 | rs1 | i=1 | reserved | imm7 |
|----|----------|------|--------|-----|-----|----------|------|
| 31 | 29 | 28 | 24 | 18 | 13 | 12 | 6  0 |

| *Suggested Assembly Language Syntax* |
|---|
| ta        *software_trap#* |
| tn        *software_trap#* |
| tne       *software_trap#*    *(synonym:* tnz*)* |
| te        *software_trap#*    *(synonym:* tz*)* |
| tg        *software_trap#* |
| tle       *software_trap#* |
| tge       *software_trap#* |
| tl        *software_trap#* |
| tgu       *software_trap#* |
| tleu      *software_trap#* |
| tcc       *software_trap#*    *(synonym:* tgeu*)* |
| tcs       *software_trap#*    *(synonym:* tlu*)* |
| tpos      *software_trap#* |
| tneg      *software_trap#* |
| tvc       *software_trap#* |
| tvs       *software_trap#* |

Description:

A Ticc instruction evaluates the integer condition codes (*icc*) according to the *cond* field of the instruction, producing either a "true" or "false" result. If "true" and no higher priority exceptions or interrupt requests are pending, then a trap_instruction trap is generated. If "false", a trap_instruction trap does not occur and the instruction behaves like a NOP.

If a trap_instruction trap is generated, the *tt* field of the Trap Base Register (TBR) is written with 128 plus the least significant seven bits of "r[*rs1*] + r[*rs2*]" if the *i* field is zero, or 128 plus the least significant seven bits of "r[*rs1*] + sign_ext(*software_trap#*)" if the *i* field is one.

After a taken Ticc, the processor enters supervisor mode, disables traps, decrements the CWP (modulo NWINDOWS), and saves PC and nPC into r[17] and r[18] (*local* registers 1 and 2) of the new window. See Chapter 7, "Traps."

Programming Note    Ticc can be used to implement breakpointing, tracing, and calls to supervisor software. It can also be used for run-time checks, such as out-of-range array indexes, integer overflow, etc.

Traps:

trap_instruction

## B.28. Read State Register Instructions

| opcode | op3 | rs1 | operation |
|--------|-----|-----|-----------|
| RDY | 101000 | 0 | Read Y Register |
| RDASR‡ | 101000 | 1 – 15 | Read Ancillary State Register (*reserved*) |
| RDASR‡ | 101000 | 16 – 31 | (*implementation-dependent*) |
| RDPSR† | 101001 | reserved | Read Processor State Register |
| RDWIM† | 101010 | reserved | Read Window Invalid Mask Register |
| RDTBR† | 101011 | reserved | Read Trap Base Register |

† privileged instruction
‡ privileged instruction if source register is privileged

Format (3):

| 10 | rd | op3 | rs1 | unused (zero) | unused(zero) |
|----|----|-----|-----|---------------|--------------|

31    29         24            18    13    12              0

| Suggested Assembly Language Syntax |
|-----|
| rd    %y,    $reg_{rd}$ |
| rd    $asr\_reg_{rs1}$, $reg_{rd}$ |
| rd    %psr, $reg_{rd}$ |
| rd    %wim, $reg_{rd}$ |
| rd    %tbr, $reg_{rd}$ |

Description:

These instructions read the specified IU state register into r[$rd$].

Note that RDY is distinguished from RDASR only by the $rs1$ field. The $rs1$ field must be zero and $op3$ = 0x28 to read the Y register.

If $rs1 \neq 0$ and $op3$ = 0x28, then an implementation-dependent ancillary state register is read. Values of $rs1$ in the range 1...14 are reserved for future versions of the architecture; values 16...31 are available for implementations to use. An RDASR instruction with $rs1$ = 15 and $rd$ = 0 is defined to be an STBAR instruction (see Section B.30 for its description). RDASR with $rs1$ = 15 and $rd \neq 0$ is reserved for future versions of the architecture.

An $rs1$ value of 1...14 in an RDASR instruction produces undefined results, but does not cause an illegal_instruction trap.

For an RDASR instruction with $rs1$ in the range 16...31, the following are implementation-dependent: the interpretation of bits 13:0 and 29:25 in the instruction, whether the instruction is privileged or not, and whether the instruction causes an illegal_instruction trap or not.

Implementation Note    Ancillary state registers may include (for example) timer, counter, diagnostic, self-test, and trap-control registers. See Appendix L, "Implementation Characteristics," for information on implemented ancillary state registers.

Traps:

privileged_instruction (except RDY)
illegal_instruction (RDASR only; implementation-dependent)

## B.29. Write State Register Instructions

| opcode | op3 | rd | operation |
|--------|-----|-----|-----------|
| WRY | 110000 | 0 | Write Y Register |
| WRASR‡ | 110000 | 1 – 15 | Write Ancillary State Register (*reserved*) |
| WRASR‡ | 110000 | 16 – 31 | (*implementation-dependent*) |
| WRPSR† | 110001 | reserved | Write Processor State Register |
| WRWIM† | 110010 | reserved | Write Window Invalid Mask Register |
| WRTBR† | 110011 | reserved | Write Trap Base Register |

† privileged instruction
‡ privileged instruction if destination register is privileged

Format (3):

| 10 | rd | op3 | rs1 | i=0 | unused(zero) | rs2 |
|----|-----|-----|-----|-----|--------------|-----|
| 31 | 29 | 24 | 18 | 13 | 12 | 4 0 |

| 10 | rd | op3 | rs1 | i=1 | simm13 |
|----|-----|-----|-----|-----|--------|
| 31 | 29 | 24 | 18 | 13 | 12 0 |

| Suggested Assembly Language Syntax |
|-----------------------------------|
| wr    reg*rs1* , reg_or_imm , %y |
| wr    reg*rs1* , reg_or_imm , asr_reg*rd* |
| wr    reg*rs1* , reg_or_imm , %psr |
| wr    reg*rs1* , reg_or_imm , %wim |
| wr    reg*rs1* , reg_or_imm , %tbr |

Description:

WRY, WRPSR, WRWIM, and WRTBR write "r[$rs1$] **xor** r[$rs2$]" if the $i$ field is zero, or "r[$rs1$] **xor** sign_ext($simm13$)" if the $i$ field is one, to the writable fields of the specified IU state register. (Note the exclusive-or operation.)

Note that WRY is distinguished from WRASR only by the $rd$ field. The $rd$ field must be zero and $op3$ = 0x30 to write the Y register.

WRASR writes a value to the ancillary state register (ASR) indicated by $rd$. The operation performed to generate the value written may be $rd$-dependent or implementation-dependent (see below). A WRASR instruction is indicated by $rd \neq 0$ and $op3$ = 0x30.

WRASR instructions with $rd$ in the range 1...15 are reserved for future versions of the architecture; executing a WRASR instruction with $rd$ in that range produces undefined results.

WRASR instructions with $rd$ in the range 16...31 are available for implementation-dependent uses. For a WRASR instruction with $rd$ in the range 16...31, the following are implementation-dependent: the interpretation of bits 18:0 in the instruction, the operation(s) performed (for example,

SPARC International, Inc.

**xor**) to generate the value written to the ASR, whether the instruction is privileged or not, and whether the instruction causes an illegal_instruction trap or not. In some existing implementations, WRASR instructions may write the Y register (see Appendix L, "Implementation Characteristics"). WRASR in new implementations must not write the Y register.

If the result of a WRPSR instruction would cause the CWP field of the PSR to point to an unimplemented window, it causes an illegal_instruction trap and does not write the PSR.

The write state register instructions are **delayed-write** instructions. That is, they may take until completion of the third instruction following the write instruction to consummate their write operation. The number of delay instructions (0 to 3) is implementation-dependent.

WRPSR appears to write the ET and PIL fields immediately with respect to interrupts.

The following paragraphs define the relationship between the writing of a field of a state register and that field's being simultaneously or subsequently accessed:

1. If any of the three instructions after a write state register instruction **writes** any field of its destination register, the subsequent contents of that field are undefined. The exception to this is that another instance of the **same** write state register instruction (e.g. a WRPSR following within three instructions of another WRPSR) will write the field as intended.

   Programming Note
   > Many instructions implicitly write the CWP or *icc* fields of the PSR. For example, SAVE, RESTORE, traps, and RETT write CWP, and many instructions write *icc*.

2. If any of the three instructions after a write state register instruction **reads** any field that was **changed** by the original write state register instruction, the contents of that field read by that instruction are undefined.

   Programming Note
   > Many instructions implicitly read CWP or *icc*. For example, CALL implicitly reads CWP; instructions that reference an integer non-global (windowed) register implicitly read CWP; SAVE, RESTORE, RETT, and traps (including Ticc) read CWP, and Bicc and Ticc read the *icc* field.

   Programming Note
   > SAVE, RESTORE and RETT implicitly read WIM. If any of them executes within three instructions after a WRWIM which changes the contents of the WIM, the occurrence of window_overflow and window_underflow traps is unpredictable.

   Programming Note
   > MULScc, RDY, SDIV, SDIVcc, UDIV, and UDIVcc implicitly read the Y register. If any of these instructions execute within three instructions after a WRY which changed the contents of the Y register, its results are undefined.

3. In some implementations, if a WRPSR instruction updates the PSR's PIL field to a new value and simultaneously sets ET to 1, an interrupt trap at a level equal to the old value of the PIL may result.

SPARC International, Inc.

Programming Note
> A pair of WRPSR instructions should be used when enabling traps and changing the value of the PIL. The first WRPSR should specify ET=0 with the new PIL value, and the second WRPSR should specify ET=1 and the new PIL value.

Programming Note
> If traps are enabled (ET=1), care must be taken if software is to disable them (ET=0). Since the "RDPSR, WRPSR" sequence is interruptible — allowing the PSR to be changed between the two instructions — this sequence is not a reliable mechanism to disable traps. Two alternatives are:
> 1) Generate a Ticc trap, the handler for which disables traps. The trap handler should verify that it was indeed "called" from supervisor mode (by examining the PS bit of the PSR) before returning from the trap to the supervisor.
> 2) Use the "RDPSR, WRPSR" sequence, but write all the interrupt and trap handlers so that before they return to the supervisor, they restore the PSR to the value it had when the interrupt handler was entered.

4. If any of the three instructions that follow a WRPSR causes a trap, the values of the S and CWP fields read from the PSR while taking the trap may be either the old or the new values.

5. If any of the three instructions that follow a WRTBR causes a trap, the trap base address (TBA) used may be either the old or the new value.

6. If any of the three instructions after any write state register instruction causes a trap, a subsequent read state register instruction in the trap handler will get the state register's new value.

Implementation Note
Ancillary state registers may include (for example) timer, counter, diagnostic, self-test, and trap-control registers. See Appendix L, "Implementation Characteristics," for information on implemented ancillary state registers.

Implementation Note
Two possible ways to cause WRPSR to appear to write ET and PIL immediately with respect to interrupts are:
- Write ET and PIL immediately (propagating forward through the pipeline as needed)
- Disable interrupts during the subsequent three instructions

Traps:

privileged_instruction (except WRY)
illegal_instruction (WRPSR, if CWP ≥ NWINDOWS)
illegal_instruction (WRASR; implementation-dependent)

SPARC International, Inc.

## B.30. STBAR Instruction

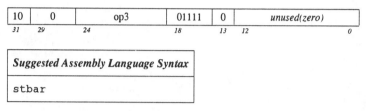

| opcode | op3 | operation |
|--------|--------|--------------|
| STBAR | 101000 | Store Barrier |

Format (3):

| 10 | 0 | op3 | 01111 | 0 | unused(zero) |
|----|---|-----|-------|---|--------------|
| 31 | 29 | 24 | 18 | 13 | 12           0 |

| Suggested Assembly Language Syntax |
|------------------------------------|
| stbar |

Description:

The store barrier instruction (STBAR) forces **all** store and atomic load-store operations issued by the processor prior to the STBAR to complete before **any** store or atomic load-store operations issued by the processor subsequent to the STBAR are executed by memory.

STBAR executes as a no-op on a machine that implements only the Strong Consistency memory model or the Total Store Ordering (TSO) memory model, and on a machine that implements the Partial Store Ordering (PSO) memory model but is running with the PSO mode disabled.

Note that the encoding of STBAR is identical to that of the RDASR instruction, except that $rs1 = 15$ and $rd = 0$.

Implementation Note

For correctness, it is sufficient for the processor to stop issuing new store and atomic load-store operations when an STBAR is encountered and resume after all stores have completed and are observed in memory by all processors. More efficient implementations may take advantage of the fact that the processor is allowed to issue store and load-store operations after the STBAR, as long as these operations are guaranteed not to be executed by memory before all the earlier stores and atomic load-stores have been executed by memory.

Traps:

(none)

SPARC International, Inc.

**B.31. Unimplemented Instruction**

| opcode | op | op2 | operation |
|--------|----|----|-----------|
| UNIMP | 00 | 000 | Unimplemented |

Format (2):

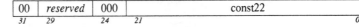

| 00 | reserved | 000 | const22 |
|----|----------|-----|---------|

31      29        24    21                                          0

| **Suggested Assembly Language Syntax** |
|----------------------------------------|
| unimp    const22 |

Description:

> The UNIMP instruction causes an illegal_instruction trap. The *const22* value is ignored by the hardware; specifically, its values are **not** reserved by the architecture for any future use.

Programming Note   This instruction can be used as part of the protocol for calling a function that is expected to return an aggregate value, such as a C-language struct or union or Pascal record. See Appendix D, "Software Considerations," for an example.

    a)    An UNIMP instruction is placed after (not in) the delay slot of the CALL instruction in the calling function.

    b)    If the called function is expecting to return a structure, it will find the size of the structure that the caller expects to be returned as the *const22* operand of the UNIMP instruction. The called function can check the opcode to make sure it is indeed UNIMP.

    c)    If the function is not going to return a structure, upon returning it attempts to execute the UNIMP instruction rather than skipping over it as it should. This causes the program to terminate. This behavior adds some run-time type checking to an interface that cannot be checked properly at compile time.

Traps:

> illegal_instruction

## B.32. Flush Instruction Memory

| opcode | op3 | operation |
|--------|------|-----------|
| FLUSH | 111011 | Flush Instruction Memory |

Format (3):

| 10 | unused (zero) | op3 | rs1 | i=0 | unused(zero) | rs2 |
|----|------|------|------|------|------|------|
| 31 | 29 | 24 | 18 | 13 | 12 | 4  0 |

| 10 | unused (zero) | op3 | rs1 | i=1 | simm13 |
|----|------|------|------|------|------|
| 31 | 29 | 24 | 18 | 13 | 12   0 |

| Suggested Assembly Language Syntax |
|------------------------------------|
| flush     address |

Description:

The FLUSH instruction ensures that subsequent instruction fetches to the target of the FLUSH by the processor executing the FLUSH appear to execute after any loads, stores, and atomic load-stores issued by that processor prior to the FLUSH.

In a multiprocessor system, FLUSH also ensures that stores and atomic load-stores to the target of the FLUSH, issued prior to the FLUSH by the processor executing the FLUSH, become visible to the instruction fetches of all other processors some time after the execution of the FLUSH.

When a processor executes a sequence of store or atomic load-stores interspersed with appropriate FLUSH and STBAR instructions, (the latter needed only for the PSO memory model), the changes appear to the instruction fetches of all processors to occur in the order in which they were made. See Chapter 6, "Memory Model," and Appendix K, "Formal Specification of the Memory Model" for a definition of what constitutes appropriate FLUSH and STBAR instructions in such a sequence.

FLUSH operates on the doubleword containing the addressed location.

A FLUSH is needed only between a store and a subsequent **instruction access** to the modified location. The memory model guarantees that **data** loads observe the results of the most recent store even if there is no intervening FLUSH. See Chapter 6, "Memory Model."

The effective virtual address operand for the FLUSH instruction is "r[$rs1$] + r[$rs2$]" if the $i$ field is zero, or "r[$rs1$] + sign_ext($simm13$)" if the $i$ field is one. The least significant two address bits of the result are unused and should be supplied as zero by software. Bit 2 of the address is ignored.

By the time five instructions subsequent to a FLUSH have executed, any internal copy of the addressed location in the issuing processor will contain

SPARC International, Inc.

the same value as the one which would be seen if read from memory. For example, the processor pipeline or instruction buffers might contain an internal copy of the addressed location. See IBuf in Chapter 6, "Memory Model." FLUSH does **not** necessarily affect such internal copies in other processors attached to the memory system.

Programming Notes

(1) FLUSH is typically used in self-modifying code.

(2) Although FLUSH provides support for self-modifying code, the use of self-modifying code is not encouraged. FLUSH may be a time-consuming operation on some implementations.

Implementation Notes

(1) FLUSH may operate on more than just the doubleword implied by the effective address. In particular, it may flush one or more containing cache lines or blocks.

(2) In a uniprocessor system with a combined I and D cache (or no cache) and a total pipeline (store buffer plus IBuf) depth of no more than five instructions, FLUSH may not need to perform any operation.

In a uniprocessor system with split I and D caches, FLUSH ensures that if both caches contain a copy of the contents of the addressed location, those cached copies eventually become consistent.

In a multiprocessor system with caches, FLUSH ensures that all cached copies of the contents of the addressed location are consistent.

Cache consistency may be implemented by any combination of invalidation, write-back of cached data, or other implementation-dependent consistency mechanisms.

(3) If FLUSH is not implemented in hardware as described above, FLUSH causes an unimplemented_FLUSH (or illegal_instruction) trap, and the function of FLUSH is performed by system software. Whether FLUSH traps or not is implementation-dependent. If it does trap, it causes an unimplemented_FLUSH or illegal_instruction trap. On implementations where unimplemented_FLUSH supports faster software emulation of FLUSH than does illegal_instruction, use of unimplemented_FLUSH is preferred. An implementation may select the trapping behavior of the FLUSH instruction based on a pin or an implementation-dependent bit in a control register.

(4) In a given implementation, FLUSH may need to flush the processor's IBuf and/or pipeline to fulfill the requirement that the IBuf and pipeline will be consistent with the cache within five instructions.

(5) The number of instructions which must execute after a FLUSH before its effect is complete is implementation-dependent, but is at most 5.

(6) See Appendix L, "Implementation Characteristics," for implementation-specific information about the FLUSH instruction.

Traps:

unimplemented_FLUSH  (*implementation-dependent*) illegal_instruction (*implementation-dependent*)

## B.33. Floating-point Operate (FPop) Instructions

| opcode | op3 | operation |
|--------|--------|------------------------|
| FPop1 | 110100 | Floating-point operate |
| FPop2 | 110101 | Floating-point operate |

Format (3):

| 10 | rd | 110100 | rs1 | opf | rs2 |
|----|----|--------|-----|-----|-----|

31    29    24              18    13          4    0

| 10 | rd | 110101 | rs1 | opf | rs2 |
|----|----|--------|-----|-----|-----|

31    29    24              18    13          4    0

Description:

The Floating-point Operate (FPop) instructions are encoded using two type 3 formats: FPop1 and FPop2. The particular floating-point operation is indicated by *opf* field. Note that the load/store floating-point instructions are not FPop instructions.

FPop1 instructions do not affect the floating-point condition codes. FPop2 instructions may affect the floating-point condition codes.

The FPop instructions support operations between integer words and single-, double-, and quad-precision floating-point operands in $f$ register(s).

All FPop instructions operate according to ANSI/IEEE Std. 754-1985 on single, double, and quad formats. See Chapter 3, "Data Formats," for definitions of the floating-point data types.

The least significant bit of an $f$ register address is unused by double-precision FPops, and the least significant 2 bits of an $f$ register address are unused by quad-precision FPop instructions. The unused register address bits are reserved and, for future compatibility, should be supplied as zeros by software. If these bits are non-zero in an FPop with a double- or quad-precision operand, it is recommended that the FPop cause an fp_exception trap with FSR.*ftt* = invalid_fp_register.

If an FPop2 (for example, FCMP, FCMPE) instruction sets the floating-point condition codes, then at least one non-FPop2 (non-floating-point-operate2) instruction must be executed between the FPop2 and a subsequent FBfcc instruction. Otherwise, the result of the FBfcc is undefined.

An FPop instruction causes an fp_disabled trap if either the EF field of the PSR is 0 or no FPU is present.

Floating-point exceptions may cause either precise or deferred traps. See Chapter 7, "Traps."

Programming Note    See Appendix G, "SPARC ABI Software Considerations," regarding use of FSQRT, FsMULd, and quad-precision floating-point instructions in SPARC ABI software.

Implementation Note    See Appendix L, "Implementation Characteristics," for information on whether FsMULd, FdMULq, and the quad-precision instructions are executed in hardware or software in the various SPARC implementations.

SPARC International, Inc.

**Convert Integer to Floating point Instructions**

| opcode | opf | operation |
|--------|-----|-----------|
| FiTOs | 011000100 | Convert Integer to Single |
| FiTOd | 011001000 | Convert Integer to Double |
| FiTOq | 011001100 | Convert Integer to Quad |

Format (3):

| 10 | rd | 110100 | unused(zero) | opf | rs2 |
|----|----|--------|--------------|-----|-----|

31  29   24        18          13         4    0

| Suggested Assembly Language Syntax |
|------------------------------------|
| fitos    $freg_{rs2}$ , $freg_{rd}$ |
| fitod    $freg_{rs2}$ , $freg_{rd}$ |
| fitoq    $freg_{rs2}$ , $freg_{rd}$ |

Description:

These instructions convert the 32-bit integer word operand in f[*rs2*] into a floating-point number in the destination format. They write the result into the *f* register(s) specified by *rd*.

FiTOs rounds according to the RD field of the FSR.

Programming Note    See Appendix G, "SPARC ABI Software Considerations," regarding use of the FiTOq instruction in SPARC ABI software.

Traps:

fp_disabled
fp_exception (NX (FiTOs only), invalid_fp_register(FiTOd, FiTOq))

SPARC International, Inc.

**Convert Floating point to Integer Instructions**

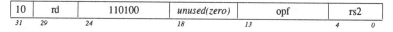

| opcode | opf | operation |
|--------|-----|-----------|
| FsTOi | 011010001 | Convert Single to Integer |
| FdTOi | 011010010 | Convert Double to Integer |
| FqTOi | 011010011 | Convert Quad to Integer |

Format (3):

| 10 | rd | 110100 | unused(zero) | opf | rs2 |
|----|----|--------|--------------|-----|-----|
| 31 | 29 | 24 | 18 | 13 | 4    0 |

| *Suggested Assembly Language Syntax* |  |
|--------|--------|
| fstoi | $freg_{rs2}$ , $freg_{rd}$ |
| fdtoi | $freg_{rs2}$ , $freg_{rd}$ |
| fqtoi | $freg_{rs2}$ , $freg_{rd}$ |

Description:

These instructions convert the floating-point operand in the $f$ register(s) specified by *rs2* into a 32-bit integer word in f[*rd*].

The result is always rounded toward zero (the RD field of the FSR register is ignored).

Programming Note    See Appendix G, "SPARC ABI Software Considerations," regarding use of the FqTOi instruction in SPARC ABI software.

Traps:

fp_disabled
fp_exception (NV, NX, invalid_fp_register(FdTOi, FqTOi))

SPARC International, Inc.

**Convert Between Floating-point Formats Instructions**

| opcode | opf | operation |
|--------|-----|-----------|
| FsTOd | 011001001 | Convert Single to Double |
| FsTOq | 011001101 | Convert Single to Quad |
| FdTOs | 011000110 | Convert Double to Single |
| FdTOq | 011001110 | Convert Double to Quad |
| FqTOs | 011000111 | Convert Quad to Single |
| FqTOd | 011001011 | Convert Quad to Double |

Format (3):

| 10 | rd | 110100 | unused(zero) | opf | rs2 |
|----|----|--------|--------------|-----|-----|
| 31 | 29 | 24 | 18 | 13 | 4 0 |

| Suggested Assembly Language Syntax | |
|---|---|
| fstod | $freg_{rs2}$ , $freg_{rd}$ |
| fstoq | $freg_{rs2}$ , $freg_{rd}$ |
| fdtos | $freg_{rs2}$ , $freg_{rd}$ |
| fdtoq | $freg_{rs2}$ , $freg_{rd}$ |
| fqtos | $freg_{rs2}$ , $freg_{rd}$ |
| fqtod | $freg_{rs2}$ , $freg_{rd}$ |

Description:

These instructions convert the floating-point operand in the $f$ register(s) specified by $rs2$ to a floating-point number in the destination format. They write the result into the $f$ register(s) specified by $rd$.

Rounding is performed according to the RD field of the FSR.

FqTOd, FqTOs, and FdTOs (the "narrowing" conversion instructions) can raise OF, UF, and NX exceptions. FdTOq, FsTOq, and FsTOd (the "widening" conversion instructions) cannot.

Any of these six instructions can trigger an NV exception if the source operand is a signaling NaN.

Programming Note    See Appendix G, "SPARC ABI Software Considerations," regarding use of the FsTOq, FdTOq, FqTOs, and FqTOd instructions in SPARC ABI software.

Traps:

fp_disabled
fp_exception (OF, UF, NV, NX, invalid_fp_register)

SPARC International, Inc.

**Floating-point Move
Instructions**

| opcode | opf | operation |
|--------|-----|-----------|
| FMOVs | 000000001 | Move |
| FNEGs | 000000101 | Negate |
| FABSs | 000001001 | Absolute Value |

Format (3):

| 10 | rd | 110100 | unused(zero) | opf | rs2 |
|----|----|--------|--------------|-----|-----|

31    29         24              18          13      4    0

| Suggested Assembly Language Syntax |
|-----------------------------------|
| fmovs    $freg_{rs2}$ , $freg_{rd}$ |
| fnegs    $freg_{rs2}$ , $freg_{rd}$ |
| fabss    $freg_{rs2}$ , $freg_{rd}$ |

Description:

FMOVs copies the contents of f[$rs2$] to f[$rd$].

FNEGs copies the contents of f[$rs2$] to f[$rd$] with the sign bit complemented.

FABSs copies the contents of f[$rs2$] to f[$rd$] with the sign bit cleared.

These instructions do not round.

Programming Note    To transfer a multiple-precision value between $f$ registers, one FMOVs instruction is required per word to be transferred.

Programming Note    If the source and destination registers ($freg_{rs2}$ and $freg_{rd}$) are the same, a single FNEGs (FABSs) instruction performs negation (absolute-value) for any operand precision, including double and quad.

If the source and destination registers are different, a double-precision negation (absolute value) is performed by an FNEGs (FABSs) and an FMOVs instruction. Similarly, a quad-precision negation (absolute value) requires an FNEGs (FABSs) and three FMOVs instructions.

See Section 3, "Data Formats," for the formats of the floating-point data types.

Traps:

fp_disabled

**Floating-point Square Root Instructions**

| opcode | opf | operation |
|--------|-----|-----------|
| FSQRTs | 000101001 | Square Root Single |
| FSQRTd | 000101010 | Square Root Double |
| FSQRTq | 000101011 | Square Root Quad |

Format (3):

| 10 | rd | 110100 | unused(zero) | opf | rs2 |
|----|-----|--------|--------------|-----|-----|
| 31 | 29 | 24 | 18 | 13 | 4   0 |

| Suggested Assembly Language Syntax |
|------------------------------------|
| fsqrts  $freg_{rs2}$ , $freg_{rd}$ |
| fsqrtd  $freg_{rs2}$ , $freg_{rd}$ |
| fsqrtq  $freg_{rs2}$ , $freg_{rd}$ |

Description:

These instructions generate the square root of the floating-point operand in the $f$ register(s) specified by the $rs2$ field. They place the result in the destination $f$ register(s) specified by the $rd$ field.

Rounding is performed according to the $rd$ field of the FSR.

Programming Note    See Appendix G, "SPARC ABI Software Considerations," regarding use of FSQRT instructions in SPARC ABI software.

Implementation Note    See Appendix L, "Implementation Characteristics," for information on whether the FSQRT instructions are executed in hardware or in software in the various SPARC implementations.

Traps:

fp_disabled
fp_exception (NV, NX, invalid_fp_register(FSQRTd, FSQRTq))

**Floating-point Add and
Subtract Instructions**

| opcode | opf | operation |
|--------|-----|-----------|
| FADDs | 001000001 | Add Single |
| FADDd | 001000010 | Add Double |
| FADDq | 001000011 | Add Quad |
| FSUBs | 001000101 | Subtract Single |
| FSUBd | 001000110 | Subtract Double |
| FSUBq | 001000111 | Subtract Quad |

Format (3):

| 10 | rd | 110100 | rs1 | opf | rs2 |
|----|----|--------|-----|-----|-----|

31    29         24           18    13          4    0

| Suggested Assembly Language Syntax |
|---|
| fadds    $freg_{rs1}$ , $freg_{rs2}$ , $freg_{rd}$ |
| faddd    $freg_{rs1}$ , $freg_{rs2}$ , $freg_{rd}$ |
| faddq    $freg_{rs1}$ , $freg_{rs2}$ , $freg_{rd}$ |
| fsubs    $freg_{rs1}$ , $freg_{rs2}$ , $freg_{rd}$ |
| fsubd    $freg_{rs1}$ , $freg_{rs2}$ , $freg_{rd}$ |
| fsubq    $freg_{rs1}$ , $freg_{rs2}$ , $freg_{rd}$ |

Description:

The floating-point add instructions add the $f$ register(s) specified by the $rs1$ field and the $f$ register(s) specified by the $rs2$ field, and write the sum into the $f$ register(s) specified by the $rd$ field.

The floating-point subtract instructions subtract the $f$ register(s) specified by the $rs2$ field from the $f$ register(s) specified by the $rs1$ field, and write the difference into the $f$ register(s) specified by the $rd$ field.

Programming Note    See Appendix G, "SPARC ABI Software Considerations," regarding use of the FADDq and FSUBq instructions in SPARC ABI software.

Traps:

fp_disabled
fp_exception (OF, UF, NX, NV ($\infty - \infty$),
          invalid_fp_register(all except FADDs and FSUBs))

SPARC International, Inc.

## Floating-point Multiply and Divide Instructions

| opcode | opf | operation |
|--------|-----|-----------|
| FMULs | 001001001 | Multiply Single |
| FMULd | 001001010 | Multiply Double |
| FMULq | 001001011 | Multiply Quad |
| FsMULd | 001101001 | Multiply Single to Double |
| FdMULq | 001101110 | Multiply Double to Quad |
| FDIVs | 001001101 | Divide Single |
| FDIVd | 001001110 | Divide Double |
| FDIVq | 001001111 | Divide Quad |

Format (3):

| 10 | rd | 110100 | rs1 | opf | rs2 |
|----|----|--------|-----|-----|-----|
| 31 | 29 | 24 | 18 | 13 | 4    0 |

| Suggested Assembly Language Syntax | |
|---|---|
| fmuls | $freg_{rs1}$ , $freg_{rs2}$ , $freg_{rd}$ |
| fmuld | $freg_{rs1}$ , $freg_{rs2}$ , $freg_{rd}$ |
| fmulq | $freg_{rs1}$ , $freg_{rs2}$ , $freg_{rd}$ |
| fsmuld | $freg_{rs1}$ , $freg_{rs2}$ , $freg_{rd}$ |
| fdmulq | $freg_{rs1}$ , $freg_{rs2}$ , $freg_{rd}$ |
| fdivs | $freg_{rs1}$ , $freg_{rs2}$ , $freg_{rd}$ |
| fdivd | $freg_{rs1}$ , $freg_{rs2}$ , $freg_{rd}$ |
| fdivq | $freg_{rs1}$ , $freg_{rs2}$ , $freg_{rd}$ |

Description:

The floating-point multiply instructions multiply the $f$ register(s) specified by the *rs1* field by the $f$ register(s) specified by the *rs2* field, and write the product into the $f$ register(s) specified by the *rd* field.

The FsMULd instruction provides the exact double-precision product of two single-precision operands, without underflow, overflow, or rounding error. Similarly, FdMULq provides the exact quad-precision product of two double-precision operands.

The floating-point divide instructions divide the $f$ register(s) specified by the *rs1* field by the $f$ register(s) specified by the *rs2* field, and write the quotient into the $f$ register(s) specified by the *rd* field.

Programming Note    See Appendix G, "SPARC ABI Software Considerations," regarding use of the FMULq, FDIVq, FsMULd, and FdMULq instructions in SPARC ABI software.

Traps:

fp_disabled
fp_exception (OF, UF, DZ (FDIV only), NV, NX,
                invalid_fp_register(all except FMULs and FDIVs))

SPARC International, Inc.

## Floating-point Compare Instructions

| opcode | opf | operation |
|--------|-----|-----------|
| FCMPs | 001010001 | Compare Single |
| FCMPd | 001010010 | Compare Double |
| FCMPq | 001010011 | Compare Quad |
| FCMPEs | 001010101 | Compare Single and Exception if Unordered |
| FCMPEd | 001010110 | Compare Double and Exception if Unordered |
| FCMPEq | 001010111 | Compare Quad and Exception if Unordered |

Format (3):

| 10 | unused(zero) | 110101 | rs1 | opf | rs2 |
|----|------|------|------|------|------|
| 31 | 29 | 24 | 18 | 13 | 4    0 |

| Suggested Assembly Language Syntax | |
|---|---|
| fcmps | $freg_{rs1}$ , $freg_{rs2}$ |
| fcmpd | $freg_{rs1}$ , $freg_{rs2}$ |
| fcmpq | $freg_{rs1}$ , $freg_{rs2}$ |
| fcmpes | $freg_{rs1}$ , $freg_{rs2}$ |
| fcmped | $freg_{rs1}$ , $freg_{rs2}$ |
| fcmpeq | $freg_{rs1}$ , $freg_{rs2}$ |

Description:

These instructions compare the $f$ register(s) specified by the *rs1* field with the $f$ register(s) specified by the *rs2* field, and set the floating-point condition codes according to the following table:

Table B-2    *Floating-point Condition Codes (fcc)*

| fcc | Relation |
|-----|----------|
| 0 | $freg_{rs1} = freg_{rs2}$ |
| 1 | $freg_{rs1} < freg_{rs2}$ |
| 2 | $freg_{rs1} > freg_{rs2}$ |
| 3 | $freg_{rs1} \, ? \, freg_{rs2}$ (unordered) |

The "compare and cause exception if unordered" (FCMPEs, FCMPEd, and FCMPEq) instructions cause an invalid (NV) exception if either operand is a signaling NaN or a quiet NaN. FCMP causes an invalid (NV) exception if either operand is a signaling NaN.

A non-FPop2 (non-floating-point-operate2) instruction must be executed between an FPop2 (FCMP or FCMPE) instruction and a subsequent FBfcc instruction. Otherwise, the result of the FBfcc is unpredictable.

Programming Note    See Appendix G, "SPARC ABI Software Considerations," regarding use of the FCMPq and FCMPEq instructions in SPARC ABI software.

Traps:
    fp_disabled
    fp_exception (NV, invalid_fp_register(all except FCMPs and FCMPEs))

## B.34. Coprocessor Operate Instructions

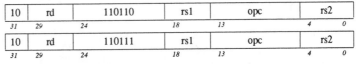

| opcode | op3 | operation |
|--------|--------|----------------------|
| CPop1 | 110110 | Coprocessor Operate |
| CPop2 | 110111 | Coprocessor Operate |

Format (3):

| 10 | rd | 110110 | rs1 | opc | rs2 |
|----|----|--------|-----|-----|-----|

31   29   24          18   13      4   0

| 10 | rd | 110111 | rs1 | opc | rs2 |
|----|----|--------|-----|-----|-----|

31   29   24          18   13      4   0

| **Suggested Assembly Language Syntax** |
|---|
| cpop1    $opc$, $creg_{rs1}$, $creg_{rs2}$, $creg_{rd}$ |
| cpop2    $opc$, $creg_{rs1}$, $creg_{rs2}$, $creg_{rd}$ |

Note    The above is a suggested "generic" assembly language syntax for these instructions, which may be used in an implementation-independent SPARC assembler. It is expected that assemblers supporting specific coprocessor implementations will (also) support syntaxes with more mnemonic instruction names and fewer operands.

Description:

The Coprocessor Operate (CPop) instructions are encoded via two type 3 formats: CPop1 and CPop2. Interpretation of the $rd$, $rs1$, $opc$, and $rs2$ fields is coprocessor-dependent. Note that the load/store coprocessor instructions are not "CPop" instructions.

CPop1 instructions do not affect the coprocessor condition codes. CPop2 instructions may affect the coprocessor condition codes.

All CPop instructions take all operands from and return all results to coprocessor registers. The data types supported by a coprocessor are coprocessor-dependent. Operand alignment within the coprocessor is coprocessor-dependent.

If the EC field of the PSR is 0 or if no coprocessor is present, a CPop instruction causes a cp_disabled trap.

The conditions under which execution of a CPop instruction causes a cp_exception trap are coprocessor-dependent.

Implementation Note    Typically, the particular coprocessor operation is indicated by the $opc$ field.

Traps:

cp_disabled
cp_exception (*coprocessor-dependent*)

# C

---

# ISP Descriptions

This Appendix provides a description of the SPARC architecture using instruction-set processor (**ISP**) notation, the semantics of which are summarized below. The ISP description assumes a sequential execution model with no instruction concurrency (except delayed branches) and all traps are precise. As pointed out elsewhere, an implementation need not conform to this model. See Chapter 7, "Traps."

## C.1. ISP Notation

The ISP notation used in this Appendix is a modified version of Bell and Newell's ISP notation, which was designed in 1971 to accurately describe ISAs and their implementations. While the semantics are intuitive, the following guidelines provide important details:

- The only data type is the **bit vector**. Variables are defined as bit vectors of particular widths, declared as **variable<n:m>**. Variable subfields can be defined, also with the **<n:m>** notation. The value of a vector is a number in a base indicated by its subscript. The default base is decimal. Arrays of vectors are declared as **array[n:m]**.

- The notation ← indicates variable assignment, and := indicates a macro definition.

- When a bit vector is assigned to another of greater length, the operand is right-justified in the destination vector and the high-order positions are zero-filled. The macro **zero_extend** is sometimes used to make this clear. Conversely, the macro **sign_extend** causes the high-order positions of the result to be filled with the highest-order (sign) bit of its operand.

- The semicolon ';' separates statements. Parentheses '()' group statements and expressions that could otherwise be interpreted ambiguously.

SPARC International, Inc.

▫ All statements are generally executed ''simultaneously''. However, if the term **next** appears, it indicates that the statement or statements that follow the **next** are executed after those that appear before the **next**. Thus, all statements between **next** phrases are executed concurrently. More precisely, this means that all expressions on the right hand sides of assignments located between **next**'s are evaluated first, after which the variables on the left hand sides are updated. (This convention emulates synchronous, clocked hardware.)

For example, if A=0 and B=0, execution of the following two statements,

```
A ← B+1;
B ← A+1;
```

results in A=1 and B=1. However,

```
A ← B+1;
next;
B ← A+1;
```

results in A=1 and B=2.

▫ The symbol ☐ designates concatenation of vectors. A comma ',' on the left side of an assignment separates quantities that are concatenated for the purpose of assignment. For example, if the 2-bit vector T2 equals 3, and X, Y, and Z are 1-bit vectors, then:

```
(X, Y, Z)  ←   0☐T2
```

results in X=0, Y=1, and Z=1.

▫ The operators '+' and '−' perform two's complement arithmetic.

▫ The major difference between the notation used here and Bell & Newell's ISP notation is that the notation used here uses the more common:

**if** cond **then** S1 **else** S2

notation, whereas Bell & Newell used:

```
(cond  →  S1,  ¬ cond  →  S2)
```

For the logical symbols, **or**, **and**, **xor**, and **not** are used instead of Bell & Newell's ∨, ∧, ⊕, and ¬.

## C.2. Processor External Interface Definition

The ISP description requires some signals and macros that portray a processor's external interface as it might appear in an implementation. This Appendix assumes the following macros and signals only for definitional purposes. The appearance of these, or any other variable in the ISP notation, does not necessarily imply their presence in a particular implementation or visibility to a user-application program.

**Interface Macros**

The macros `memory_read` and `memory_write` define a memory interface without assuming any particular implementation-specific signals:

```
(load_data, MAE) ← memory_read(addr_space, address)

MAE ← memory_write(addr_space, address, byte_mask,
                        store_data)
```

`memory_read` accesses the word in memory selected by both the 32-bit address `address` and the 8-bit address space identifier `addr_space`, and writes the 32-bit value into `load_data`. If a `memory_read` generates an exception, the 1-bit string `MAE` is written to 1, otherwise it is written to 0.

`memory_write` is defined as follows:

```
memory_write(addr_space, address, byte_mask, store_data) := (
     sync := store_barrier_pending or (not PSO_mode);
     MAE ← external_memory_write(sync, addr_space, address,
                                   byte_mask, store_data)
     store_barrier_pending ← 0;
);
```

`external_memory_write` stores all or part of the argument `store_data` into the word selected by `address` and address space identifier `addr_space`. `byte_mask` is a 4-bit string that encodes which of the 4 bytes are to be written into the addressed word. (The MSB corresponds to byte 0 and the LSB to byte 3). If its parameter `sync` is true, `external_memory_write` ensures that the current write to memory will be allowed to complete only after all previous writes have been completed by memory.

If a `memory_read` generates an exception, the 1-bit string `MAE` is written to 1, otherwise it is written to 0. If there is an exception, `memory_write` does not change the memory or an MMU, except possibly in the case of a "non-resumable machine-check error", as allowed by the default trap model.

**Interface Signals**

The interface signals described in this section are logically (if not physically) present in a SPARC implementation.

The naming convention used identifies signals logically sent from the bus to the processor (that is, IU) with a "bp_" prefix, and identifies those logically sent from the processor to the bus with a "pb_" prefix.

`bp_IRL<3:0>`  This external signal presents an asynchronous interrupt request to the processor. Level 0 indicates that no interrupt is being requested, and levels 1 through 15 request interrupts, with level 15 having the highest priority. Level 15 is non-maskable, unless all traps are disabled.

`bp_reset_in`  This signal indicates that the external system is requesting a reset. The processor responds by entering reset_mode and clearing `pb_error`.

SPARC International, Inc.

| | |
|---|---|
| `pb_error` | The processor asserts this signal when it is in error_mode. |
| `pb_block_ldst_word` | The processor asserts this signal to ensure that the memory system will not process another SWAP or LDSTUB operation to the same memory word. |
| `pb_block_ldst_byte` | The processor asserts this signal to ensure that the memory system will not process another SWAP or LDSTUB operation to the same memory byte. |
| `bp_FPU_present` | This signal indicates that an FPU is present. |
| `bp_FPU_exception` | The floating-point unit asserts this signal to cause an fp_exception trap. |
| `bp_FPU_cc<1:0>` | These are the condition codes for the floating-point branch instruction (FBfcc), from the *fcc* field of the floating-point status register (FSR). |
| `bp_CP_present` | This signal indicates that a coprocessor is present. |
| `bp_CP_exception` | The coprocessor asserts this signal to cause a cp_exception trap. |
| `bp_CP_cc<1:0>` | The coprocessor supplies these condition codes for the coprocessor branch instruction (CBccc). |

## C.3. Register Field Definitions

```
PSR<31:0>;                          { Processor State Register }
        impl                        := PSR<31:28>;
        ver                         := PSR<27:24>;
        icc                         := PSR<23:20>;
                N                       := PSR<23>;
                Z                       := PSR<22>;
                V                       := PSR<21>;
                C                       := PSR<20>;
        reserved_PSR                := PSR<19:14>;
        EC                          := PSR<13>;
        EF                          := PSR<12>;
        PIL                         := PSR<11:8>;
        S                           := PSR<7>;
        PS                          := PSR<6>;
        ET                          := PSR<5>;
        CWP                         := PSR<4:0>;


TBR<31:0>;                          { Trap Base Register }
        TBA                         := TBR<31:12>;
        tt                          := TBR<11:4>;
        zero                        := TBR<3:0>;


FSR<31:0>;                          { Floating-Point State Register }
```

SPARC International, Inc.

```
RD                    := FSR<31:30>;
unused0               := FSR<29:28>;
TEM                   := FSR<27:23>;
        NVM               := FSR<27>;
        OFM               := FSR<26>;
        UFM               := FSR<25>;
        DZM               := FSR<24>;
        NXM               := FSR<23>;
NS                    := FSR<22>;
reserved_FSR          := FSR<21:20>;
ver                   := FSR<19:17>;
ftt                   := FSR<16:14>;
qne                   := FSR<13>;
unused1               := FSR<12>;
fcc                   := FSR<11:10>;
aexc                  := FSR<9:5>;
        nva               := FSR<9>;
        ofa               := FSR<8>;
        ufa               := FSR<7>;
        dza               := FSR<6>;
        nxa               := FSR<5>;
cexc                  := FSR<4:0>;
        nvc               := FSR<4>;
        ofc               := FSR<3>;
        ufc               := FSR<2>;
        dzc               := FSR<1>;
        nxc               := FSR<0>;
```

```
G[1:7]<31:0>;                    { Global Registers }
R[0:(16×NWINDOWS)−1]<31:0>;      { Windowed Registers }
f[0:31]<31:0>;                   { Floating-Point Registers }
WIM<31:0>;                       { Window Invalid Mask Register }
Y<31:0>;                         { Y Register }
PC<31:0>;                        { Program Counter }
nPC<31:0>;                       { Next Program Counter }
```

SPARC International, Inc.

```
r[n] := if  (n = 0)
            then   0
            else if (1 ≤ n ≤ 7)
                then  G[n]              { globals }
                else  R[((n–8)+(CWP×16)) modulo (16×NWINDOWS)] ;  { windowed registers }

ASR[ 1:15]<31:0>;                       { Implementation-independent Ancillary State Registers }
ASR[16:31]<31:0>;                       { Implementation-dependent  Ancillary State Registers }

IEEE_754_exception      := 1;              { Floating-point trap types }
unfinished_FPop         := 2;
unimplemented_FPop      := 3;
sequence_error          := 4;
hardware_error          := 5;
invalid_fp_register     := 6;
```

## C.4. Instruction Field Definitions

The numbers in braces are the widths of the fields in bits.

```
instruction<31:0> ;
     op                {2} := instruction<31:30>;
     op2               {3} := instruction<24:22>;
     op3               {6} := instruction<24:19>;
     opf               {9} := instruction<13:5>;
     opc               {9} := instruction<13:5>;
     asi               {8} := instruction<12:5>;
     i                 {1} := instruction<13>;
     rd                {5} := instruction<29:25>;
     a                 {1} := instruction<29>;
     cond              {4} := instruction<28:25>;
     rs1               {5} := instruction<18:14>;
     rs2               {5} := instruction<4:0>;
     simm13           {13} := instruction<12:0>;
     shcnt             {5} := instruction<4:0>;
     disp30           {30} := instruction<29:0>;
     disp22           {22} := instruction<21:0>;
     software_trap#    {7} := instruction<6:0>;
```

## C.5. Processor States and Instruction Dispatch

According to this description, the processor can be in one of three states: execute_mode, reset_mode, or error_mode. (Note that the IU or FPU could have more states depending on the degree of instruction concurrency and the presence of deferred or interrupting traps.)

The processor is defined to be in reset_mode when bp_reset_in is asserted. The processor remains in reset_mode until bp_reset_in is reset, at which point it enters execute_mode and begins executing at address 0 with *addr_space* = 9.

While in execute_mode, the processor checks for interrupt requests and exception traps before reading the instruction given by the program counter. If the previous instruction was not an annulling control transfer, the instruction is dispatched.  A dispatched instruction is either executed or raises an exception.

The processor can enter the `error_mode` state from any state except `reset_mode` if an exception trap is generated while traps are disabled (ET = 0).

According to this description, the processor remains in `error_mode` until `bp_reset_in` is asserted. (An implementation can assert `bp_reset_in` whenever `pb_error` is detected in order to cause a reset trap.)

```
while (reset_mode = 1) (
    if (bp_reset_in = 0) then (
        reset_mode ← 0;
        execute_mode ← 1;
        trap ← 1;
        reset_trap ← 1
    )
);
```

```
while (error_mode = 1)  (
    if (bp_reset_in = 1) then (
        error_mode ← 0;
        reset_mode ← 1;
        pb_error ← 0
    )
);
```

SPARC International, Inc.

```
while (execute_mode = 1) (
    if (bp_reset_in = 1) then (
        execute_mode ← 0;
        reset_mode ← 1;
        break    { out of  while (execute_mode = 1)  loop }
    ) else if ((ET = 1) and ((bp_IRL = 15) or (bp_IRL > PIL))) then (
        trap ← 1;
        interrupt_level ← bp_IRL
    );
    next;

    if (trap = 1) then   execute_trap;    { See Section C.8 }

    if (execute_mode = 1) then (              { execute_trap may have set execute_mode to 0 }

        { the following code emulates the delayed nature of the write-state-register instructions }
        PSR ← PSR'; PSR' ← PSR''; PSR'' ← PSR'''; PSR''' ← PSR'''';
        ASR ← ASR'; ASR' ← ASR''; ASR'' ← ASR'''; ASR''' ← ASR'''';
        TBR ← TBR'; TBR' ← TBR''; TBR'' ← TBR'''; TBR''' ← TBR'''';
        WIM ← WIM'; WIM' ← WIM''; WIM'' ← WIM'''; WIM''' ← WIM'''';
         Y  ←   Y';  Y' ←   Y'';  Y'' ←   Y''';  Y''' ←    Y'''';
        next;

        addr_space := (if (S = 0) then 8 else 9);
        (instruction, MAE) ← memory_read(addr_space, PC);
        next;

        if ( (MAE = 1) and (annul = 0) ) then (
            trap ← 1;
            instruction_access_exception ← 1
        ) else (
            if (annul = 0) then (
                dispatch_instruction ;    { See Section C.6 }
                next;
                if (FPop1 or FPop2) then (
                    complete_fp_execution    { See Section C.7 }
                )
                next;
                if ( (trap = 0) and
                    not (CALL or RETT or JMPL or
                      Bicc or FBfcc or CBccc or Ticc) ) then (
                    PC ← nPC;
                    nPC← nPC + 4
                )
            ) else { annul ≠ 0 } (
                annul ← 0;
                PC ← nPC;
                nPC ← nPC + 4
            )
        )
    )
);
```

## C.6. Instruction Dispatch

The `dispatch_instruction` macro determines if the instruction is an FPop or CPop and generates an fp_disabled or cp_disabled trap if appropriate. Otherwise, the instruction is executed according to the ISP definitions given below.

Unused bit patterns in the *op*, *op2*, *op3*, *opf*, and *i* fields of instructions cause illegal_instruction traps. Other fields that are defined to be *unused* are ignored and do not cause traps.

```
illegal_IU_instr := (
    if ( ( (op = 00₂) and (op2 = 000₂) ) { UNIMP instruction }
        or
        ( ((op=11₂) or (op=10₂)) and (op3= unassigned ) )
        ) then 1 else 0
);


dispatch_instruction := (
    if (illegal_IU_instr = 1) then (
        trap ← 1;
        illegal_instruction ← 1
    );
    if ((FPop1 or FPop2 or FBfcc) and ((EF = 0) or (bp_FPU_present = 0))) then (
        trap ← 1;
        fp_disabled ← 1
    );
    if (CPop1 or CPop2 or CBccc) and ((EC = 0) or (bp_CP_present = 0))) then (
        trap ← 1;
        cp_disabled ← 1
    );
    next;
    if (trap = 0) then (
        { code for specific instruction, defined below }
    );
);
```

## C.7. Floating-point Execution

The `complete_fp_execution` macro checks for floating-point traps and maintains the Floating-point State Register (FSR).

```
complete_fp_execution := (

    if (trap = 0) then (          { no traps so far }

        if (bp_FPU_present = 0) then (   { no FPU is present }
            trap ← 1;
            fp_exception ← 1;
            ftt ← unimplemented_FPop;

        ) else if (c = 0) then (          { not finished }
            trap ← 1;
            fp_exception ← 1;
            ftt ← unfinished_FPop;

        ) else (                       { FPU present; FPop executed and finished }

            if ( (texc and TEM) ≠ 0) then (  { floating-point trap }
                cexc ← most_significant_bit_of(texc and TEM);
                trap ← 1;
                fp_exception ← 1;
                ftt ← IEEE_754_exception;
            ) else (                        { no floating-point trap }
                cexc ← texc;
                aexc ← (aexc or texc);

                if (single_result = 1) then (
                    f[rd] ← sresult;
                )

                if (double_result = 1) then (
                    (f[rd<4:1>□0₂], f[rd<4:1>□1₂]) ← dresult;
                )

                if (quad_result = 1) then (
                    (f[rd<4:2>□00₂], f[rd<4:2>□01₂],
                     f[rd<4:2>□10₂], f[rd<4:2>□11₂]) ← qresult;
                )

                if (compare = 1) then (
                    fcc ← tfcc;
                )

                ftt ← 0;
            )
        )
    )
);
```

## C.8. Traps

The `execute_trap` macro selects the highest-priority trap and then causes a trap. See Chapter 7, "Traps."

```
execute_trap := (

    select_trap;          { see below }
    next;

    if (error_mode = 0) then (
        ET ← 0;
        PS ← S;
        CWP ← (CWP - 1) modulo NWINDOWS;

        next;
        if (annul = 0) then (
            r[17] ← PC;
            r[18] ← nPC;
        ) else { annul ≠ 0 } (
            r[17] ← nPC;
            r[18] ← nPC + 4;
            annul ← 0;
        )

        next;
        S ← 1;
        if (reset_trap = 0) then (
            PC ← TBR;
            nPC ← TBR + 4
        ) else { reset_trap = 1 } (
            PC ← 0;
            nPC ← 4;
            reset_trap ← 0;
        )
    )
);


select_trap := (

    if (reset_trap = 1) then { ignore ET, and leave tt unchanged }
    else if (ET = 0) then (
        execute_mode ← 0;
        error_mode ← 1 )
    else if (data_store_error = 1) then tt ← 00101011₂
    else if (instruction_access_error = 1) then tt ← 00100001₂
    else if (r_register_access_error = 1) then tt ← 00100000₂
    else if (instruction_access_exception = 1) then tt ← 00000001₂
    else if (privileged_instruction = 1) then tt ← 00000011₂
    else if (illegal_instruction = 1) then tt ← 00000010₂
    else if (fp_disabled = 1) then tt ← 00000100₂
    else if (cp_disabled = 1) then tt ← 00100100₂
```

```
    else if (unimplemented_FLUSH = 1) then tt ← 00100101₂
    else if (window_overflow = 1) then tt ← 00000101₂
    else if (window_underflow = 1) then tt ← 00000110₂
    else if (mem_address_not_aligned = 1) then tt ← 00000111₂
    else if (fp_exception = 1) then tt ← 00001000₂;
    else if (cp_exception = 1) then tt ← 00101000₂;
    else if (data_access_error = 1) then tt ← 00101001₂
    else if (data_access_exception = 1) then tt ← 00001001₂
    else if (tag_overflow = 1) then tt ← 00001010₂
    else if (division_by_zero = 1) then tt ← 00101010₂
    else if (trap_instruction = 1) then tt ← 1₂▯ticc_trap_type
    else if (interrupt_level > 0) then tt ← 0001₂▯interrupt_level;

next;

    trap ← 0;
    instruction_access_exception ← 0;
    illegal_instruction ← 0;
    privileged_instruction ← 0;
    fp_disabled ← 0;
    cp_disabled ← 0;
    window_overflow ← 0;
    window_underflow ← 0;
    mem_address_not_aligned ← 0;
    fp_exception ← 0;
    cp_exception ← 0;
    data_access_exception ← 0;
    tag_overflow ← 0;
    division_by_zero ← 0;
    trap_instruction ← 0;
    interrupt_level ← 0
);
```

## C.9.  Instruction Definitions

This section contains the ISP definitions of the SPARC architecture instructions. These complement the instruction descriptions in Appendix B, "Instruction Definitions."

### Load Instructions

```
if (LDD or LD or LDSH or LDUH or LDSB or LDUB
        or LDDF or LDF or LDFSR or LDDC or LDC or LDCSR) then (
        address ← r[rs1] + (if (i = 0) then r[rs2] else sign_extend(simm13));
        addr_space ← (if (S = 0) then 10 else 11)
) else if (LDDA or LDA or LDSHA or LDUHA or LDSBA or LDUBA) then (
        if (S = 0) then (
            trap ← 1;
            privileged_instruction ← 1
        ) else if (i = 1) then (
            trap ← 1;
            illegal_instruction ← 1
        ) else (
            address ← r[rs1] + r[rs2];
            addr_space ← asi
        )
)
next;
if (trap = 0) then (
        if ( (LDF or LDDF or LDFSR) and ((EF = 0) or (bp_FPU_present = 0))  then (
            trap ← 1;
            fp_disabled ← 1
        ) else if ( (LDC or LDDC or LDCSR) and ((EC = 0) or (bp_CP_present = 0)) then (
            trap ← 1;
            cp_disabled ← 1
        ) else if ( ( (LDD or LDDA or LDDF or LDDC) and (address<2:0> ≠ 0)) or
            ((LD or LDA or LDF or LDFSR or LDC or LDCSR) and (address<1:0> ≠ 0)) or
            ((LDSH or LDSHA or LDUH or LDUHA) and address<0> ≠ 0) ) then (
            trap ← 1;
            mem_address_not_aligned ← 1
        ) else if (LDDF and (rd<0> ≠ 0)) then (
            trap ← 1;
            fp_exception ← 1;
            ftt ← invalid_fp_register
        ) else if ((LDF or LDDF or LDFSR) and (an FPU sequence error is detected)) then (
            trap ← 1;
            fp_exception ← 1;
            ftt ← sequence_error
        ) else if ((LDC or LDDC or LDCSR) and (a CP sequence error is detected)) then (
            trap ← 1;
            cp_exception ← 1;
            { possibly additional implementation-dependent actions }
        )
);
next;
if (trap = 0) then (
        (data, MAE) ← memory_read(addr_space, address);
        next;
        if (MAE = 1) then (
```

SPARC International, Inc.

```
                                trap ← 1;
                                data_access_exception ← 1
                    ) else (
                        if (LDSB or LDSBA or LDUB or LDUBA) then (
                            if      (address<1:0> = 0)    then byte ← data<31:24>
                            else if (address<1:0> = 1)    then byte ← data<23:16>
                            else if (address<1:0> = 2)    then byte ← data<15: 8>
                            else if (address<1:0> = 3)    then byte ← data< 7: 0>;
                            next;
                            if (LDSB or LDSBA) then
                                    word0 ← sign_extend_byte(byte)
                            else
                                    word0 ← zero_extend_byte(byte)
                        ) else if (LDSH or LDSHA or LDUH or LDUHA) then (
                            if      (address<1:0> = 0)    then halfword ← data<31:16>
                            else if (address<1:0> = 2)    then halfword ← data<15: 0>;
                            next;
                            if (LDSH or LDSHA) then
                                    word0 ← sign_extend_halfword(halfword)
                            else
                                    word0 ← zero_extend_halfword(halfword)
                        ) else
                            word0 ← data
                    )
        );
        next;
        if (trap = 0) then (
                if ( (rd ≠ 0) and (LD or LDA or LDSH or LDSHA
                    or LDUHA or LDUH or LDSB or LDSBA or LDUB or LDUBA) ) then
                        r[rd] ← word0
            else if (LDF ) then f[rd] ← word0
            else if (LDC ) then { implementation-dependent actions }
            else if (LDFSR) then FSR ← word0
            else if (LDCSR) then CSR ← word0
            else if (LDD or LDDA) then r[rd and 11110₂] ← word0
            else if (LDDF) then f[rd and 11110₂] ← word0
            else if (LDDC) then { implementation-dependent actions }
        );
        next;
        if ((trap = 0) and (LDD or LDDA or LDDF or LDDC)) then (
            (word1, MAE) ← memory_read(addr_space, address + 4);
            next;
            if (MAE = 1) then (         { MAE = 1 only due to a "non-resumable machine-check error" }
                    trap ← 1;
                    data_access_exception ← 1 )
            else if (LDD or LDDA) then r[rd or 1] ← word1
            else if (LDDF) then f[rd or 1] ← word1
            else if (LDDC) then { implementation-dependent actions }
        );
```

**Store Instructions**

```
if ( (S = 0) and (STDA or STA or STHA or STBA or STDFQ or STDCQ) ) then (
    trap ← 1;
    privileged_instruction ← 1
) else if ((i = 1) and (STDA or STA or STHA or STBA)) then (
    trap ← 1;
    illegal_instruction ← 1
);
next;
if (trap = 0) then (
    if (STD or ST or STH or STB or STF or STDF
        or STFSR or STDFQ or STCSR or STC or STDC or STDCQ) then (
        address ← r[rs1] + (if (i = 0) then r[rs2] else sign_extend(simm13));
        addr_space ← (if (S = 0) then 10 else 11)
    ) else if (STDA or STA or STHA or STBA) then (
        address ← r[rs1] + r[rs2];
        addr_space ← asi
    );
    if ((STF or STDF or STFSR or STDFQ) and
        ((EF = 0) or (bp_FPU_present = 0)) ) then (
        trap ← 1;
        fp_disabled ← 1
    );
    if ((STC or STDC or STCSR or STDCQ) and
        ((EC = 0) or (bp_CP_present = 0)) ) then (
        trap ← 1;
        cp_disabled ← 1
    )
);
next;
if (trap = 0) then (
    if ((STH or STHA) and (address<0> ≠ 0)) then (
        trap ← 1;                    { misaligned half-word address }
        mem_address_not_aligned ← 1
    );
    if ((ST or STA or STF or STFSR or STC or STCSR) and (address<1:0> ≠ 0)) then (
        trap ← 1;                    { misaligned full-word address }
        mem_address_not_aligned ← 1
    );
    if ((STD or STDA or STDF or STDFQ or STDC or STDCQ) and (address<2:0>≠0)) then (
        trap ← 1;                    { misaligned double-word address }
        mem_address_not_aligned ← 1
    ) else (
        if (STDFQ and ((implementation has no floating-point queue) or (FSR.qne = 0))) then (
            trap ← 1;
            fp_exception ← 1;
            ftt ← sequence_error;
        );
        if (STDCQ and (implementation has no coprocessor queue)) then (
            trap ← 1;
            cp_exception ← 1;
            { possibly additional implementation-dependent actions }
        );
```

```
                    if (STDF and (rd<0> ≠ 0)) then (
                        trap ← 1;
                        fp_exception ← 1;
                        ftt ← invalid_fp_register
                    )
            )
);
next;
if (trap = 0) then (
    if (STF) then ( byte_mask ← 1111₂; data0 ← f[rd] )
    else if (STC) then ( byte_mask ← 1111₂; data0 ← implementation_dependent_value )
    else if (STDF) then ( byte_mask ← 1111₂; data0 ← f[rd and 11110₂] )
    else if (STDC) then ( byte_mask ← 1111₂; data0 ← implementation_dependent_value )
    else if (STD or STDA) then ( byte_mask ← 1111₂; data0 ← r[rd and 11110₂] )
    else if (STDFQ) then ( byte_mask ← 1111₂; data0 ← implementation_dependent_value )
    else if (STDCQ) then ( byte_mask ← 1111₂; data0 ← implementation_dependent_value )
    else if (STFSR) then (
        while ((FSR.qne = 1) and (trap = 0)) (
            { wait for pending floating-point instructions to complete }
        )
        next;
        byte_mask ← 1111₂; data0 ← FSR
    ) else if (STCSR) then (
        { implementation-dependent actions }
        byte_mask ← 1111₂; data0 ← CSR
    ) else if (ST or STA) then ( byte_mask ← 1111₂; data0 = r[rd] )
    else if (STH or STHA) then (
        if (address<1:0> = 0) then (
            byte_mask ← 1100₂; data0 ← shift_left_logical(r[rd], 16) )
        else if (address<1:0> = 2) then (
            byte_mask ← 0011₂; data0 ← r[rd] )
    ) else if (STB or STBA) then (
        if (address<1:0> = 0) then (
            byte_mask ← 1000₂; data0 ← shift_left_logical(r[rd], 24) )
        else if (address<1:0> = 1) then (
            byte_mask ← 0100₂; data0 ← shift_left_logical(r[rd], 16) )
        else if (address<1:0> = 2) then (
            byte_mask ← 0010₂; data0 ← shift_left_logical(r[rd], 8) )
        else if (address<1:0> = 3) then (
            byte_mask ← 0001₂; data0 ← r[rd] )
    );
);
next;
if (trap = 0) then (
    MAE ← memory_write(addr_space, address, byte_mask, data0);
    next;
    if (MAE = 1) then (
        trap ← 1;
        data_access_exception ← 1
    )
);
next;
if ((trap = 0) and (STD or STDA or STDF or STDC or STDFQ or STDCQ)) then (
```

SPARC International, Inc.

```
if (STD or STDA) then ( data1  ← r[rd or 00001₂] )
else if (STDF ) then ( data1  ← f[rd or 00001₂] )
else if (STDC ) then ( data1  ← implementation_dependent_value )
else if (STDFQ) then ( data1  ← implementation_dependent_value )
else if (STDCQ) then ( data1  ← implementation_dependent_value )
next;
MAE ← memory_write(addr_space, address + 4, 1111₂, data1);
next;
if (MAE = 1) then (          { MAE = 1 only due to a "non-resumable machine-check error" }
     trap ← 1;
     data_access_exception ← 1
)
);
```

**Atomic Load-Store Unsigned**
**Byte Instructions**

```
if (LDSTUB) then (
        address ← r[rs1] + (if (i = 0) then r[rs2] else sign_extend(simm13));
        addr_space ← (if (S = 0) then 10 else 11)
) else if (LDSTUBA) then (
        if (S = 0) then (
                trap ← 1;
                privileged_instruction ← 1
        ) else if (i = 1) then (
                trap ← 1;
                illegal_instruction ← 1
        ) else (
                address ← r[rs1] + r[rs2];
                addr_space ← asi
        )
);
next;
if (trap = 0) then (
        while ( (pb_block_ldst_byte = 1) or (pb_block_ldst_word = 1) ) (
                { wait for lock(s) to be lifted }
                { an implementation actually need only block when another LDSTUB or SWAP
                  is pending on the same byte in memory as the one addressed by this LDSTUB }
        );
        next;
        pb_block_ldst_byte ← 1;
        next;
        (data, MAE) ← memory_read(addr_space, address);
        next;
        if (MAE = 1) then (
                trap ← 1;
                data_access_exception ← 1
        )
)
next;
if (trap = 0) then (
        if      (address<1:0> = 0) then ( byte_mask ← 1000₂)
        else if (address<1:0> = 1) then ( byte_mask ← 0100₂)
        else if (address<1:0> = 2) then ( byte_mask ← 0010₂)
        else if (address<1:0> = 3) then ( byte_mask ← 0001₂)
        ;
        next;
        MAE ← memory_write(addr_space, address, byte_mask, FFFFFFFF₁₆);
        next;
        pb_block_ldst_byte ← 0;
        if (MAE = 1) then (          { MAE = 1 only due to a "non-resumable machine-check error" }
                trap ← 1;
                data_access_exception ← 1
        ) else (
                if      (address<1:0> = 0) then word ← zero_extend_byte(data<31:24>)
                else if (address<1:0> = 1) then word ← zero_extend_byte(data<23:16>)
                else if (address<1:0> = 2) then word ← zero_extend_byte(data<15:8>)
                else if (address<1:0> = 3) then word ← zero_extend_byte(data<7:0>);
                next;
```

SPARC International, Inc.

```
            if (rd ≠ 0) then r[rd] ← word
    )
);
```

**Swap Register with Memory Instructions**

```
if (SWAP) then (
        address ← r[rs1] + (if (i = 0) then r[rs2] else sign_extend(simm13));
        addr_space ← (if (S = 0) then 10 else 11)
) else if (SWAPA) then (
    if (S = 0) then (
        trap ← 1;
        privileged_instruction ← 1
    ) else if (i = 1) then (
        trap ← 1;
        illegal_instruction ← 1
    ) else (
        address ← r[rs1] + r[rs2];
        addr_space ← asi
    )
);
next;
if (trap = 0) then (
    temp ← r[rd];
    while ( (pb_block_ldst_byte = 1) or (pb_block_ldst_word = 1) ) (
            { wait for lock(s) to be lifted }
            { an implementation actually need only block when another SWAP is pending on
              the same word in memory as the one addressed by this SWAP, or a LDSTUB is
              pending on any byte of the word in memory addressed by this SWAP }
    );
    next;
    pb_block_ldst_word ← 1;
    next;
    (word, MAE) ← memory_read(addr_space, address);
    next;
    if (MAE = 1) then (
        trap ← 1;
        data_access_exception ← 1
    )
next;
if (trap = 0) then (
    MAE ← memory_write(addr_space, address, 1111₂, temp);
    next;
    pb_block_ldst_word ← 0;
    if (MAE = 1) then (        { MAE = 1 only due to a "non-resumable machine-check error" }
        trap ← 1;
        data_access_exception ← 1
    ) else (
        if (rd ≠ 0) then r[rd] ← word
    )
);
```

SPARC International, Inc.

**Logical Instructions**

```
operand2 := if (i = 0) then r[rs2] else sign_extend(simm13);

if (AND or ANDcc) then result ← r[rs1] and operand2
else if (ANDN or ANDNcc) then result ← r[rs1] and not operand2
else if (OR or ORcc) then result ← r[rs1] or operand2
else if (ORN or ORNcc) then result ← r[rs1] or not operand2
else if (XOR or XORcc) then result ← r[rs1] xor operand2
else if (XNOR or XNORcc) then result ← r[rs1] xor not operand2;
next;
if (rd ≠ 0) then r[rd] ← result;
if (ANDcc or ANDNcc or ORcc or ORNcc or XORcc or XNORcc) then (
    N ← result<31>;
    Z ← if (result = 0) then 1 else 0;
    V ← 0;
    C ← 0
);
```

**SETHI Instruction**

```
if (rd ≠ 0) then (
    r[rd]<31:10> ← imm22;
    r[rd]<9:0> ← 0
)
```

**NOP Instruction**

*{ No Operation }*

**Shift Instructions**

```
shift_count := if (i = 0) then r[rs2]<4:0> else shcnt;

if (SLL and (rd ≠ 0) ) then
    r[rd] ← shift_left_logical(r[rs1], shift_count)
else if (SRL and (rd ≠ 0) ) then
    r[rd] ← shift_right_logical(r[rs1], shift_count)
else if (SRA and (rd ≠ 0) ) then
    r[rd] ← shift_right_arithmetic(r[rs1], shift_count)
```

**Add Instructions**

```
operand2 := if (i = 0) then r[rs2] else sign_extend(simm13);

if (ADD or ADDcc) then
        result ← r[rs1] + operand2;
else if (ADDX or ADDXcc) then
        result ← r[rs1] + operand2 + C;
next;
if (rd ≠ 0) then
        r[rd] ← result;
if (ADDcc or ADDXcc) then (
    N ← result<31>;
    Z ← if (result = 0) then 1 else 0;
    V ← (r[rs1]<31> and operand2<31> and (not result<31>)) or
        ((not r[rs1]<31>) and (not operand2<31>) and result<31>);
    C ← (r[rs1]<31> and operand2<31>) or
        ((not result<31>) and (r[rs1]<31> or operand2<31>))
);
```

**Tagged Add Instructions**

```
operand2 := if (i = 0) then r[rs2] else sign_extend(simm13);

result ← r[rs1] + operand2;
next;
temp_V ← (r[rs1]<31> and operand2<31> and (not result<31>)) or
        ((not r[rs1]<31>) and (not operand2<31>) and result<31>) or
        (r[rs1]<1:0> ≠ 0 or operand2<1:0> ≠ 0);
next;
if (TADDccTV and (temp_V = 1)) then (
    trap ← 1;
    tag_overflow ← 1
) else (
    N ← result<31>;
    Z ← if (result = 0) then 1 else 0;
    V ← temp_V;
    C ← (r[rs1]<31> and operand2<31>) or
        ((not result<31>) and (r[rs1]<31> or operand2<31>));
    if (rd ≠ 0) then
        r[rd] ← result;
);
```

## Subtract Instructions

```
operand2 := if (i = 0) then r[rs2] else sign_extend(simm13);

if (SUB or SUBcc) then
    result ← r[rs1] - operand2;
else if (SUBX or SUBXcc) then
    result ← r[rs1] - operand2 - C;
next;
if (rd ≠ 0) then
    r[rd] ← result;
if (SUBcc or SUBXcc) then (
    N ← result<31>;
    Z ← if (result = 0) then 1 else 0;
    V ← (r[rs1]<31> and (not operand2<31>) and (not result<31>)) or
        ((not r[rs1]<31>) and operand2<31> and result<31>);
    C ← ((not r[rs1]<31>) and operand2<31>) or
        (result<31> and ((not r[rs1]<31>) or operand2<31>))
);
```

## Tagged Subtract Instructions

```
operand2 := if (i = 0) then r[rs2] else sign_extend(simm13);

result ← r[rs1] - operand2;
next;
temp_V ← (r[rs1]<31> and (not operand2<31>) and (not result<31>)) or
        ((not r[rs1]<31>) and operand2<31> and result<31>) or
        (r[rs1]<1:0> ≠ 0 or operand2<1:0> ≠ 0);
next;
if (TSUBccTV and (temp_V = 1)) then (
    trap ← 1;
    tag_overflow ← 1
) else (
    N ← result<31>;
    Z ← if (result = 0) then 1 else 0;
    V ← temp_V;
    C ← ((not r[rs1]<31>) and operand2<31>) or
        (result<31> and ((not r[rs1]<31>) or operand2<31>));
    if (rd ≠ 0) then
        r[rd] ← result;
);
```

**Multiply Step Instruction**

```
operand1 := (N xor V) ☐ (r[rs1]<31:1>);
operand2 :=  (
        if (Y<0> = 0) then 0
        else if (i = 0) then r[rs2] else sign_extend(simm13)
);

result ← operand1 + operand2;
Y ← r[rs1]<0> ☐ Y<31:1>;
next;
if (rd ≠ 0) then (
        r[rd] ← result;
)
N ← result<31>;
Z ← if (result = 0) then 1 else 0;
V ← (operand1<31> and operand2<31> and (not result<31>)) or
        ((not operand1<31>) and (not operand2<31>) and result<31>);
C ← (operand1<31> and operand2<31>) or
        ((not result<31>) and (operand1<31> or operand2<31>))
```

**Multiply Instructions**

```
operand2 := if (i = 0) then r[rs2] else sign_extend(simm13);

if (UMUL or UMULcc) then   (Y, result) ← multiply_unsigned(r[rs1], operand2)
else if (SMUL or SMULcc) then   (Y, result) ← multiply_signed(r[rs1], operand2)
next;
if (rd ≠ 0) then (
        r[rd] ← result;
)
if (UMULcc or SMULcc) then (
        N ← result<31>;
        Z ← if (result = 0) then 1 else 0;
        V ← 0
        C ← 0
);
```

SPARC International, Inc.

**Divide Instructions**

```
operand2 := if (i = 0) then r[rs2] else sign_extend(simm13);

next;
if (operand2 = 0) then (
    trap ← 1;
    division_by_zero ← 1
) else (
    if (UDIV or UDIVcc) then (
        temp_64bit ← divide_unsigned(Y[]r[rs1], operand2);
        next;
        result ← temp_64bit<31:0>;
        temp_V ← if (temp_64bit<63:32> = 0) then 0 else 1;
    ) else if (SDIV or SDIVcc) then (
        temp_64bit ← divide_signed(Y[]r[rs1], operand2)
        next;
        result ← temp_64bit<31:0>;
        temp_V ← if ( (temp_64bit<63:31> = 0) or
                      (temp_64bit<63:31> = (2³³ − 1)) ) then 0 else 1;
    ) ;
    next;

    if (temp_V) then (
        { result overflowed 32 bits; return largest appropriate integer }
        if (UDIV or UDIVcc) then result ← 2³² − 1;
        else if (SDIV or SDIVcc) then (
            if (temp_64bit > 0) then result ← 2³¹ − 1;
            else  result ← −2³¹
        )
    );
    next;

    if (rd ≠ 0) then (
        r[rd] ← result
    ) ;
    if (UDIVcc or SDIVcc) then (
        N ← result<31>;
        Z ← if (result = 0) then 1 else 0;
        V ← temp_V;
        C ← 0
    )
);
```

## SAVE and RESTORE
## Instructions

```
operand2 := if (i = 0) then r[rs2] else sign_extend(simm13);

if (SAVE) then (
     new_cwp ← (CWP - 1) modulo NWINDOWS;
     next;
     if ((WIM and 2^new_cwp) ≠ 0) then (
          trap ← 1;
          window_overflow ← 1
     ) else (
          result ← r[rs1] + operand2;      { operands from old window }
          CWP ← new_cwp
     )
) else if (RESTORE) then (
     new_cwp ← (CWP + 1) modulo NWINDOWS;
     next;
     if ((WIM and 2^new_cwp) ≠ 0) then (
          trap ← 1;
          window_underflow ← 1
     ) else (
          result ← r[rs1] + operand2;      { operands from old window }
          CWP ← new_cwp
     )
);
next;
if ((trap = 0) and (rd ≠ 0)) then
     r[rd] ← result                  { destination in new window }
```

SPARC International, Inc.

**Branch on Integer Condition Instructions**

```
eval_icc := (
    if (BNE)   then (if (Z = 0) then 1 else 0);
    if (BE)    then (if (Z = 1) then 1 else 0);
    if (BG)    then (if ((Z or (N xor V)) = 0) then 1 else 0);
    if (BLE)   then (if ((Z or (N xor V)) = 1) then 1 else 0);
    if (BGE)   then (if ((N xor V) = 0) then 1 else 0);
    if (BL)    then (if ((N xor V) = 1) then 1 else 0);
    if (BGU)   then (if ((C = 0) and (Z = 0)) then 1 else 0);
    if (BLEU)  then (if ((C = 1) or (Z = 1)) then 1 else 0);
    if (BCC)   then (if (C = 0) then 1 else 0);
    if (BCS)   then (if (C = 1) then 1 else 0);
    if (BPOS)  then (if (N = 0) then 1 else 0);
    if (BNEG)  then (if (N = 1) then 1 else 0);
    if (BVC)   then (if (V = 0) then 1 else 0);
    if (BVS)   then (if (V = 1) then 1 else 0);
    if (BA)    then 1;
    if (BN)    then 0
);
PC ← nPC;
if (eval_icc = 1) then (
    nPC ← PC + sign_extend(disp22☐00₂);
    if (BA and (a = 1)) then
        annul ← 1           { only for annulling Branch-Always }
) else (
    nPC ← nPC + 4;
    if (a = 1) then
        annul ← 1           { only for annulling branches other than BA }
)
```

SPARC International, Inc.

**Floating-Point Branch on**
**Condition Instructions**

```
E := if (fcc = 0) then 1 else 0;
L := if (fcc = 1) then 1 else 0;
G := if (fcc = 2) then 1 else 0;
U := if (fcc = 3) then 1 else 0;

eval_fcc := (
        if (FBU)   then (if (U) then 1 else 0);
        if (FBG)   then (if (G) then 1 else 0);
        if (FBUG)  then (if (G or U) then 1 else 0);
        if (FBL)   then (if (L) then 1 else 0);
        if (FBUL)  then (if (L or U) then 1 else 0);
        if (FBLG)  then (if (L or G) then 1 else 0);
        if (FBNE)  then (if (L or G or U) then 1 else 0);
        if (FBE)   then (if (E) then 1 else 0);
        if (FBUE)  then (if (E or U) then 1 else 0);
        if (FBGE)  then (if (E or G) then 1 else 0);
        if (FBUGE) then (if (E or G or U) then 1 else 0);
        if (FBLE)  then (if (E or L) then 1 else 0);
        if (FBULE) then (if (E or L or U) then 1 else 0);
        if (FBO)   then (if (E or L or G) then 1 else 0);
        if (FBA)   then 1;
        if (FBN)   then 0
);

PC ← nPC;
if (eval_fcc = 1) then (
        nPC ← PC + sign_extend(disp22▯ 00₂);
        if (FBA and (a = 1)) then
                annul ← 1          { only for annulling F.P. Branch-Always }
) else (
        nPC ← nPC + 4;
        if (a = 1) then
                annul ← 1          { only for annulling branches other than FBA }
)
```

SPARC International, Inc.

**Coprocessor Branch on**
**Condition Instructions**

```
C0 := if (bp_CP_cc<1:0> = 0) then 1 else 0;
C1 := if (bp_CP_cc<1:0> = 1) then 1 else 0;
C2 := if (bp_CP_cc<1:0> = 2) then 1 else 0;
C3 := if (bp_CP_cc<1:0> = 3) then 1 else 0;

eval_bp_CP_cc := (
        if (CB3)    then (if (C3) then 1 else 0);
        if (CB2)    then (if (C2) then 1 else 0);
        if (CB23)   then (if (C2 or C3) then 1 else 0);
        if (CB1)    then (if (C1) then 1 else 0);
        if (CB13)   then (if (C1 or C3) then 1 else 0);
        if (CB12)   then (if (C1 or C2) then 1 else 0);
        if (CB123)  then (if (C1 or C2 or C3) then 1 else 0);
        if (CB0)    then (if (C0) then 1 else 0);
        if (CB03)   then (if (C0 or C3) then 1 else 0);
        if (CB02)   then (if (C0 or C2) then 1 else 0);
        if (CB023)  then (if (C0 or C2 or C3) then 1 else 0);
        if (CB01)   then (if (C0 or C1) then 1 else 0);
        if (CB013)  then (if (C0 or C1 or C3) then 1 else 0);
        if (CB012)  then (if (C0 or C1 or C2) then 1 else 0);
        if (CBA) then 1;
        if (CBN) then 0
);

PC ← nPC;
if (eval_bp_CP_cc = 1) then (
        nPC ← PC + sign_extend(disp22▯00₂);
        if (CBA and (a = 1)) then
                annul ← 1        { only for annulling C.P. Branch-Always }
) else (
        nPC ← nPC + 4;
        if (a = 1) then
                annul ← 1        { only for annulling branches other than CBA }
)
```

**CALL Instruction**

```
r[15] ← PC;
PC ← nPC;
nPC ← PC + disp30▯00₂
```

**Jump and Link Instruction**

```
jump_address ← r[rs1] + (if (i = 0) then r[rs2] else sign_extend(simm13));
next;
if (jump_address<1:0> ≠ 0) then (
        trap ← 1;
        mem_address_not_aligned ← 1
) else (
        if (rd ≠ 0) then r[rd] ← PC;
        PC ← nPC;
        nPC ← jump_address
)
```

SPARC International, Inc.

**Return from Trap Instruction**

```
new_cwp ← (CWP + 1) modulo NWINDOWS;
address ← r[rs1] + (if (i = 0) then r[rs2] else sign_extend(simm13));
next;
if (ET = 1) then (
        trap ← 1;
        if (S = 0) then privileged_instruction ← 1
        else { S ≠ 0 } illegal_instruction ← 1
) else if (S = 0) then (
        trap ← 1;
        privileged_instruction ← 1;
        tt ← 00000011₂;    { trap type for privileged_instruction }
        execute_mode ← 0;
        error_mode   ← 1
) else if ((WIM and 2^new_cwp) ≠ 0) then (
        trap ← 1;
        window_underflow ← 1;
        tt ← 00000110₂;    { trap type for window_underflow }
        execute_mode ← 0;
        error_mode   ← 1
) else if (address<1:0> ≠ 0) then (
        trap ← 1;
        mem_address_not_aligned ← 1;
        tt ← 00000111₂;    { trap type for mem_address_not_aligned }
        execute_mode ← 0;
        error_mode   ← 1
) else (
        ET ← 1;
        PC ← nPC;
        nPC ← address;
        CWP ← new_cwp;
        S ← PS
)
```

**Trap on Integer Condition Instructions**

```
trap_eval_icc := (
     if (TNE)  then (if (Z = 0) then 1 else 0);
     if (TE)   then (if (Z = 1) then 1 else 0);
     if (TG)   then (if ((Z or (N xor V)) = 0) then 1 else 0);
     if (TLE)  then (if ((Z or (N xor V)) = 1) then 1 else 0);
     if (TGE)  then (if ((N xor V) = 0) then 1 else 0);
     if (TL)   then (if ((N xor V) = 1) then 1 else 0);
     if (TGU)  then (if ((C = 0) and (Z = 0)) then 1 else 0);
     if (TLEU) then (if ((C = 1) or (Z = 1)) then 1 else 0);
     if (TCC)  then (if (C = 0) then 1 else 0);
     if (TCS)  then (if (C = 1) then 1 else 0);
     if (TPOS) then (if (N = 0) then 1 else 0);
     if (TNEG) then (if (N = 1) then 1 else 0);
     if (TVC)  then (if (V = 0) then 1 else 0);
     if (TVS)  then (if (V = 1) then 1 else 0);
     if (TA)   then 1;
     if (TN)   then 0
);

trap_number := r[rs1] + (if (i = 0) then r[rs2] else sign_extend(software_trap#));

if (Ticc) then (
     if (trap_eval_icc = 1) then (
          trap ← 1;
          trap_instruction ← 1;
          ticc_trap_type ← trap_number<6:0>
     ) else (
          PC ← nPC;
          nPC ← nPC + 4
     )
);
```

**Read State Register Instructions**

```
if ((RDPSR or RDWIM or RDTBR
   or (RDASR and (privileged_ASR(rs1) = 1))) and (S = 0)) then (
     trap ← 1;
     privileged_instruction ← 1
) else if (illegal_instruction_ASR(rs1) = 1) then (
     trap ← 1;
     illegal_instruction ← 1
) else if (rd ≠ 0) then (
     if        (RDY)   then  r[rd] ← Y
     else if (RDASR) then  r[rd] ← ASR[rs1]
     else if (RDPSR) then  r[rd] ← PSR
     else if (RDWIM) then  r[rd] ← WIM
     else if (RDTBR) then  r[rd] ← TBR;
);
```

**Write State Register**
**Instructions**

```
operand2 := if (i = 0) then r[rs2] else sign_extend(simm13);
result := r[rs1] xor operand2;

if (WRY) then (
        Y'''' ← result
) else if (WRASR) then (
    if ( (privileged_ASR(rd) = 1) and (S = 0) ) then (
            trap ← 1;
            privileged_instruction ← 1
    ) else if (illegal_instruction_ASR(rd) = 1) then (
            trap ← 1;
            illegal_instruction ← 1
    ) else (
            ASR[rd]'''' ← result
    )
) else if (WRPSR) then (
    if (S = 0) then (
            trap ← 1;
            privileged_instruction ← 1
    ) else if (result<4:0> ≥ NWINDOWS) then (
            trap ← 1;
            illegal_instruction ← 1
    ) else (
            PSR'''' ← result
            { but ET and PIL appear to be written immediately,
              with respect to interrupts}
    )
) else if (WRWIM) then (
    if (S = 0) then (
            trap ← 1;
            privileged_instruction ← 1
    ) else (
            WIM'''' ← result
            { but don't write bits corresponding to non-existent windows }
    )
) else if (WRTBR) then (
    if (S = 0) then (
            trap ← 1;
            privileged_instruction ← 1
    ) else (
            TBR''''<31:12> ← result<31:12>
    )
);
```

**Store Barrier Instruction**

```
store_barrier_pending ← 1 ;
next ;
```

**Unimplemented Instruction**

```
trap ← 1 ;
illegal_instruction ← 1
```

**Flush Instruction Memory**

```
address := r[rs1] + (if (i = 0) then r[rs2] else sign_extend(simm13));
flush_cache_line(address);          { See Appendix L for definition }
flush_Ibuf_and_pipeline(address);   { See Appendix L for definition }
```

{ *If the FLUSH instruction is unimplemented, one of either illegal_instruction trap*
*or unimplemented_FLUSH trap (at the implementer's discretion) will result.* }

## C.10. Floating-Point Operate Instructions

The multiple-precision FPops use the following notation to indicate *f register* alignment. The recommended (but not required) practice of trapping on FPop's with misaligned registers is assumed below:

```
misaligned_fp_reg_trap := (
    trap ← 1;
    fp_exception ← 1;
    ftt ← invalid_fp_register
);
```

{ *double precision* }

```
rs1E  := if (rs1<0> = 0) then  rs1<4:1>[ ]0₂  else  misaligned_fp_reg_trap;
rs1O  := if (rs1<0> = 0) then  rs1<4:1>[ ]1₂  else  misaligned_fp_reg_trap;
rs2E  := if (rs1<0> = 0) then  rs2<4:1>[ ]0₂  else  misaligned_fp_reg_trap;
rs2O  := if (rs1<0> = 0) then  rs2<4:1>[ ]1₂  else  misaligned_fp_reg_trap;
rdE   := if (rs1<0> = 0) then   rd<4:1>[ ]0₂  else  misaligned_fp_reg_trap;
rdO   := if (rs1<0> = 0) then   rd<4:1>[ ]1₂  else  misaligned_fp_reg_trap;
```

{ *quad precision* }

```
rs1EE := if (rs1<1:0> = 0) then rs1<4:2>[ ]00₂  else  misaligned_fp_reg_trap;
rs1EO := if (rs1<1:0> = 0) then rs1<4:2>[ ]01₂  else  misaligned_fp_reg_trap;
rs1OE := if (rs1<1:0> = 0) then rs1<4:2>[ ]10₂  else  misaligned_fp_reg_trap;
rs1OO := if (rs1<1:0> = 0) then rs1<4:2>[ ]11₂  else  misaligned_fp_reg_trap;
rs2EE := if (rs1<1:0> = 0) then rs2<4:2>[ ]00₂  else  misaligned_fp_reg_trap;
rs2EO := if (rs1<1:0> = 0) then rs2<4:2>[ ]01₂  else  misaligned_fp_reg_trap;
rs2OE := if (rs1<1:0> = 0) then rs2<4:2>[ ]10₂  else  misaligned_fp_reg_trap;
rs2OO := if (rs1<1:0> = 0) then rs2<4:2>[ ]11₂  else  misaligned_fp_reg_trap;
 rdEE := if (rs1<1:0> = 0) then  rd<4:2>[ ]00₂  else  misaligned_fp_reg_trap;
 rdEO := if (rs1<1:0> = 0) then  rd<4:2>[ ]01₂  else  misaligned_fp_reg_trap;
 rdOE := if (rs1<1:0> = 0) then  rd<4:2>[ ]10₂  else  misaligned_fp_reg_trap;
 rdOO := if (rs1<1:0> = 0) then  rd<4:2>[ ]11₂  else  misaligned_fp_reg_trap;
```

Most of the floating-point routines defined below (or not defined since they are implementation-dependent) return:

(1)   A single, double, or quad result (`sresult, dresult, qresult`)

(2)   A 5-bit exception vector (`texc`) similar to the *cexc* field of the FSR, or a 2-bit condition code vector (`tfcc`) identical to the *fcc* field of the FSR

(3)   A completion status bit (`c`), which indicates whether the arithmetic unit was able to complete the operation

**Convert Integer to Floating-Point Instructions**

```
if (FiTOs) then
        (sresult, texc, c) ← cvt_int_to_single(f[rs2])
else if (FiTOd) then
        (dresult, texc, c) ← cvt_int_to_double(f[rs2])
else if (FiTOq) then
        (qresult, texc, c) ← cvt_int_to_quad(f[rs2]) ;
```

**Convert Floating-Point to Integer**

```
if (FsTOi) then
        (result, texc, c) ← cvt_single_to_int(f[rs2])
else if (FdTOi) then
        (result, texc, c) ← cvt_double_to_int(f[rs2E]□f[rs2O])
else if (FqTOi) then
        (result, texc, c) ← cvt_quad_to_int(
                        f[rs2EE]□f[rs2EO]□f[rs2OE]□f[rs2OO]) ;
```

**Convert Between Floating-Point Formats Instructions**

```
if (FsTOd) then
        (dresult, texc, c) ← cvt_single_to_double(f[rs2])
else if (FsTOq) then
        (qresult, texc, c) ← cvt_single_to_quad(f[rs2])
else if (FdTOs) then
        (sresult, texc, c) ← cvt_double_to_single(f[rs2E]□f[rs2O])
else if (FdTOq) then
        (qresult, texc, c) ← cvt_double_to_quad(f[rs2E]□f[rs2O])
else if (FqTOs) then
        (sresult, texc, c) ← cvt_quad_to_sgl(
                        f[rs2EE]□f[rs2EO]□f[rs2OE]□f[rs2OO])
else if (FqTOd) then
        (dresult, texc, c) ← cvt_quad_to_dbl(
                        f[rs2EE]□f[rs2EO]□f[rs2OE]□f[rs2OO]);
```

**Floating-Point Move Instructions**

```
if (FMOVs) then
        sresult ← f[rs2]
else if (FNEGs) then
        sresult ← f[rs2] xor 80000000₁₆
else if (FABSs) then
        sresult ← f[rs2] and 7FFFFFFF₁₆ ;
texc ← 0;
c ← 1
```

**Floating-Point Square Root Instructions**

```
if (FSQRTs) then
        (sresult, texc, c) ← sqrt_single(f[rs2])
else if (FSQRTd) then
        (dresult, texc, c) ← sqrt_double(f[rs2E]□f[rs2O])
else if (FSQRTq) then
        (qresult, texc, c) ← sqrt_quad(f[rs2EE]□f[rs2EO]□f[rs2OE]□f[rs2OO]) ;
```

**Floating-Point Add and Subtract Instructions**

```
if (FADDs) then
        (sresult, texc, c) ← add_single(f[rs1], f[rs2])
else if (FSUBs) then
        (sresult, texc, c) ← sub_single(f[rs1], f[rs2])
else if (FADDd) then
        (dresult, texc, c) ← add_double(f[rs1E]☐f[rs1O], f[rs2E]☐f[rs2O])
else if (FSUBd) then
        (dresult, texc, c) ← sub_double(f[rs1E]☐f[rs1O], f[rs2E]☐f[rs2O])
else if (FADDq) then
        (qresult, texc, c) ← add_quad(f[rs1EE]☐f[rs1EO]☐f[rs1OE]☐f[rs1OO],
                f[rs2EE]☐f[rs2EO]☐f[rs2OE]☐f[rs2OO])
else if (FSUBq) then
        (qresult, texc, c) ← sub_quad(f[rs1EE]☐f[rs1EO]☐f[rs1OE]☐f[rs1OO],
                f[rs2EE]☐f[rs2EO]☐f[rs2OE]☐f[rs2OO]) ;
```

**Floating-Point Multiply and Divide Instructions**

```
if (FMULs) then
        (sresult, texc, c) ← mul_single(f[rs1], f[rs2])
else if (FDIVs) then
        (sresult, texc, c) ← div_single(f[rs1], f[rs2])
else if (FMULd) then
        (dresult, texc, c) ← mul_double(f[rs1E]☐f[rs1O], f[rs2E]☐f[rs2O])
else if (FsMULd) then
        (dresult, texc, c) ← mul_single_to_double(f[rs1], f[rs2])
else if (FDIVd) then
        (dresult, texc, c) ← div_double(f[rs1E]☐f[rs1O], f[rs2E]☐f[rs2O])
else if (FMULq) then
        (qresult, texc, c) ← mul_quad(f[rs1EE]☐f[rs1EO]☐f[rs1OE]☐f[rs1OO],
                        f[rs2EE]☐f[rs2EO]☐f[rs2OE]☐f[rs2OO])
else if (FdMULq) then
        (qresult, texc, c) ← mul_double_to_quad(f[rs1E]☐f[rs1O],
                        f[rs2E]☐f[rs2O])
else if (FDIVq) then
        (qresult, texc, c) ← div_quad(f[rs1EE]☐f[rs1EO]☐f[rs1OE]☐f[rs1OO],
                        f[rs2EE]☐f[rs2EO]☐f[rs2OE]☐f[rs2OO]) ;
```

**Floating-Point Compare Instructions**

```
if (FCMPs) then
        (tfcc, texc, c) ← compare_single(f[rs1], f[rs2])
else if (FCMPd) then
        (tfcc, texc, c) ← compare_double(f[rs1E]□f[rs1O], f[rs2E]□f[rs2O])
else if (FCMPq) then
        (tfcc, texc, c) ← compare_quad(f[rs1EE]□f[rs1EO]□f[rs1OE]□f[rs1OO],
                f[rs2EE]□f[rs2EO]□f[rs2OE]□f[rs2OO])
else if (FCMPEs) then
        (tfcc, texc, c) ← compare_e_single(f[rs1], f[rs2]);
else if (FCMPEd) then
        (tfcc, texc, c) ← compare_e_double(f[rs1E]□f[rs1O], f[rs2E]□f[rs2O])
else if (FCMPEq) then
        (tfcc, texc, c) ← compare_e_quad(
                        f[rs1EE]□f[rs1EO]□f[rs1OE]□f[rs1OO],
                        f[rs2EE]□f[rs2EO]□f[rs2OE]□f[rs2OO]) ;
```

# D

## Software Considerations

This appendix describes how software can use the SPARC architecture effectively. **It describes software conventions that have proven useful, assumptions that compilers may make about the resources available, and how compilers can use those resources.** It does not discuss how supervisor software (an operating system) may use the architecture.

The goal of minimizing average procedure-call overhead is a prime motivation for many of the software conventions described in this appendix.

**D.1. Registers**

Register usage is typically a critical resource allocation issue for compilers. The SPARC architecture provides windowed integer registers (*in*, *out*, *local*), global integer registers, floating-point registers, and (in some implementations) coprocessor registers.

*In* **and** *Out* **Registers**

The *in* and *out* registers are used primarily for passing parameters to subroutines and receiving results from them, and for keeping track of the memory stack. When a procedure is called, the caller's *outs* become the callee's *ins*.

One of a procedure's *out* registers (%o6) is used as its stack pointer, %sp. It points to an area in which the system can store %r16 ... %r31 (%l0 ... %l7 and %i0 ... %i7) when the register file overflows (window_overflow trap), and is used to address most values located on the stack. See Figure D-2. A trap[2] can occur at any time, which may precipitate a subsequent window_overflow trap, during which the contents of the user's register window at the time of the original trap are spilled to the memory to which its %sp points.

A procedure may store temporary values in its *out* registers, with the exception of %sp, with the understanding that those values are volatile across procedure calls. %sp cannot be used for temporary values for the reasons described in the *Register Windows and* %sp section below.

Up to six parameters[3] may be passed by placing them in *out* registers %o0...%o5;

---

[2] E.g., due to an error in executing an instruction (for example, a mem_address_not_aligned trap), or due to any type of external interrupt.

[3] Six is more than adequate, since the overwhelming majority of procedures in system code take fewer than six parameters. According to the studies cited by Weicker (Weicker, R.P., Dhrystone: A Synthetic

SPARC International, Inc.

additional parameters are passed in the memory stack. The stack pointer is implicitly passed in %o6, and a CALL instruction places its own address in %o7[4].

When an argument is a data aggregate[5] being passed by value, the caller first makes a temporary copy of the data aggregate in its stack frame, then passes a pointer to the copy in the argument *out* register (or on the stack, if it is the 7th or later argument).

After a callee is entered and its SAVE instruction has been executed, the caller's *out* registers are accessible as the callee's *in* registers.

The caller's stack pointer %sp (%o6) automatically becomes the current procedure's frame pointer %fp (%i6) when the SAVE instruction is executed.

The callee finds its first six parameters in %i0 ... %i5, and the remainder (if any) on the stack.

For each passed-by-value data aggregate, the callee finds a pointer to a copy of the aggregate in its argument list. The compiler must arrange for an extra dereferencing operation each time such an argument is referenced in the callee.

If the callee is passed fewer than six parameters, it may store temporary values in the unused *in* registers.

If a register parameter (in %i0 ... %i5) has its address taken in the called procedure, the callee stores that parameter's value on the memory stack. The parameter is then accessed in that memory location for the lifetime of the pointer(s) which contains its address (or for the lifetime of the procedure, if the compiler doesn't know the pointer's lifetime).

The six words available on the stack for saving the first six parameters are deliberately contiguous in memory with those in which additional parameters may be passed. This supports constructs such as C's *varargs*[6], for which the callee copies to the stack the register parameters which must be addressable.

A function returns a scalar integer value by writing it into its *in*s (which are the caller's *out*s), starting with %i0. A scalar floating-point value is returned in the floating-point registers, starting with %f0. Aggregate values are returned using the mechanism described in the *Functions Returning Aggregate Values* section of this appendix.

---

Systems Programming Benchmark, *CACM* 27:10, October 1984), at least 97% (measured statically) take fewer than six parameters. The average number of parameters did not exceed 2.1, measured either statically or dynamically, in any of these studies.

[4] If a JMPL instruction is used in place of a CALL for consistency it can (explicitly) place its address in %o7.

[5] Some examples of data aggregates are C language structs and unions, and Pascal records.

[6] *Varargs* is the means by which variable-length argument lists are passed to C procedures.

A procedure's return address, normally the address of the instruction just after the CALL's delay-slot instruction, is simply calculated as $i7 + 8$ [7].

### *Local* Registers

The *local*s are used for automatic[8] variables, and for most temporary values. For access efficiency, a compiler may also copy parameters (i.e. those past the sixth) from the memory stack into the *local*s and use them from there.

If an automatic variable's address is taken, the variable's value must be stored in the memory stack, and be accessed there for the lifetime of the pointer(s) which contains its address (or for the lifetime of the procedure, if the compiler doesn't know the pointer's lifetime).

See Section D.7 for methods of allocating more or fewer than 8 registers for local values.

### Register Windows and %sp

Some caveats about the use of %sp and the SAVE and RESTORE instructions are appropriate. **It is essential that:**

- %sp *always* contain the correct value, so that when (and if) a register window overflow/underflow trap occurs, the register window can be correctly stored to or reloaded from memory [9].

- User (non-supervisor) code uses SAVE and RESTORE instructions carefully. In particular, "walking" the call chain through the register windows using RESTOREs, expecting to be able to return to where one started using SAVEs does not work as one might suppose. This fails because the "next" register window (in the "SAVE direction") is reserved for use by trap handlers. Since non-supervisor code cannot disable traps, a trap could write over the contents of a user register window which has "temporarily" been RESTORE'd[10]. The safe method is to flush the register windows out to user memory (the stack) in supervisor state using a software trap designed for that purpose. Then, user code can safely "walk" the call chain through user memory, instead of through the register windows.

The rule-of-thumb which will avoid such problems is to consider all memory below %sp on the user's stack, and the contents of all register windows "below" the current one to be volatile.

---

[7] For convenience, SPARC assemblers may provide a "ret" (return) synthetic instruction which generates a "jmpl %i7 + 8, %g0" hardware instruction.

[8] In the C language, "auto" is the storage class of a local variable whose lifetime is no longer than that of its containing procedure.

[9] The SAVE instruction is typically used to generate a new %sp while shifting to a new register window, all in one atomic operation. When SAVE is used this way, synchronization of the two operations should not be a problem.

[10] Another reason this fails is that user code has no way to determine how many register windows are implemented by the hardware.

SPARC International, Inc.

**_Global_ Registers**

Unlike the *ins*, *locals*, and *outs*, the *globals* are not part of any register window. The *globals* are a set of eight registers with global scope, like the register sets of more traditional processor architectures. The *globals* (except %g0) are conventionally assumed to be volatile across procedure calls. However, if they were used on a per-procedure basis and expected to be nonvolatile across procedure calls, either the caller or the callee would have to take responsibility for saving and restoring their contents.

Global register %g0 has a "hardwired" value of zero. It always reads as zero, and writes to it have no effect.

The *global* registers, other than %g0, can be used for temporaries, global variables, or global pointers — either user variables, or values maintained as part of the program's execution environment.

For example, one could use *globals* in the execution environment by establishing a convention that global scalars are addressed via offsets from a global base register. In the general case, memory accessed at an arbitrary address requires two instructions, e.g.:

```
sethi   %hi(address),reg
ld      [reg+%lo(address)],reg
```

Use of a global base register for frequently accessed global values would provide faster (single-instruction) access to $2^{13}$ bytes of those values, e.g.:

```
ld      [%gn+offset],reg
```

Additional global registers could be conscripted to provide single-instruction access to correspondingly more global values.

The current convention is that the global registers (except %g0) are assumed to be volatile across procedure calls. The convention used by the SPARC Application Binary Interface (ABI) is that %g1 is assumed to be volatile across procedure calls, %g2 ... %g4 are reserved for use by the application program (for example, as global register variables), and %g5 ... %g7 are assumed to be nonvolatile and reserved for (as-yet-undefined) use by the execution environment.

**Floating-Point Registers**

There are thirty-two 32-bit floating-point registers. Floating-point registers are accessed with different instructions than the integer registers; their contents can be moved among themselves, and to or from memory.

Like the global registers, the floating-point registers must be managed by software. Compilers use the floating-point registers for user variables and compiler temporaries and return floating-point function values in them. Existing compilers **do not** pass parameters in them.

Across a procedure call, either the caller must save its live floating-point registers, or the callee must save the ones it is going to use and restore them before returning. Current compilers use the "caller-save" convention.

| | | | |
|---|---|---|---|
| | %i7 | (%r31) | return address − 8 † |
| | %fp, %i6 | (%r30) | frame pointer † |
| | %i5 | (%r29) | incoming param 6 † |
| *in* | %i4 | (%r28) | incoming param 5 † |
| | %i3 | (%r27) | incoming param 4 † |
| | %i2 | (%r26) | incoming param 3 † |
| | %i1 | (%r25) | incoming param 2 † |
| | %i0 | (%r24) | incoming param 1 / return value to caller † |
| | %l7 | (%r23) | local 7 † |
| | %l6 | (%r22) | local 6 † |
| | %l5 | (%r21) | local 5 † |
| *local* | %l4 | (%r20) | local 4 † |
| | %l3 | (%r19) | local 3 † |
| | %l2 | (%r18) | local 2 † |
| | %l1 | (%r17) | local 1 † |
| | %l0 | (%r16) | local 0 † |
| | %o7 | (%r15) | temporary value / address of CALL instruction ‡ |
| | %sp, %o6 | (%r14) | stack pointer † |
| | %o5 | (%r13) | outgoing param 6 ‡ |
| *out* | %o4 | (%r12) | outgoing param 5 ‡ |
| | %o3 | (%r11) | outgoing param 4 ‡ |
| | %o2 | (%r10) | outgoing param 3 ‡ |
| | %o1 | (%r9 ) | outgoing param 2 ‡ |
| | %o0 | (%r8 ) | outgoing param 1 / return value from callee ‡ |
| | %g7 | (%r7 ) | global 7 (SPARC ABI: use reserved) |
| | %g6 | (%r6 ) | global 6 (SPARC ABI: use reserved) |
| | %g5 | (%r5 ) | global 5 (SPARC ABI: use reserved) |
| *global* | %g4 | (%r4 ) | global 4 (SPARC ABI: global register variable §) |
| | %g3 | (%r3 ) | global 3 (SPARC ABI: global register variable §) |
| | %g2 | (%r2 ) | global 2 (SPARC ABI: global register variable §) |
| | %g1 | (%r1 ) | temporary value ‡ |
| | %g0 | (%r0 ) | 0 |
| *state* | %y | | Y register (used in multiplication/division) ‡ |
| | (*icc* field of %psr) | | Integer condition codes ‡ |
| | (*fcc* field of %fsr) | | Floating-point condition codes ‡ |
| | (*ccc* field of %csr) | | Coprocessor condition codes ‡ |
| | %f31 | | floating-point value ‡ |
| *floating* | : | | : |
| *point* | : | | : |
| | %f0 | | floating-point value ‡ |

† assumed by caller to be preserved across a procedure call
‡ assumed by caller to be destroyed (volatile) across a procedure call
§ should not be used in SPARC ABI library code

Figure D-1    *SPARC Register Set, as Seen by a User-Mode Procedure*

SPARC International, Inc.

## D.2. The Memory Stack

Space on the memory stack, called a "stack frame", is normally allocated for each procedure.

Under certain conditions, optimization may enable a leaf[11] procedure to use its caller's stack frame instead of one of its own. In that case, the procedure allocates no space of its own for a stack frame. The following description of the memory stack applies to all procedures, except leaf procedures which have been optimized in this way.

The following are *always* allocated at compile time in every procedure's stack frame:

- 16 words, always starting at %sp, for saving the procedure's *in* and *local* registers, should a register window overflow occur

The following are allocated at compile time in the stack frames of non-leaf procedures:

- One word, for passing a "hidden" (implicit) parameter. This is used when the caller is expecting the callee to return a data aggregate by value; the hidden word contains the address of stack space allocated (if any) by the caller for that purpose See Section D.4.

- Six words, into which the callee may store parameters that must be addressable

Space is allocated as needed in the stack frame for the following at compile time:

- Outgoing parameters beyond the sixth

- All automatic arrays, automatic data aggregates, automatic scalars which must be addressable, and automatic scalars for which there is no room in registers

- Compiler-generated temporary values (typically when there are too many for the compiler to keep them all in registers)

- Floating-point registers being saved across calls (occurs if floating-point instructions are used by a procedure)

Space can be allocated dynamically (at runtime) in the stack frame for the following:

- Memory allocated using the alloca() function of the C library

Addressable automatic variables on the stack are addressed with negative offsets relative to %fp; dynamically allocated space is addressed with positive offsets from the pointer returned by alloca(); everything else in the stack frame is addressed with positive offsets relative to %sp.

---

[11] See Section D.5, Leaf Procedure Optimization.

The stack pointer %sp must always be doubleword-aligned. This allows window overflow and underflow trap handlers to use the more efficient STD and LDD instructions to store and reload register windows.

When a non-leaf procedure is active, its stack frame appears as in Figure D-2.

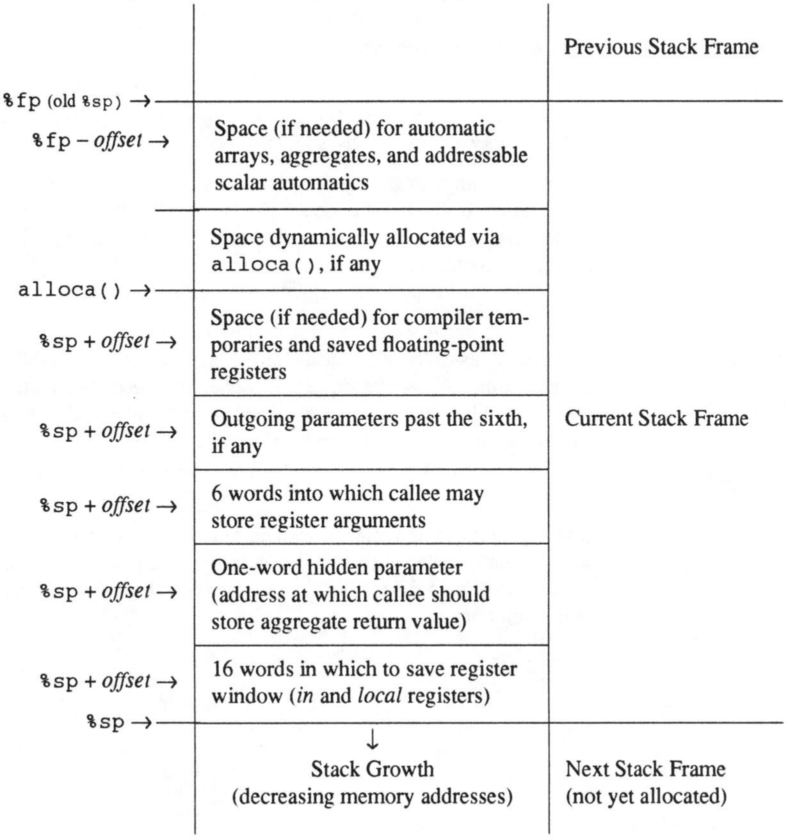

| | | Previous Stack Frame |
|---|---|---|
| %fp (old %sp) → | | |
| %fp − *offset* → | Space (if needed) for automatic arrays, aggregates, and addressable scalar automatics | |
| | Space dynamically allocated via alloca( ), if any | |
| alloca( ) → | | |
| %sp + *offset* → | Space (if needed) for compiler temporaries and saved floating-point registers | |
| %sp + *offset* → | Outgoing parameters past the sixth, if any | Current Stack Frame |
| %sp + *offset* → | 6 words into which callee may store register arguments | |
| %sp + *offset* → | One-word hidden parameter (address at which callee should store aggregate return value) | |
| %sp + *offset* → | 16 words in which to save register window (*in* and *local* registers) | |
| %sp → | | |
| | ↓ Stack Growth (decreasing memory addresses) | Next Stack Frame (not yet allocated) |

Figure D-2    *The User Stack Frame*

SPARC International, Inc.

### D.3. Functions Returning Aggregate Values

Some programming languages, including C, some dialects of Pascal, and Modula-2, allow the user to define a function returning an aggregate value. Examples include a C struct or union, or a Pascal record. Since such a value may not fit into the registers, another value-returning protocol must be defined to return the result in memory.

Reentrancy and efficiency considerations require that the memory used to hold such a return value be allocated by the function's caller. The address of this memory area is passed as the one-word hidden parameter mentioned in the section *The Memory Stack* above.

Because of the lack of type safety in the C language, a function should not assume that its caller is expecting an aggregate return value and has provided a valid memory address. Thus, some additional handshaking is required.

When a procedure expecting an aggregate return value from a called function is compiled, an UNIMP instruction is placed after the delay-slot instruction following the CALL to the function in question. The immediate field in this UNIMP instruction contains the low-order twelve bits of the size (in bytes) of the area allocated by the caller for the aggregate value expected to be returned.

When the aggregate-returning function is about to store its value in the memory allocated by its caller, it first tests for the presence of this UNIMP instruction in its caller's instruction stream. If it is found, the callee assumes the hidden parameter to be valid, stores its return value at the given address, and returns control to the instruction following the caller's UNIMP instruction. If the UNIMP instruction is not found, the hidden parameter is assumed **not** to be valid and no value is returned.

On the other hand, if a scalar-returning function is called when an aggregate return value is expected (which is clearly a software error), the function returns as usual, executing the UNIMP instruction, which causes an unimplemented-instruction trap.

## D.4.  Tagged Arithmetic

The tagged add/subtract instructions assume tagged-format data, in which a tag occupies the two low-order bits of each operand.  If either of the two operands has a nonzero tag, or if arithmetic overflow occurs, the operation sets the PSR's overflow bit.  Some variants of the tagged arithmetic instructions cause a tag_overflow exception instead of setting the overflow bit.

Tagged arithmetic operations are used regularly in languages with dynamically typed data, such as Lisp and Smalltalk.

One possible model for tagging is to use a tag value of 0 for integers, and a tag value of 3 for pointers to pairs of words (that is, list cells).  Using this model, suppose that p is a tagged pointer to a list cell (that is, p has "3" in its low-order two bits).  Since load/store instructions execute successfully only with properly aligned addresses, if p is a list cell with a tag of "3" (a pointer), a load/store word instruction with an address specifier of "p - 3" or "p + 1" will succeed, accessing the first or second word (respectively) of the list cell. If p is not a pointer (that is, contains a tag other than 3), such a load/store will cause a mem_address_not_aligned trap.  This scheme can be used to test for unexpected data types.

The non-trapping versions of the tagged arithmetic instructions typically incur the overhead of a following "branch on overflow" instruction, plus execution of code to deal with the overflow when the overflow condition occurs.  The trapping versions incur no per-instruction overhead, but have the overhead of a tag_overflow trap when overflow occurs.  So, the choice of whether to use the trapping or non-trapping versions of the tagged arithmetic instructions depends on two factors:

- The overhead of a tag_overflow trap

- The relative frequency of overflow in tagged arithmetic operations

If the trapping overhead is small and tag overflow occurs infrequently, the trapping versions of the tagged arithmetic instructions provide the best performance.  If trapping overhead is high and tag overflow occurs frequently enough, use of the non-trapping tagged arithmetic instructions is recommended.

SPARC International, Inc.

## D.5. Leaf Procedure Optimization

A **leaf procedure** is one that is a "leaf" in the program's call graph; that is, one that does not call (e.g. via CALL or JMPL) any other procedures.

Each procedure, including leaf procedures, normally uses a SAVE instruction to allocate a stack frame and obtain a register window for itself, and a corresponding RESTORE instruction to deallocate it. The time costs associated with this are:

- Possible generation of register-window overflow/underflow traps at runtime. This only happens occasionally[12], but when either underflow or overflow does occur, it costs dozens of machine cycles to process.

- The two cycles expended by the SAVE and RESTORE instructions themselves

There are also space costs associated with this convention, the cumulative cache effects of which may not be negligible. The space costs include:

- The space occupied on the stack by the procedure's stack frame

- The two words occupied by the SAVE and RESTORE instructions

Of the above costs, the trap-processing cycles are typically the most significant.

Some leaf procedures can be made to operate *without* their own register window or stack frame, using their caller's instead. This can be done when the candidate leaf procedure meets all of the following conditions[13]:

- Contains no references to `%sp`, except in its SAVE instruction

- Contains no references to `%fp`

- Refers to (or can be made to refer to) no more than 8 of the 32 integer registers[14], inclusive of `%o7` (the "return address").

If a procedure conforms to the above conditions, it can be made to operate using its caller's stack frame and registers — an optimization that saves both time and space. When optimized, such a procedure is known as an **optimized leaf procedure**. It may only safely use registers that its caller already assumes to be volatile across a procedure call, namely, `%o0 ... %o5`, `%o7`, and `%g1`[15].

---

[12] The frequency of overflow and underflow traps depends on the software application, and upon the number of register windows (*NWINDOWS*) implemented in hardware. In a multitasking UNIX workstation environment, SPARC processors with 7 register windows in hardware have been observed to spend approximately 3% of total cycles in register-window overflow and underflow trap handling. Simulations indicate that the frequency of such traps approximately halve with the availability of *each* of the next few additional register windows in hardware, e.g. a processor with 8 register windows in hardware should spend about 1.5% of its cycles in overflow/underflow handling.

[13] Although slightly less restrictive conditions could be used, the optimization would become more complex to perform and the incremental gain would usually be small.

[14] Or 14 of the 32 registers, if SPARC ABI compliance isn't required.

[15] `%g1 ... %g7` if SPARC ABI compliance isn't required.

The optimization can be performed at the assembly language level using the following steps:

- Change all references to registers in the procedure to registers that the caller assumes volatile across the call:

    - Leave references to %o7 unchanged.

    - Leave any references to %g0 ... %g7 unchanged.

    - Change %i0 ... %i5 to %o0 ... %o5, respectively. If an *in* register is changed to an *out* register that was already referenced in the original unoptimized version of the procedure, all original references to that *out* register must be changed to refer to an unused *out* or *global* register.

    - Change references to each *local* register into references to any register among %o0 ... %o5 or %g1 [16] that remains unused.

- Delete the SAVE instruction. If it was in a delay slot, replace it with a NOP instruction. If its destination register was not %g0 or %sp, convert the SAVE into the corresponding ADD instruction instead of deleting it.

- If the RESTORE's implicit addition operation is used for a productive purpose (such as setting up the procedure's return value), convert the RESTORE to the corresponding ADD instruction. Otherwise, the RESTORE is only used for stack and register-window deallocation; replace it with a NOP instruction (it is probably in the delay slot of the RET, and so cannot be deleted).

- Change the RET (return) synthetic instruction to RETL (return-from-leaf-procedure synthetic instruction).

- Perform any optimizations newly made possible, such as combining instructions, or filling the delay slot of the RETL with a productive instruction.

After the above changes, there should be no SAVE or RESTORE instructions, and no references to *in* or *local* registers in the procedure body. All original references to *in*s are now to *out*s. All other register references are to either %g1 [16], or other *out*s.

Costs of optimizing leaf procedures in this way include:

- Additional intelligence in the peephole optimizer to recognize and optimize candidate leaf procedures.

- Additional intelligence in debuggers to properly report the call chain and the stack traceback for optimized leaf procedures[17].

---

[16] %g1 ... %g7 if SPARC ABI compliance isn't required.

[17] A debugger can recognize an optimized leaf procedure by scanning it, noting the absence of a SAVE instruction. Compilers often constrain the SAVE, if present, to appear within the first few instructions of a procedure; in such a case, only those instruction positions need be examined.

## D.6. Example Code

This section illustrates common parameter-passing conventions and gives a simple example of leaf-procedure optimization.

The following code fragment shows a simple procedure call with a value returned, and the procedure itself:

```
! CALLER:
!    int i;                              /* compiler assigns "i" to register %17 */
!    i = sum3( 1, 2, 3 );
        ...
        mov     1, %o0              ! first arg to sum3 is 1
        mov     2, %o1              ! second arg to sum3 is 2
        call    sum3               ! the call to sum3
        mov     3, %o2             ! last parameter to sum3 in delay slot
        mov     %o0, %17           ! copy return value to %17 (variable "i")
        ...


#define SA(x)      (((x)+7)&(~0x07))   /* rounds "x" up to doubleword boundary */
#define MINFRAME ((16+1+6)*4)          /* minimum size frame */

! CALLEE:
!    int sum3( a, b, c )
!                  int a, b, c;    /* args received in %i0, %i1, and %i2 */
!    {
!              return  a+b+c;
!    }

sum3:
        save    %sp,-SA(MINFRAME),%sp ! set up new %sp; alloc min. stack frame
        add     %i0, %i1, %17      ! compute sum in local %17
        add     %17, %i2, %17      !   (or %i0 could have been used directly)
        ret                        ! return from sum3, and...
        restore %17, 0, %o0        !   move result into output reg & restore
```

Since "sum3" does not call any other procedures (i.e., it is a "leaf" procedure), it can be optimized to become:

```
sum3:
        add     %o0, %o1, %o0      !
        retl                       ! (must use RETL, not RET,
        add     %o0, %o2, %o0      !    to return from leaf procedure)
```

**D.7. Register Allocation Within a Window**

The usual SPARC software convention is to allocate eight registers (%l0–%l7) for local values. A compiler could allocate more registers for local values at the expense of having fewer *outs*/*ins* available for argument passing.

For example, if instead of assuming that the boundary between local values and input arguments is between r[23] and r[24] (%l7 and %i0), software could by convention assume that the boundary is between r[25] and r[26] (%i1 and %i2). This would provide 10 registers for local values and 6 "in"/"out" registers.

The following table illustrates this:

|  | Standard Register Model | "10-Local" Register Model | Arbitrary Register Model |
|---|:---:|:---:|:---:|
| registers for local values | 8 | 10 | $n$ |
| "in"/"out" registers: | | | |
| reserved for %sp/%fp | 1 | 1 | 1 |
| reserved for return address | 1 | 1 | 1 |
| available for arg passing | 6 | 4 | $14-n$ |
| total "ins"/"outs" | 8 | 6 | $16-n$ |

**D.8. Other Register
Window Usage Models**

So far, this appendix has described SPARC software conventions that are appropriate for use in a general-purpose multitasking computer system. However, SPARC is used in many other applications, notably those that are embedded and/or provide real-time capabilities. In such applications, other schemes for allocation of SPARC's register windows might be more nearly optimal than the one described above in this appendix.

The intent of this section is not to enumerate all possible register-window organization schemes, but to trigger the reader's imagination by providing a few examples of modifications that could be made to the standard SPARC software conventions. Readers can then design register-usage schemes appropriate to the specific needs of their applications of SPARC processors.

In the general-purpose computer system application of SPARC discussed above in this appendix[18], procedure calls are assumed to be frequent relative to both context switches and User-Supervisor state transitions. A primary goal in this application is to minimize *total* overhead, which includes time spent in both context switches and procedure calls. As more register windows are shared among competing processes, total procedure call time decreases (due to execution of fewer window overflow and underflow traps), while total context-switch time may increase (the average number of register windows saved during a context switch increases). The task is to strike a balance to minimize the sum of these two factors[19].

In other applications, different software conventions for use of memory and SPARC's windowed registers might be more nearly optimal. Such situations may occur, for example, where any of the following are of high importance:

- Minimal *average* context-switch time

- A *constant* (or small worst-case deterministic) context-switch time

- A *constant* (or small worst-case deterministic) procedure-call time

- A large number of register windows (say, ≥14) available in a given SPARC implementation

To better meet goals such as the above, modifications could be made to the software conventions described above. These employ creative uses of SPARC's flexible procedure-calling mechanism[20] and its windowed register set. A few possible modifications to the software conventions follow.

---

[18] For example, most UNIX-based systems.

[19] Since existing SPARC implementations (as of early 1990) have only 7 or 8 register windows, context-switch time has not yet become a significant factor. With 20 or more register windows available in some future SPARC implementations, the optimal allocation of register window resources under UNIX will no longer be to share all windows among all processes and the kernel.

[20] The procedure-calling mechanism is flexible because the procedure-calling and return instructions, CALL (or JMPL) and RET, are distinct from the stack and register-window management instructions, SAVE and RESTORE.

[A]  Divide the register file into "supervisor state" register windows and "user state" register windows. In cases in which user/supervisor state transitions are frequent, this would reduce register-window overflow/underflow overhead.

To be effective, this would require a SPARC implementation with $\geq$ 14 register windows in hardware (a minimum of 7 windows each for user and supervisor code). Empirical measurements show that the number of window overflow and underflow traps in typical user code approximately halves for each window added, up to about 12 windows. In a UNIX system, system calls (supervisor code) often involve deep (sometimes $\geq$ 20) and "narrow" (few instructions between CALLs) call chains. Such behavior is atypical of user code. This suggests that if a SPARC implementation running UNIX has more than 14 windows, additional windows might be most effectively allocated for supervisor use[21].

[B]  Using multiple 1's in the Window Invalid Mask (WIM), partition the register file into groups of (at least two) windows each. Assign each group of register windows to an executing task. This would be useful for real-time processing, where extremely fast context switches are desired; a context switch would mainly consist of loading a new stack pointer, resetting the CWP to the new task's block of register windows, and saving/restoring whatever subset of the global registers is assumed to be nonvolatile. In particular, note that *no* window registers would need to be loaded or stored during a context switch.

This method assumes that only a few tasks are present and, in the simplest case, that all tasks share one address space[22]. The number of hardware register windows required is a function of the number of windows reserved for the supervisor, the number of windows reserved for each task, and the number of tasks. Register windows could be allocated to tasks unequally, if appropriate.

[C]  Avoid using the normal register-window mechanism, by not using SAVE and RESTORE instructions. Software would effectively see 32 general-purpose registers instead of SPARC's usual windowed register file. In this mode, SPARC would operate like processors with more traditional (flat) register architectures. Procedure call times would be more deterministic (due to lack of underflow/overflow traps), but for most types of software, average procedure call time would significantly increase, due to increased memory traffic for parameter passing and saving/restoring local variables.

Existing SPARC compilers would require modification to produce code to make use of this register organization.

---

[21]  Use of a preemptable kernel may complicate this.

[22]  Either the processor uses physical addressing (no MMU), or all tasks' user address spaces are mapped identically.

SPARC International, Inc.

It would be awkward, at best, to attempt to mix (link) code using the SAVE/RESTORE convention with code not using it in the same process. If both conventions *were* used in the same system, two versions of each library would be required.

It would be possible to run user code with one register-usage convention and supervisor code with another. With sufficient intelligence in the supervisor, user processes with different register conventions could be run simultaneously[23].

---

[23] Although technically possible, this is not to suggest that there would be significant utility in mixing user processes with differing register-usage conventions.

# E

# Example Integer Multiplication and Division Routines

This appendix contains routines a SPARC system might use to perform integer multiplication, division, and remaindering in the absence of the implementation of multiply (SMUL, SMULcc, UMUL, UMULcc) or divide (SDIV, SDIVcc, UDIV, UDIVcc) instructions in hardware. These routines are written in the assembly language accepted by Sun Microsystems' SPARC assembler[24].

Programming Note   These sample routines do not set the integer condition codes identically to the integer multiply and divide instructions. They require modification to do so.

Programming Note   The routines in this appendix were written prior to definition of the SPARC ABI. See Appendix G, "SPARC ABI Software Considerations." They may or may not implement SPARC ABI-compliant versions of .mul, .umul, .div, .udiv, .rem, and .urem; their compliance has not been verified.

If they are compliant with the SPARC ABI, software which calls them and which is desired to remain ABI-compliant should only rely on the ABI-defined interfaces to these routines. For example, a caller should ignore the state of the condition codes upon return from .mul.

---

[24] For details, see Sun's *Sun-4 Assembly Language Reference Manual*.

SPARC International, Inc.

## E.1.  Signed Multiplication

```
/*
 * Procedure to perform a 32-bit by 32-bit multiply.
 * Pass the multiplicand in %i0, and the multiplier in %i1.
 * The least significant 32 bits of the result are returned in %i0,
 * and the most significant in %i1.
 *
 * This code has an optimization built-in for short (less than 13-bit)
 * multiplies.  Short multiplies require 26 or 27 instruction cycles, and
 * long ones require 47 to 51 instruction cycles.  For two nonnegative numbers
 * (the most common case) a long multiply takes 47 instruction cycles.
 *
 * This code indicates that overflow has occurred by clearing the Z condition
 * code upon return [note that this is different from condition codes set
 * by the SMULcc and UMULcc instructions].  The following call sequence
 * would be used if one wished to deal with overflow (and did not require
 * the calling software to be SPARC ABI-compliant):
 *
 *        call      .mul
 *        nop                            ! (or set up last parameter here)
 *        bnz       overflow_code  ! (or tnz to overflow handler)
 *
 * Note that this is a leaf routine; i.e. it calls no other routines and does
 * all of its work in the out registers.  Thus, the usual SAVE and RESTORE
 * instructions are not needed.
 */

        .global .mul
.mul:
        mov       %o0, %y        ! multiplier to Y register
        andncc    %o0, 0xfff, %g0! mask out lower 12 bits
        be        mul_shortway   ! can do it the short way
        andcc     %g0, %g0, %o4  ! zero the partial product and clear N and V conditions
        !
        ! long multiply
        !
        mulscc    %o4, %o1, %o4  ! first iteration of 33
        mulscc    %o4, %o1, %o4
        mulscc    %o4, %o1, %o4
        mulscc    %o4, %o1, %o4
        mulscc    %o4, %o1, %o4
        mulscc    %o4, %o1, %o4
        mulscc    %o4, %o1, %o4
        mulscc    %o4, %o1, %o4
        mulscc    %o4, %o1, %o4
        mulscc    %o4, %o1, %o4
        mulscc    %o4, %o1, %o4
        mulscc    %o4, %o1, %o4
        mulscc    %o4, %o1, %o4
        mulscc    %o4, %o1, %o4
        mulscc    %o4, %o1, %o4
        mulscc    %o4, %o1, %o4
```

```
        mulscc    %o4, %o1, %o4
        mulscc    %o4, %o1, %o4
        mulscc    %o4, %o1, %o4
        mulscc    %o4, %o1, %o4
        mulscc    %o4, %o1, %o4
        mulscc    %o4, %o1, %o4
        mulscc    %o4, %o1, %o4
        mulscc    %o4, %o1, %o4
        mulscc    %o4, %o1, %o4
        mulscc    %o4, %o1, %o4
        mulscc    %o4, %o1, %o4
        mulscc    %o4, %o1, %o4
        mulscc    %o4, %o1, %o4
        mulscc    %o4, %o1, %o4
        mulscc    %o4, %o1, %o4  ! 32nd iteration
        mulscc    %o4, %g0, %o4  ! last iteration only shifts
        !
        ! If %o0 (multiplier) was negative, the result is:
        !    (%o0 * %o1) + %o1 * (2**32)
        ! We fix that here.
        !
        tst       %o0
        rd        %y, %o0
        bge       1f
        tst       %o0               ! for when we check for overflow

        sub       %o4, %o1, %o4  ! bit 33 and up of the product are in
                                    ! %o4, so we don't have to shift %o1
        !
        ! We haven't overflowed if:
        !    low-order bits are nonnegative and high-order bits are 0
        !    low-order bits are negative    and high-order bits are all 1
        !
        ! If you are not interested in detecting overflow,
        ! replace the four following instructions (bge, addcc, retl, subcc) with:
        !          1:   retl
        !               mov       %o4, %o1
        !
1:
        bge       2f               ! if low-order bits were nonnegative.
        addcc     %o4, %g0, %o1  ! return most sig. bits of prod and set
                                    ! Z appropriately (for nonnegative product)
        retl                       ! leaf-routine return
        subcc     %o4, -1, %g0   ! set Z if high order bits are -1 (for negative product)
2:
        retl                       ! leaf-routine return
        nop
        !
        ! short multiply
        !
mul_shortway:
        mulscc    %o4, %o1, %o4  ! first iteration of 13
```

```
mulscc    %o4, %o1, %o4
mulscc    %o4, %o1, %o4
mulscc    %o4, %o1, %o4
mulscc    %o4, %o1, %o4
mulscc    %o4, %o1, %o4
mulscc    %o4, %o1, %o4
mulscc    %o4, %o1, %o4
mulscc    %o4, %o1, %o4
mulscc    %o4, %o1, %o4
mulscc    %o4, %o1, %o4
mulscc    %o4, %o1, %o4    ! 12th iteration
mulscc    %o4, %g0, %o4    ! last iteration only shifts

rd        %y, %o5
sll       %o4, 12, %o0    ! left shift middle bits by 12 bits
srl       %o5, 20, %o5    ! right shift low bits by 20 bits
!
! We haven't overflowed if:
!    low-order bits are nonnegative and high-order bits are 0
!    low-order bits are negative    and high-order bits are -1
!
! if you are not interested in detecting overflow,
! replace the following code with:
!
!         or        %o5, %o0, %o0
!         retl
!         mov       %o4, %o1
!
orcc      %o5, %o0, %o0    ! merge for true product
bge       3f               ! if low-order bits were nonnegative.
sra       %o4, 20, %o1     ! right shift high bits by 20 bits
                           ! and put into  %o1
retl                       ! leaf-routine return
subcc     %o1, -1, %g0     ! set Z if high order bits are -1 (for
                           ! negative product)
3:
retl                       ! leaf-routine return
addcc     %o1, %g0, %g0    ! set Z if high order bits are 0
```

SPARC International, Inc.

## E.2.  Unsigned Multiplication

```
/*
 * Procedure to perform a 32 by 32 unsigned multiply.
 * Pass the multiplier in %o0, and the multiplicand in %o1.
 * The least significant 32 bits of the result will be returned in %o0,
 * and the most significant in %o1.
 *
 * This code has an optimization built-in for short (less than 13 bit)
 * multiplies. Short multiplies require 25 instruction cycles, and long ones
 * require 46 or 48 instruction cycles.
 *
 * This code indicates that overflow has occurred, by leaving the Z condition
 * code clear. The following call sequence would be used if you wish to
 * deal with overflow:
 *
 *      call       .umul
 *      nop                       ! (or set up last parameter here)
 *      bnz        overflow_code  ! (or tnz to overflow handler)
 *
 * Note that this is a leaf routine; i.e. it calls no other routines and does
 * all of its work in the out registers.  Thus, the usual SAVE and RESTORE
 * instructions are not needed.
 */
        .global    .umul
.umul:
        or         %o0, %o1, %o4  ! logical or of multiplier and multiplicand
        mov        %o0, %y        ! multiplier to Y register
        andncc     %o4, 0xfff, %o5! mask out lower 12 bits
        be         mul_shortway   ! can do it the short way
        andcc      %g0, %g0, %o4  ! zero the partial product and clear N and V conditions
        !
        ! long multiply
        !
        mulscc     %o4, %o1, %o4  ! first iteration of 33
        mulscc     %o4, %o1, %o4
        mulscc     %o4, %o1, %o4
        mulscc     %o4, %o1, %o4
        mulscc     %o4, %o1, %o4
        mulscc     %o4, %o1, %o4
        mulscc     %o4, %o1, %o4
        mulscc     %o4, %o1, %o4
        mulscc     %o4, %o1, %o4
        mulscc     %o4, %o1, %o4
        mulscc     %o4, %o1, %o4
        mulscc     %o4, %o1, %o4
        mulscc     %o4, %o1, %o4
        mulscc     %o4, %o1, %o4
        mulscc     %o4, %o1, %o4
        mulscc     %o4, %o1, %o4
        mulscc     %o4, %o1, %o4
        mulscc     %o4, %o1, %o4
        mulscc     %o4, %o1, %o4
        mulscc     %o4, %o1, %o4
```

```
        mulscc    %o4, %o1, %o4
        mulscc    %o4, %o1, %o4
        mulscc    %o4, %o1, %o4
        mulscc    %o4, %o1, %o4
        mulscc    %o4, %o1, %o4
        mulscc    %o4, %o1, %o4
        mulscc    %o4, %o1, %o4
        mulscc    %o4, %o1, %o4
        mulscc    %o4, %o1, %o4
        mulscc    %o4, %o1, %o4
        mulscc    %o4, %o1, %o4
        mulscc    %o4, %o1, %o4
        mulscc    %o4, %o1, %o4  ! 32nd iteration
        mulscc    %o4, %g0, %o4  ! last iteration only shifts
        /*
         * Normally, with the shift and add approach, if both numbers are
         * nonnegative, you get the correct result.  With 32-bit twos-complement
         * numbers, -x can be represented as ((2 - (x/(2**32))) mod 2) * 2**32.
         * To avoid a lot of 2**32's, we can just move the radix point up to be
         * just to the left of the sign bit.  So:
         *
         *    x *  y   = (xy) mod 2
         *   -x *  y   = (2 - x) mod 2 * y = (2y - xy) mod 2
         *    x * -y   = x * (2 - y) mod 2 = (2x - xy) mod 2
         *   -x * -y   = (2 - x) * (2 - y) = (4 - 2x - 2y + xy) mod 2
         *
         * For signed multiplies, we subtract (2**32) * x from the partial
         * product to fix this problem for negative multipliers (see .mul in
         * Section 1.
         * Because of the way the shift into the partial product is calculated
         * (N xor V), this term is automatically removed for the multiplicand,
         * so we don't have to adjust.
         *
         * But for unsigned multiplies, the high order bit wasn't a sign bit,
         * and the correction is wrong.  So for unsigned multiplies where the
         * high order bit is one, we end up with xy - (2**32) * y.  To fix it
         * we add y * (2**32).
         */
        tst       %o1
        bge       1f
        nop
        add       %o4, %o0, %o4
1:
        rd        %y, %o0        ! return least sig. bits of prod
        retl                     ! leaf-routine return
        addcc     %o4, %g0, %o1  ! delay slot; return high bits and set
                                 ! zero bit appropriately
        !
        ! short multiply
        !
mul_shortway:
        mulscc    %o4, %o1, %o4  ! first iteration of 13
        mulscc    %o4, %o1, %o4
```

```
mulscc     %o4, %o1, %o4
mulscc     %o4, %o1, %o4
mulscc     %o4, %o1, %o4
mulscc     %o4, %o1, %o4
mulscc     %o4, %o1, %o4
mulscc     %o4, %o1, %o4
mulscc     %o4, %o1, %o4
mulscc     %o4, %o1, %o4
mulscc     %o4, %o1, %o4
mulscc     %o4, %o1, %o4  ! 12th iteration
mulscc     %o4, %g0, %o4  ! last iteration only shifts

rd         %y, %o5
sll        %o4, 12, %o4   ! left shift partial product by 12 bits
srl        %o5, 20, %o5   ! right shift product by 20 bits
or         %o5, %o4, %o0  ! merge for true product
!
! The delay instruction (addcc) moves zero into %o1,
! sets the zero condition code, and clears the other conditions.
! This is the equivalent result to a long umultiply which doesn't overflow.
!
retl                      ! leaf-routine return
addcc      %g0, %g0, %o1
```

SPARC International, Inc.

## E.3. Division

Integer division implemented in software or microcode is usually done by a method such as the non-restoring algorithm, which provides one digit of quotient per step. A W-by-W digit division of radix-B digits is most easily achieved using $2 \times W$-digit arithmetic. This section develops the recommended division algorithm in steps. Program 6 is the final version.

**Program 1**

A binary-radix, 16-digit version of this method is illustrated by the C language function in Program 1, which performs an unsigned division producing the quotient in Q and the remainder in R.

```
#include <stdio.h>
#include <assert.h>

#define W 16     /* maximum number of bits in the dividend & divisor */

unsigned short
divide( dividend, divisor )
    unsigned  short dividend, divisor;
{
    long int       R;     /* partial remainder -- need 2*W bits */
    unsigned short Q;     /* partial quotient */
    int            iter;

    R = dividend;
    Q = 0;
    for ( iter = W; iter >= 0; iter -= 1 )
    {
        assert( ((Q*divisor)+R) == dividend );

        if (R >= 0)
        {
            R -= divisor <<iter;
            Q += 1<<iter;
        }
        else /* R < 0 */
        {
            R += divisor <<iter;
            Q -= 1<<iter;
        }
    }

    if ( R < 0 )
    {
        R += divisor;
        Q -= 1;
    }
    return Q;
}
```

**Program 2**

In the simple form shown above, this method has two drawbacks:

❑ It requires an accumulator 2×W bits wide.

❑ It always requires W steps.

These problems may be overcome by estimating the quotient before the actual division is carried out. This can cut the time required for a division from $O(W)$ to $O(\log_B(\text{quotient}))$. Program 2 illustrates how this estimate may be used to reduce the number of divide steps required and the size of the accumulator.

```
#include <stdio.h>
#include <assert.h>

#define W 32 /* maximum number of bits in a divisor or dividend */

#define Big_value (unsigned)(1<<(W-2)) /* 2 ^ (W-1) */

int
estimate_log_quotient( dividend, divisor )
        unsigned dividend, divisor;
{
        unsigned log_quotient;

        for (log_quotient = 0;  log_quotient < W;  log_quotient += 1 )
        {
                if ( ((divisor << log_quotient) > Big_value) ||
                    ((divisor << log_quotient) >= dividend ) )
                {
                        break;
                }
        }

        return log_quotient;
}

unsigned
divide( dividend, divisor )
        unsigned dividend, divisor;
{
        int         R;          /* remainder */
        unsigned int Q;         /* quotient  */
        int         iter;

        R = dividend;
        Q = 0;
        for ( iter = estimate_log_quotient(dividend, divisor);
              iter >= 0;  iter -= 1)
        {
                assert( ((Q*divisor)+R) == dividend );

                if (R >= 0)
                {
```

**SPARC International, Inc.**

```
                        R -= divisor <<iter;
                        Q  += 1<<iter;
                }
                else /* R < 0 */
                {
                        R += divisor <<iter;
                        Q  -= 1<<iter;
                }
        }

        if ( R < 0 )
        {
                R += divisor;
                Q -= 1;
        }
        return Q;
}
```

**Program 3**

Another way to reduce the number of division steps required is to choose a larger base, $B'$. This is only feasible if the cost of the radix-$B'$ inner loop does not exceed the cost of the radix-$B$ inner loop by more than $\log_B (B')$. When $B' = B^N$ for some integer $N$, a radix-$B'$ inner loop can easily be constructed from the radix-$B$ inner loop by arranging an $N$-high, $B$-ary decision tree. Programs 3 and 4 illustrate how this can be done. Program 3 uses $N$-level recursion to show the principle, but the overhead of recursion in this example far outweighs the loop overhead saved by reducing the number of steps required. Program 4 shows how run-time recursion can be eliminated if $N$ is fixed at two.

```
#include <stdio.h>
#include <assert.h>

#define W 32 /* bits in a word */

int B,              /* number base of division (must be a power of 2) */
    N;              /* log2(B) */
#define WB   (W/N)  /* base B digits in a word */
#define Big_value (unsigned)(B<<(WB-2)) /* B ^ (WB-1) */

int Q, /* partial quotient */
    R, /* partial remainder */
    V; /* multiple of the divisor */
int
estimate_log_quotient( dividend, divisor )
      unsigned dividend, divisor;
{
      unsigned log_quotient;

      for (log_quotient = 0;  log_quotient < WB;  log_quotient += 1 )
      {
              if ( ((divisor << (log_quotient*N)) >  Big_value) ||
                  ((divisor << (log_quotient*N)) >= dividend ) )
              {
                    break;
              }
      }

      return log_quotient;
}


int
compute_digit( level, quotient_digit )
      int level, quotient_digit;
{
      if (R >= 0)
      {
              R -= V << level;
              quotient_digit += 1<<level;
      }
      else /* R < 0 */
      {
```

```
                        R += V << level;
                        quotient_digit -= 1<<level;
        }

        if (level > 0)
        {
                return compute_digit( level-1, quotient_digit );
        }
        else    return quotient_digit;
}


unsigned
divide( dividend, divisor )
        unsigned dividend, divisor;
{
        int iter;

        B = (1<<(N));
        R = dividend;
        Q = 0;
        for ( iter = estimate_log_quotient(dividend, divisor);
              iter >= 0;   iter -= 1)
        {
                assert( ((Q*divisor)+R) == dividend );

                V = divisor << (iter*N);
                Q += compute_digit(N-1, 0) << (iter*N);
        }
        if ( R < 0 )
        {
                R += divisor;
                Q -= 1;
        }
        return Q;
}
```

**Program 4**

```
#include <stdio.h>
#include <assert.h>

#define W 32    /* bits in a word */

#define B 4     /* number base of division (must be a power of 2) */
#define N 2     /* log2(B)*/
#define WB  (W/N)    /* base B digits in a word */
#define Big_value (unsigned)(B<<(WB-2)) /* B ^ WB-1 */

int
estimate_log_quotient( dividend, divisor )
        unsigned dividend, divisor;
{

        unsigned log_quotient;

        for (log_quotient = 0;  log_quotient < WB;  log_quotient += 1 )
        {
                if ( ((divisor << (log_quotient*N)) > Big_value) ||
                    ((divisor << (log_quotient*N)) >= dividend ) )
                {
                    break;
                }
        }

        return log_quotient;
}


int
unsigned
divide( dividend, divisor )
        unsigned dividend, divisor;
{

        int Q, /* partial quotient */
            R, /* partial remainder */
            V; /* multiple of the divisor */
        int iter;

        R = dividend;
        Q = 0;
        for ( iter = estimate_log_quotient(dividend, divisor);
              iter >= 0;  iter -= 1)
        {
                assert( ((Q*divisor)+R) == dividend );

                V = divisor << (iter*N);

                /* N-deep, B-wide decision tree */
                if ( R >= 0 )
                {
                        R -= V<<1;
```

```
                              if ( R >= 0 )
                              {
                                      R -= V;
                                      Q += 3 <<(N*iter);
                              }
                              else /* R < 0 */
                              {
                                      R += V;
                                      Q += 1 <<(N*iter);
                              }
                      }
                      else /* R < 0 */
                      {
                              R += V<<1;
                              if ( R >= 0 )
                              {
                                      R -= V;
                                      Q -= 1 <<(N*iter);
                              }
                              else /* R < 0 */
                              {
                                      R += V;
                                      Q -= 3 <<(N*iter);
                              }
                      }
              }

              if ( R < 0 )
              {
                      R += divisor;
                      Q -= 1;
              }

              return Q;
      }
```

**Program 5**

At the risk of losing even more clarity, several of the bookkeeping operations can be optimized away, as shown in Program 5.

```c
#include <stdio.h>
#include <assert.h>

#define W 32    /* bits in a word */

#define B 4     /* number base of division (must be a power of 2) */
#define N 2     /* log2(B)*/
#define WB  (W/N)    /* base B digits in a word */
#define Big_value (unsigned)(B<<(WB-2)) /* B ^ WB-1 */


int
unsigned
divide( dividend, divisor )
        unsigned dividend, divisor;
{

        int Q, /* partial quotient */
            R, /* partial remainder */
            V; /* multiple of the divisor */
        int iter;

        R = dividend;
        Q = 0;
        V = divisor;

        for ( iter = 0;  (V <= Big_value) && (V <= dividend);  iter += 1 )
        {
                V <<= N;
        }

        for ( V <<= (N-1);  iter >= 0;  iter -= 1 )
        {
                Q <<= N;
                assert( ((Q*(1<<(iter*N))*divisor)+R) == dividend );

                /* N-deep, B-wide decision tree */
                if ( R >= 0 )
                {
                        R -= V;
                        V >>= 1;
                        if ( R >= 0 )
                        {
                                R -= V;
                                V >>= 1;
                                Q += 3 ;
                        }
                        else /* R < 0 */
                        {
                                R += V;
```

SPARC International, Inc.

```
                                V >>= 1;
                                Q += 1 ;
                        }
                }
                else /* R < 0 */
                {
                        R += V;
                        V >>= 1;
                        if ( R >= 0 )
                        {
                                R -= V;
                                V >>= 1;
                                Q -= 1;
                        }
                        else /* R < 0 */
                        {
                                R += V;
                                V >>= 1;
                                Q -= 3;
                        }
                }
        }

        if ( R < 0 )
        {
                R += divisor;
                Q -= 1;
        }

        return Q;
}
```

**Program 6**

Program 6 is the recommended method for software division on SPARC (in the absence of hardware divide instructions).

The depth of the decision tree — two in the preceding examples — is controlled by the constant N, and is currently set to three, based on empirical evidence. The decision tree is not explicitly coded, but defined by the recursive m4 macro DEVELOP_QUOTIENT_BITS. Other differences include:

□ Handling of signed and unsigned operands

□ More care taken to avoid overflow for very large quotients or divisors

□ Special tests made for division by zero and zero quotient

□ Provision for conditional compilation for either division or remaindering

Note that this routine sets the condition codes differently from those set by any of the SDIV or UDIV instructions.

Assembly language code suitable for input to a SPARC assembler can be obtained by processing this code with the **m4** and **cpp** preprocessors, in turn.

```
/*
 * Division/Remainder
 *
 * Input is:
 *   dividend -- the thing being divided
 *   divisor  -- how many ways to divide it
 * Important parameters:
 *   N -- how many bits per iteration we try to get
 *        as our current guess: define(N, 3)
 *   WORDSIZE -- how many bits altogether we're talking about:
 *        obviously: define(WORDSIZE, 32)
 * A derived constant:
 *   TOPBITS -- how many bits are in the top "decade" of a number:
 *        define(TOPBITS, eval( WORDSIZE - N*((WORDSIZE-1)/N) ) )
 * Important variables are:
 *   Q -- the partial quotient under development -- initially 0
 *   R -- the remainder so far -- initially == the dividend
 *   ITER -- number of iterations of the main division loop which will
 *        be required. Equal to CEIL( lg2(quotient)/N )
 *        Note that this is log_base_(2^N) of the quotient.
 *   V -- the current comparand -- initially divisor*2^(ITER*N-1)
 * Cost:
 *   current estimate for non-large dividend is
 *        CEIL( lg2(quotient) / N ) x ( 10 + 7N/2 ) + C
 *   a large dividend is one greater than 2^(31-TOPBITS) and takes a
 *   different path, as the upper bits of the quotient must be developed
 *   one bit at a time.
 *   This uses the m4 and cpp macro preprocessors.
 */

#include "sw_trap.h"

define(dividend, '%i0')
define(divisor, '%i1')
```

SPARC International, Inc.

```
define(Q,  '%i2')
define(R,  '%i3')
define(ITER,   '%l0')
define(V,  '%l1')
define(SIGN,   '%l2')
define(T, '%l3')    ! working variable
define(SC,'%l4')
/*
 * This is the recursive definition of how we develop quotient digits.
 * It takes three important parameters:
 *    $1 -- the current depth, 1<=$1<=N
 *    $2 -- the current accumulation of quotient bits
 *    N  -- max depth
 * We add a new bit to $2 and either recurse or insert the bits in the quotient.
 * Dynamic input:
 *    R -- current remainder
 *    Q -- current quotient
 *    V -- current comparand
 *    cc -- set on current value of R
 * Dynamic output:
 *    R', Q', V', cc'
 */

define(DEVELOP_QUOTIENT_BITS,
 `      !depth $1, accumulated bits $2
        bl   L.$1.eval(2^N+$2)
        srl  V,1,V
        ! remainder is nonnegative
        subcc R,V,R
        ifelse( $1, N,
 `        b    9f
            add  Q, ($2*2+1), Q
 ',`        DEVELOP_QUOTIENT_BITS( incr($1), `eval(2*$2+1)')
 ')
L.$1.eval(2^N+$2):              ! remainder is negative
        addcc R,V,R
        ifelse( $1, N,
 `        b    9f
            add  Q, ($2*2-1), Q
 ',`        DEVELOP_QUOTIENT_BITS( incr($1), `eval(2*$2-1)')
 ')
        ifelse( $1, 1, `9:')
')
ifelse( ANSWER, `quotient', `
        .global   .div, .udiv
.udiv:    ! UNSIGNED DIVIDE
        save %sp,-64,%sp
        b    divide
        mov  0,SIGN               ! result always nonnegative

.div:     ! SIGNED DIVIDE
        save %sp,-64,%sp
        orcc divisor,dividend,%g0  ! are either dividend or divisor negative
```

```
        bge   divide                  ! if not, skip this junk
        xor   divisor,dividend,SIGN ! record sign of result in sign of SIGN
        tst   divisor
        bge   2f
        tst   dividend
        !     divisor < 0
        bge   divide
        neg   divisor
        2:
        !     dividend < 0
        neg   dividend
        !     FALL THROUGH
', `
        .global   .rem, .urem
.urem:    ! UNSIGNED REMAINDER
        save  %sp,-64,%sp            ! do this for debugging
        b     divide
        mov   0,SIGN                 ! result always nonnegative

.rem:! SIGNED REMAINDER
        save  %sp,-64,%sp            ! do this for debugging
        orcc divisor,dividend,%g0 ! are either dividend or divisor negative
        bge   divide                  ! if not, skip this junk
        mov   dividend,SIGN          ! record sign of result in sign of SIGN
        tst   divisor
        bge   2f
        tst   dividend
        !     divisor < 0
        bge   divide
        neg   divisor
        2:
        !     dividend < 0
        neg   dividend
        !     FALL THROUGH
')


divide:
        ! Compute size of quotient, scale comparand.
        orcc divisor,%g0,V          ! movcc    divisor,V
        te    ST_DIV0               ! if divisor = 0
        mov   dividend,R
        mov   0,Q
        sethi %hi(1<<(WORDSIZE-TOPBITS-1)),T
        cmp   R,T
        blu   not_really_big
        mov   0,ITER
        !
        ! Here, the dividend is >= 2^(31-N) or so.  We must be careful here,
        ! as our usual N-at-a-shot divide step will cause overflow and havoc.
        ! The total number of bits in the result here is N*ITER+SC, where
        ! SC <= N.
        ! Compute ITER in an unorthodox manner: know we need to Shift V into
```

SPARC International, Inc.

```
        ! the top decade: so don't even bother to compare to R.
        1:
                cmp   V,T
                bgeu  3f
                mov   1,SC
                sll   V,N,V
                b     1b
                inc   ITER
        !
        ! Now compute SC
        !
        2:      addcc V,V,V
                bcc   not_too_big ! bcc    not_too_big
                add   SC,1,SC
                        !
                        ! We're here if the divisor overflowed when Shifting.
                        ! This means that R has the high-order bit set.
                        ! Restore V and subtract from R.
                        sll   T,TOPBITS,T ! high order bit
                        srl   V,1,V ! rest of V
                        add   V,T,V
                        b     do_single_div
                        dec   SC
        not_too_big:
        3:      cmp   V,R
                blu   2b
                nop
                be    do_single_div
                nop
        ! V > R: went too far: back up 1 step
        !       srl   V,1,V
        !       dec   SC
        ! do single-bit divide steps
        !
        ! We have to be careful here. We know that R >= V, so we can do the
        ! first divide step without thinking.  BUT, the others are conditional,
        ! and are only done if R >= 0.  Because both R and V may have the high-
        ! order bit set in the first step, just falling into the regular
        ! division loop will mess up the first time around.
        ! So we unroll slightly...
        do_single_div:
                deccc SC
                bl    end_regular_divide
                nop
                sub   R,V,R
                mov   1,Q
                b     end_single_divloop
                nop
        single_divloop:
                sll   Q,1,Q
                bl    1f
                srl   V,1,V
                ! R >= 0
```

```
            sub  R,V,R
            b    2f
            inc  Q
      1:    ! R < 0
            add  R,V,R
            dec  Q
      2:
      end_single_divloop:
            deccc SC
            bge   single_divloop
            tst   R
            b     end_regular_divide
            nop


not_really_big:
1:
      sll  V,N,V
      cmp  V,R
      bleu 1b
      inccc ITER
      be   got_result
      dec  ITER
do_regular_divide:

      ! Do the main division iteration
      tst  R
      ! Fall through into divide loop
divloop:
      sll  Q,N,Q
      DEVELOP_QUOTIENT_BITS( 1, 0 )
end_regular_divide:
      deccc ITER
      bge   divloop
      tst   R
      bge   got_result
      nop
      ! non-restoring fixup here
ifelse( ANSWER, 'quotient',
`     dec  Q
',`   add  R,divisor,R
')


got_result:
      tst SIGN
      bge 1f
      restore
      ! answer < 0
      retl             ! leaf-routine return
ifelse( ANSWER, 'quotient',
`     neg  %o2,%o0   ! quotient  <- -Q
',`   neg  %o3,%o0   ! remainder <- -R
')
```

```
1:   retl            ! leaf-routine return
ifelse( ANSWER, `quotient',
`    mov  %o2,%o0   ! quotient  <-  Q
',`  mov  %o3,%o0   ! remainder <-  R
')
```

# F

## Opcodes and Condition Codes

This Appendix lists the SPARC instruction opcodes and condition codes.

Table F-1    *op[1:0]*

| op [1:0] | | | |
|---|---|---|---|
| 0 | 1 | 2 | 3 |
| **See Table F-2** | **CALL** | **See Table F-3** | **See Table F-4** |

Table F-2    *op2[2:0] (op=0, empty columns eliminated)*

| op2 [2:0] | | | | |
|---|---|---|---|---|
| 0 | 2 | 4 | 6 | 7 |
| UNIMP | Bicc **See Table F-7** | SETHI NOP† | FBfcc **See Table F-7** | CBccc **See Table F-7** |

† *rd=0, imm22=0*

Table F-3    *op3[5:0] (op=2)*

| | | op3 [5:4] | | | |
|---|---|---|---|---|---|
| | | 0 | 1 | 2 | 3 |
| op3 [3:0] | 0 | ADD | ADDcc | TADDcc | WRASR†<br>WRY‡ |
| | 1 | AND | ANDcc | TSUBcc | WRPSR |
| | 2 | OR | ORcc | TADDccTV | WRWIM |
| | 3 | XOR | XORcc | TSUBccTV | WRTBR |
| | 4 | SUB | SUBcc | MULScc | FPop1<br>**See Table F-5** |
| | 5 | ANDN | ANDNcc | SLL | FPop2<br>**See Table F-6** |
| | 6 | ORN | ORNcc | SRL | CPop1 |
| | 7 | XNOR | XNORcc | SRA | CPop2 |
| | 8 | ADDX | ADDXcc | RDASR*<br>RDY**<br>STBAR*** | JMPL |
| | 9 | | | RDPSR | RETT |
| | A | UMUL | UMULcc | RDWIM | Ticc<br>**See Table F-7** |
| | B | SMUL | SMULcc | RDTBR | FLUSH |
| | C | SUBX | SUBXcc | | SAVE |
| | D | | | | RESTORE |
| | E | UDIV | UDIVcc | | |
| | F | SDIV | SDIVcc | | |

† $rd \neq 0$
‡ $rd = 0$
* $rs1 \neq 0$
** $rs1 = 0$
*** $rs1 = 15, rd = 0$

SPARC International, Inc.

Table F-4    *op3[5:0] (op=3)*

|  |  | op3 [5:4] | | | |
|  |  | 0 | 1 | 2 | 3 |
| op3 [3:0] | 0 | LD | LDA | LDF | LDC |
|  | 1 | LDUB | LDUBA | LDFSR | LDCSR |
|  | 2 | LDUH | LDUHA |  |  |
|  | 3 | LDD | LDDA | LDDF | LDDC |
|  | 4 | ST | STA | STF | STC |
|  | 5 | STB | STBA | STFSR | STCSR |
|  | 6 | STH | STHA | STDFQ | STDCQ |
|  | 7 | STD | STDA | STDF | STDC |
|  | 8 |  |  |  |  |
|  | 9 | LDSB | LDSBA |  |  |
|  | A | LDSH | LDSHA |  |  |
|  | B |  |  |  |  |
|  | C |  |  |  |  |
|  | D | LDSTUB | LDSTUBA |  |  |
|  | E |  |  |  |  |
|  | F | SWAP | SWAPA |  |  |

Table F-5     *opf[8:0] (op=2, op3=0x34=FPop1, empty rows eliminated)*

| | | |
|---|---|---|
| | 01 | FMOVs |
| | 05 | FNEGs |
| | 09 | FABSs |
| | 29 | FSQRTs |
| | 2A | FSQRTd |
| | 2B | FSQRTq |
| | 41 | FADDs |
| | 42 | FADDd |
| | 43 | FADDq |
| | 45 | FSUBs |
| | 46 | FSUBd |
| | 47 | FSUBq |
| | 49 | FMULs |
| | 4A | FMULd |
| | 4B | FMULq |
| opf | 4D | FDIVs |
| [8:0] | 4E | FDIVd |
| | 4F | FDIVq |
| | 69 | FsMULd |
| | 6E | FdMULq |
| | C4 | FiTOs |
| | C6 | FdTOs |
| | C7 | FqTOs |
| | C8 | FiTOd |
| | C9 | FsTOd |
| | CB | FqTOd |
| | CC | FiTOq |
| | CD | FsTOq |
| | CE | FdTOq |
| | D1 | FsTOi |
| | D2 | FdTOi |
| | D3 | FqTOi |

SPARC International, Inc.

Table F-6    *opf[8:0] (op=2, op3=0x35=FPop2, empty rows eliminated)*

| | | |
|---|---|---|
| | 51 | FCMPs |
| | 52 | FCMPd |
| opf | 53 | FCMPq |
| [8:0] | 55 | FCMPEs |
| | 56 | FCMPEd |
| | 57 | FCMPEq |

Table F-7    *cond[3:0]*

| | | Bicc | FBfcc | CBccc | Ticc |
|---|---|---|---|---|---|
| | | op=0 op2=2 | op=0 op2=6 | op=0 op2=7 | op=2 op3=0x3A |
| | 0 | BN | FBN | CBN | TN |
| | 1 | BE | FBNE | CB123 | TE |
| | 2 | BLE | FBLG | CB12 | TLE |
| | 3 | BL | FBUL | CB13 | TL |
| | 4 | BLEU | FBL | CB1 | TLEU |
| | 5 | BCS | FBUG | CB23 | TCS |
| | 6 | BNEG | FBG | CB2 | TNEG |
| cond | 7 | BVS | FBU | CB3 | TVS |
| [3:0] | 8 | BA | FBA | CBA | TA |
| | 9 | BNE | FBE | CB0 | TNE |
| | A | BG | FBUE | CB03 | TG |
| | B | BGE | FBGE | CB02 | TGE |
| | C | BGU | FBUGE | CB023 | TGU |
| | D | BCC | FBLE | CB01 | TCC |
| | E | BPOS | FBULE | CB013 | TPOS |
| | F | BVC | FBO | CB012 | TVC |

SPARC International, Inc.

# G

---

# SPARC ABI Software Considerations

The SPARC Application Binary Interface (ABI) is a software specification developed by SPARC International and AT&T. SPARC International's SCD 2.0 is a superset of the SPARC ABI. Software that conforms to this specification will produce the same results on every SPARC ABI-compliant computer system. This enables the distribution of "shrink-wrapped" software for SPARC systems.

**G.1. SPARC International, Inc.**

SPARC International is committed to directing the evolution of SPARC microprocessor architecture and systems operating environments. This is accomplished by establishing and publishing SPARC Compliance Definitions (SCD) and migration guidelines. SCDs allow system vendor and ISV members to accelerate development of binary compatible SPARC/UNIX(R) systems and software.

**G.2. SCD 1.0 and SCD 2.0**

SCD 1.0 and SCD 2.0 provide openly agreed-upon standard definitions. This makes it possible for SPARC International members to design compliant products with a minimum time to market.

SCD 1.0 compliance is the formal beginning of migration to SCD 2.0, which is based on the industry-standard UNIX System V Release 4 operating system from AT&T. Smooth migration results in many benefits including increased market opportunity for participating vendors.

The SPARC ABI standard applies to SPARC systems that are designed to execute wide-distribution software application packages. Other types of SPARC-based systems (e.g. real-time systems, embedded systems, systems running proprietary operating systems) may borrow software conventions from the ABI, but have no need to conform to it.

The ABI specifies for application software, among other things:

- The instruction set that the application may use.

- The system call and general library routines that the application may assume are available (for dynamic linking) on the system on which it is executed.

- Numerous software conventions, such as data alignment, usage of registers, stack frame layout, parameter-passing methods, and function call/return sequences (with which those described in Appendix D, "Software Considerations," are compatible).

SPARC International, Inc.

Those interested in the complete specification of the SPARC ABI should refer to two documents available from Prentice Hall: *System V Application Binary Interface* [25] (ISBN 0-13-877598-2) and *System V Application Binary Interface, SPARC Processor Supplement* (ISBN 0-13-877630-x).

## G.3.  SPARC ABI Software

ABI software, by its nature, is intended to be run on the full range of systems that are SPARC ABI-compliant. This range may encompass machines with vastly different performance characteristics, leading to tradeoffs in how code is generated for such software. This appendix describes factors to be considered when generating code for SPARC ABI software.

Note that the word "systems" in this appendix refers to SPARC-based computer systems (counted by installed base in the field, totaling in the hundreds of thousands), not to SPARC processor implementations (which total one or two dozen so far).

## G.4.  Register Usage

Register usage in SPARC ABI software is described in *System V Application Binary Interface, SPARC Processor Supplement*. Register usage specified in this document's Appendix D, "Software Considerations," (excluding Section D.8, "Other Register Window Usage Models") conforms to the ABI. ABI-conformant software may not use the "alternative" methods of configuring register windows and of allocating registers within windows mentioned in Section D.8.

## G.5.  The Memory Stack

The stack layout expected in SPARC ABI software is described in *System V Application Binary Interface, SPARC Processor Supplement*. The stack-frame layout specified in this document's Appendix D, "Software Considerations," conforms to the SPARC ABI.

## G.6.  Instruction Set

The SPARC ABI is based on the full SPARC instruction set, per this version of the SPARC Architecture manual. An ABI-compliant system correctly executes any (non-privileged) SPARC instruction in a user application program. Other than execution speed, it is transparent to the user application program whether instructions are executed in hardware or trapped and emulated in software.

There is a group of instructions that are relatively new to the SPARC architecture; their frequent use in ABI software should be considered with care. These instructions are being implemented in hardware in some new SPARC implementations, although they are emulated in software in some systems currently in the field[26]. These instructions are:

- SWAP
- Integer multiply instructions (SMUL, SMULcc, UMUL, UMULcc)

---

[25] Note that despite the document title, the ABI only requires a target system to provide a subset of UNIX System V functionality.

[26] This is the case as of mid-1990. It will change over time, as more systems in which these instructions are implemented in hardware are shipped.

SPARC International, Inc.

- Integer divide instructions (SDIV, SDIVcc, UDIV, UDIVcc)

- Floating-point square-root instructions (FSQRTs, FSQRTd, FSQRTq)

- FsMULd

- All quad-precision floating-point instructions, including FdMULq

Plus, there is one new SPARC instruction which (correctly) executes as a no-op on systems currently in the field. On some future systems, it will not be a no-op:

- Store Barrier (STBAR)

Consult Appendix L, "Implementation Characteristics," to determine which SPARC implementations support these instructions in hardware, and their instruction timings.

Programmers who write in SPARC assembly language and designers of SPARC code generators for compilers explicitly choose which SPARC instructions they will use. When choosing instructions for use in an ABI program, the tradeoffs involved in using the above SPARC instructions should be considered.

**Note that the presence or absence of these instructions in most SPARC ABI applications will have little effect on the applications' performance since most applications use them infrequently.** This section offers recommendations on how these instructions can be most effectively utilized in current SPARC ABI applications.

Explicit use of these instructions in ABI code can obtain higher performance from SPARC machines that implement them in hardware, at the expense of performance degradation on machines that implement them in software. Conversely, avoiding use of these instructions will prevent performance degradation on machines that implement them in software [26], and obtain good but not-quite-optimal performance from SPARC machines that implement them in hardware.

The history of the new SPARC instructions is described below, along with recommendations for their use in SPARC ABI software.

**SWAP instruction**

The SWAP instruction was added in Version 7 of the SPARC architecture. Some systems in the field do not implement this instruction in hardware.

When an atomic synchronization primitive is needed in ABI code, LDSTUB should be used in preference to SWAP.

**MUL instructions**

The integer multiply instructions (SMUL, SMULcc, UMUL, UMULcc) are new in Version 8 of the SPARC architecture. Some SPARC systems in the field emulate these instructions in software.

Recommended use of MUL instructions in SPARC ABI programs:

□ *To obtain good integer multiplication performance across all systems:*
Call the multiplication library routines .mul and .umul (which are dynamically linked from the host's libraries at execution time) for signed and unsigned multiplication, respectively. On systems with multiplication implemented in hardware, those routines should make use of the hardware multiply instructions. On systems with multiplication not implemented in hardware, those routines should use MULScc to perform efficient stepwise multiplication. This imposes no performance degradation on most systems in the field, and only slight degradation (a few cycles per multiplication) for machines that implement the multiply instructions in hardware.

□ *In the rare application that is integer-multiply-intensive, for which optimal performance on systems which implement multiply instructions in hardware is desired at the cost of performance degradation on most systems:*
Use in-line multiply instructions (SMUL, SMULcc, UMUL, and UMULcc). Such code may test the N or Z condition codes after SMULcc or UMULcc instructions but should **not** test the V or C condition codes, as their specification may change in a future revision to the architecture.

**DIV instructions**

The integer divide instructions (SDIV, SDIVcc, UDIV, UDIVcc) are new in Version 8 of the SPARC architecture. Some SPARC systems in the field emulate these instructions in software.

Recommended use of DIV instructions in SPARC ABI programs:

□ *To obtain good integer division performance across all systems:*
Call the division library routines .div and .udiv (which are dynamically linked from the host's libraries at execution time) for signed and unsigned division, respectively. On systems with division implemented in hardware, those routines should make use of the hardware divide instructions. On systems with division not implemented in hardware, those routines should perform stepwise division in software. This would impose no performance degradation on most systems in the field, and only slight degradation (a few cycles per division) for machines which implement the divide instructions in hardware.

□ *In the rare application which is integer-divide-intensive, for which optimal performance on systems which implement divide instructions in hardware is desired, at the cost of performance degradation on most systems:*
Use in-line divide instructions (SDIV, SDIVcc, UDIV, and UDIVcc).

**FSQRTs, FSQRTd instructions**

The single and double-precision floating-point square root instructions (FSQRTs, FSQRTd) were added in Version 7 of the SPARC architecture. Some SPARC systems in the field emulate these instructions in software, but most systems implement them in hardware.

It is recommended that SPARC ABI programs use the FSQRTs and FSQRTd instructions directly.

**FsMULd instruction**

The floating-point multiply single-to-double instruction (FsMULd) is new in Version 8 of the SPARC architecture. Some SPARC systems in the field emulate this instruction in software.

Recommended use of FsMULd instruction in SPARC ABI programs:

□ *If FsMULd is used infrequently (on a dynamic basis):*
Use the FsMULd instruction in-line.

□ *If FsMULd is used heavily (on a dynamic basis), and reasonable performance across all systems is preferred over optimal performance on the fastest systems:*
Convert the operands to double precision in scratch registers, then calculate the result with the FMULd instruction.
For example,

```
        fsmuld  %f20,%f21,%f8
```

might be replaced by:

```
        fstod   %f20,%f0
        fstod   %f23,%f2
        fmuld   %f0,%f2,%f8
```

This provides reasonable performance on machines with hardware support for FsMULd, while not penalizing those without it with the overhead of trapping and emulating the instructions in supervisor software.

□ *If FsMULd is used heavily (on a dynamic basis), and optimal performance on systems which implement FsMULd in hardware is desired at the cost of performance degradation on most systems:*
Use the FsMULd instruction in-line.

**Quad-precision floating-point instructions**

The quad-precision floating-point instructions are new in Version 8 of the SPARC architecture. Most SPARC systems in the field emulate these instructions in software.

It is recommended that SPARC ABI programs use double-precision floating-point instructions when execution speed is critical and double precision provides sufficient accuracy.

When full quad-precision arithmetic is required, the following choices are recommended:

□ *To obtain good quad-precision performance across all systems:*
Call the quad-precision library routines (which are dynamically linked from the host's libraries at execution time). The correspondence between quad-precision instructions and quad-precision library routines is presented in the following table. See the AT&T *System V Application Binary Interface, SPARC Processor Supplement* document for detailed routine descriptions.

Table G-1    *Quad-Precision Instruction - ABI routine Correspondence*

| SPARC Instruction(s) | Corresponding SPARC ABI routine(s) |
| --- | --- |
| FiTOq | _Q_itoq |
| FqTOi | _Q_qtoi |
| FsTOq | _Q_stoq |
| FqTOs | _Q_qtos |
| FdTOq | _Q_dtoq |
| FqTOd | _Q_qtod |
| FSQRTq | _Q_sqrt |
| FADDq | _Q_add |
| FSUBq | _Q_sub |
| FMULq | _Q_mul |
| FdMULq | — |
| FDIVq | _Q_div |
| FCMPq | _Q_cmp, _Q_feq, _Q_fne |
| FCMPEq | _Q_cmpe, _Q_fgt, _Q_fge, _Q_flt, _Q_fle |
| FNEGs + 3 FMOVs | _Q_neg |
| — | _Q_utoq |
| — | _Q_qtou |

On systems with quad-precision arithmetic implemented in hardware, these routines can make use of the hardware quad-precision instructions. On systems with quad-precision arithmetic not implemented in hardware, these routines emulate quad-precision arithmetic in software. This imposes no performance degradation on most systems in the field, and only slight degradation (a few cycles per instruction) for machines which implement quad-precision instructions in hardware.

□ *In the rare application which uses quad-precision floating-point arithmetic intensively and for which optimal performance on systems which implement quad-precision instructions in hardware is desired at the cost of performance degradation on most systems:*
Use in-line quad-precision floating-point instructions.

**Coprocessor instructions**

By their nature, coprocessor instructions are implementation-dependent. Therefore, they may not be explicitly used in SPARC ABI application code.

Note that application code may still benefit from the presence of a specialized coprocessor, because dynamically linked library code on the run-time host system may make use of coprocessor instructions.

| | |
|---|---|
| **Read/Write ASR instructions** | The operation of RDASR and WRASR instructions on ASR registers 1...15 is not currently defined. The operation of RDASR and WRASR instructions on ASR registers 16...31 is defined to be implementation-dependent. Therefore, none of the RDASR or WRASR instructions may be explicitly used in SPARC ABI application code. |

If some of these instructions are supported in a particular SPARC-based system implementation, dynamically linked ABI library code could make use of these instructions (transparently to ABI application code), but ABI application code cannot.

| | |
|---|---|
| **STBAR instruction** | The STBAR instruction may be used in SPARC ABI software. On existing systems which implement the Strong Consistency memory model, STBAR (correctly) executes as a no-op. Since STBAR doesn't trap when executed on machines currently in the field, there is no performance penalty for its execution on those machines. |

STBAR instructions are superfluous in SPARC ABI software, since the memory model for the 1990 SPARC ABI is TSO. See Chapter 6, "Memory Model." However, SPARC ABI software intended to execute correctly under both the TSO **and** PSO memory models must use STBAR where needed. See Appendix J, "Programming with the Memory Model."

## G.7. Self-Modifying Code

Code which writes into its own instruction space or the instruction space of another process (e.g. via shared memory) is called "self-modifying code". For each word stored in ABI software which may later be executed as an instruction, a FLUSH instruction must be issued referencing that location after the word is stored and before it is executed.

Although FLUSH provides support for self-modifying code, the use of self-modifying code is strongly discouraged. However, some operations (such as current implementations of dynamic linking) rely upon self-modifying code.

Note that FLUSH may be a time-consuming operation on some implementations.

See Appendix J, "Programming with the Memory Model" and the FLUSH instruction page in Appendix B for more information.

Note that if a FLUSH instruction causes an invalid-address fault, supervisor software will handle it; ABI user software will never see a SIGSEGV or SIGBUS signal from execution of a FLUSH instruction.

## G.8. Non-Standard Floating-Point Operation

By definition, use of the non-standard mode of floating-point operation by software will likely produce results which will vary across implementations. Therefore, ABI-compliant software must not enable it (that is, must not set FSR.NS to 1 via a LDFSR instruction).

SPARC International, Inc.

## G.9. Instruction Scheduling

Instruction scheduling is the process of (re-)ordering instructions in the instruction stream to improve performance. This function is typically performed in an optimization phase of compilation.

Any architecturally valid sequence of instructions executes correctly on any SPARC implementation. However, the performance obtained from a particular processor may be enhanced (sometimes substantially) by reordering instructions to take advantage of that processor's microarchitecture. Such a reordering may cause a degree of performance degradation on some other implementations.

Use of instruction scheduling strategies that obtain optimal performance on specific SPARC-based systems, at the expense of other SPARC-based systems, would be contrary to the spirit of the SPARC ABI. However, there are some basic instruction scheduling strategies that improve performance across almost all SPARC implementations, with little or no cost on those that do not benefit from them.
The most important strategies are:

□ *Filling Delay Slots*
Replace NOP's in the delay slots of control-transfer instructions with useful instructions.

□ *Spacing Out Floating-Point Instructions*
Intersperse integer instructions in sequences of floating-point instructions, where possible, to take advantage of the asynchronous execution of integer and floating-point instructions in most SPARC implementations.

Secondary strategies which may be helpful include:

□ *Making Consecutive Instructions Independent*
It is preferable for each instruction to be independent of the instruction that executes immediately before it. Rearrangement of instructions can often increase the occurrence of consecutive instructions that are independent. It can be especially helpful to separate instruction pairs where the first instruction is a load, and the following instruction reads the register that is the destination of the load.

□ *Avoiding Consecutive Stores*
Rearrange code to reduce the incidence of consecutive store operations. On machines in which the memory system has shallow store buffers, this can increase throughput.

Note that all instruction scheduling strategies can be made more effective by code generation and global optimization policies, such as loop unrolling, that increase the size of basic blocks (that is, reduce the frequency of control transfers).

# H

## SPARC Reference MMU Architecture

### H.1. Introduction

This appendix describes the SPARC Reference MMU Architecture, a memory management architecture for use with SPARC processors. The architecture is designed so that single-chip MMU implementations can provide general-purpose memory management that efficiently supports a large number of processes running a wide variety of applications.

The Reference MMU Architecture serves as a guideline for system implementors, describing how a preferred MMU for SPARC-based systems should behave. Actual Reference MMU implementations may employ different pinouts and different internal organizations. The Reference MMU Architecture primarily describes (for software) a common architecture for memory management. This appendix is not a data sheet for hardware engineering purposes, but is a guide to implementors and users.

One goal of the Reference MMU Architecture is to promote standardization. Use of a standard MMU architecture by manufacturers will reduce the time taken to port an operating system to new hardware and reduce the likelihood of introducing new hardware bugs. The portability of user-level and application programs is not affected by the MMU design.

### H.2. Overview

The Reference MMU Architecture can be implemented as a single chip in CMOS, Bi-CMOS, ECL, or GaAs, or even on the same chip as the CPU in some technologies. The MMU uses three levels of page tables in main memory to store full translation information, and page table entries are cached in the MMU to provide quick translation. Among the features offered by the MMU are:

- 32-bit virtual address

- 36-bit physical address

- Fixed 4K-byte page size

- Support for sparse address spaces with 3-level map

- Support for large linear mappings (4K, 256K, 16M, 4G bytes)

- Support for multiple contexts

- Page-level protections

- Hardware miss processing

SPARC International, Inc.

The Reference MMU Architecture specifies both the behavior of the MMU hardware and the organization and contents of the tables in main memory required to support it.

**H.3. Software Architecture**    A SPARC Reference MMU provides three primary functions:

1) It performs address translation from the virtual addresses of each running process to physical addresses in main memory. This mapping is done in units of 4K-byte pages so that, for example, an 8-megabyte process does not need to be located in a contiguous section of main memory. Any virtual page can be mapped into any available physical page.

2) It provides memory protection, so a process cannot read or write the address space of another process. This is necessary for most operating systems to allow multiple processes to safely reside in physical memory at the same time.

3) It implements virtual memory. The page tables track which pages are in main memory; the MMU signals a page fault if a memory reference occurs to a page not currently resident.

Figure H-1    *Block Diagram of System with MMU*

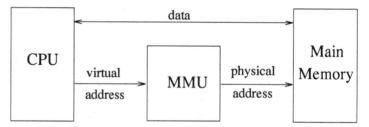

The MMU translates virtual addresses from the CPU into physical addresses, as shown above in Figure H-1. A 32-bit virtual address is translated to a 36-bit physical address, providing for a 64-gigabyte physical address space to support large physical memories and memory mapping of 32-bit busses (for example, VME or MultiBus II). A physical address is logically composed of an offset into a 4K-byte page and a Physical Page Number as follows:

Figure H-2    *Composition of a Physical Address*

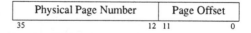

Pages are always aligned on 4K-byte boundaries; hence, the lower-order 12 bits of a physical address are always the same as the low-order 12 bits of the virtual address, and do not require translation. For every valid virtual page resident in memory there is a corresponding Page Table Entry that contains the physical page number for that virtual page. Translating a virtual address to a physical address replaces the virtual page number with the physical page number.

All the address translation information required by the SPARC Reference MMU resides in physically addressed data structures in main memory. The MMU fetches translations from these data structures, as required, by accessing main memory. Mapping a virtual address space is accomplished by up to three levels of page tables, in order to efficiently support sparse addressing. The first and second levels of these tables typically (though not necessarily) contain descriptors (called Page Table Descriptors) which point to the next-level tables. A third-level table entry is always a Page Table Entry (PTE) which points to a physical page. A first- or second-level entry may also be a PTE. A representation of the full three levels of mapping is shown below:

Figure H-3    *Reference MMU three-level mapping*

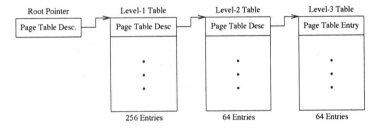

The Root Pointer Page Table Descriptor is unique to each context and is found in the Context Table. See Section H.3.1, "Contexts."

A virtual address is divided into fields as follows:

Figure H-4    *Composition of a Virtual Address*

| Index 1 | Index 2 | Index 3 | Page Offset |
|---|---|---|---|
| 31      24 | 23      18 | 17      12 | 11           0 |

Each index field provides an offset into the corresponding level of page table. A full set of tables is rarely required, as the virtual address space is usually sparsely populated. In some cases, the full three levels of page tables are not required to obtain the Page Table Entry. This happens when a 256K, 16M, or 4G-byte section of linear memory is mapped with a single Page Table Entry. See the description of Page Table Entries in Section H.3.3 for details.

CPU memory references would be too slow if each one required following the three levels of page tables in main memory in order to translate a virtual address to a physical address. Consequently, Page Table Entries are cached in the MMU's Page Descriptor Cache, or PDC (often called a translation lookaside buffer, or TLB). The cached entries are usually all that is needed to perform a translation, reducing significantly the need to fetch translation information from main memory.

Figure H-5    *Block Diagram of Reference MMU*

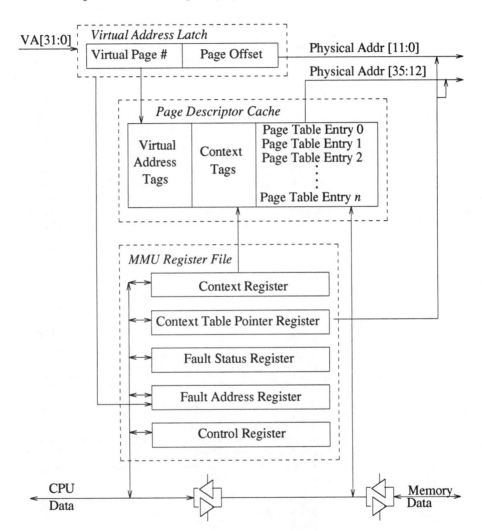

Figure H-5 is a simplified block diagram of the major components of a possible MMU implementation. The virtual address comes in to the MMU and is latched in an internal register. It is then compared with the virtual address tags stored in the PDC. A match against one of the tags indicates that the correct Page Table Entry is already stored in the MMU, and the physical address is generated directly.

If there is no match, miss processing occurs. During miss processing, the MMU automatically takes over the address and data busses from the CPU, and fetches Page Table Descriptors until it reaches the needed Page Table Entry, or incurs an error. That Page Table Entry is then cached in the MMU, translation occurs, and the original memory request continues from the latched address. Memory access permissions are checked for each translation; if the requested access violates those permissions, a trap is generated. If an error occurs, the appropriate status information is stored in the Fault Status Register and the Fault Address Regsiter, and a fault is generated to the processor.

**Contexts**

The SPARC Reference MMU can retain translations for several process address spaces at the same time. This speeds up context switching between processes. Each address space is identified by a "context" number, which may also be used by the system to maintain several processes in a virtual cache. The management of multiple contexts, including the assignment of contexts to processes, the reclamation of unused contexts and the reassignment of contexts, is the responsibility of the memory management software. Context numbers are used to index into the Context Table in main memory to find the root of the page table hierarchy (Root Pointer Page Table Descriptor) of Figure H-3 for a process, as follows:

Figure H-6    *Reference MMU Context Table*

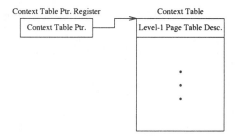

At any one time only one address space is active. The current active address space is identified by its context number. This provides the offset into the Context Table used to retrieve the pointer to the Level-1 Page Table for the address space.

The size of the context table is implementation-dependent. See the discussion of the Context Register in the following text.

**Page Table Descriptors**

A Page Table Descriptor (PTD) contains the physical address of a page table, and defines the format of entries in the Context Table, Level-1 Page Tables, and Level-2 Page Tables. A PTD is defined as follows:

Figure H-7    *Composition of a Page Table Descriptor*

| PTP | ET |
|-----|----|

31                                    2  1  0

Field definitions:

**PTP**   Page Table Pointer — Physical address of the base of a next-level page table. The PTP appears on bits 35 through 6 of the physical address bus during miss processing. The page table pointed to by a PTP must be aligned on a boundary equal to the size of the page table. The sizes of the three levels of page tables are summarized below:

| Level | Page Table Size (bytes) |
|-------|-------------------------|
| 1 | 1024 |
| 2 | 256 |
| 3 | 256 |

**ET**   Entry Type — This field differentiates a PTD from a PTE. For a PTD, it must contain the value 1.

The possible values in the ET field and their meanings are as follows:

| ET | Entry Type |
|----|------------|
| 0 | Invalid |
| 1 | Page Table Descriptor |
| 2 | Page Table Entry |
| 3 | Reserved |

"Invalid" means that the corresponding range of virtual addresses is not currently mapped to physical addresses.

**Page Table Entry**   A Page Table Entry (PTE) specifies both the physical address of a page and its access permissions. A PTE is defined as follows:

Figure H-8    *Composition of a Page Table Entry*

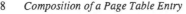

| PPN | C | M | R | ACC | ET |
|-----|---|---|---|-----|----|

31                        8  7  6  5  4      2  1  0

Field definitions:

**PPN**   Physical Page Number — The high-order 24 bits of the 36-bit physical address of the page. The PPN appears on bits 35 through 12 of the physical address bus when a translation completes.

SPARC International, Inc.

**C**      Cacheable — If this bit is one, the page is cacheable by an instruction and/or data cache.

> Programming Note
>> All Input/Output (I/O) locations mapped by the MMU should have the C bit in their corresponding PTEs set to 0.

**M**      Modified — This bit is set to one by the MMU when the page is accessed for writing (except when the access is via a Reference MMU Pass-Through ASI. See Appendix I, "Suggested ASI Assignments for SPARC Systems.")

**R**      Referenced — This bit is set to one by the MMU when the page is accessed (except when the access is via a Reference MMU Pass-Through ASI. See Appendix I, "Suggested ASI Assignments for SPARC Systems.")

**ACC**    Access Permissions — These bits indicate whether access to this page is allowed for the transaction being attempted. The Address Space Identifier used in an access determines whether it is a data access or an instruction access, and whether the access is being attempted by user or supervisor software. The ACC field has the following interpretation:

| | Accesses Allowed | |
| --- | --- | --- |
| ACC | User access (ASI = 0x8 or ASI = 0xA) | Supervisor access (ASI = 0x9 or ASI = 0xB) |
| 0 | Read Only | Read Only |
| 1 | Read/Write | Read/Write |
| 2 | Read/Execute | Read/Execute |
| 3 | Read/Write/Execute | Read/Write/Execute |
| 4 | Execute Only | Execute Only |
| 5 | Read Only | Read/Write |
| 6 | No Access | Read/Execute |
| 7 | No Access | Read/Write/Execute |

**ET**     Entry Type — This field differentiates a PTE from a PTD. See Section H.3.2, "Page Table Descriptors," above. For a PTE, it must contain the value 2.

If a PTE is found in the Context Table or a Level-1 or Level-2 Page Table, the address translation process stops and that PTE is used. Virtual addresses, from the first virtual address corresponding to the PTE through the last virtual address corresponding to the PTE, are mapped linearly to physical addresses as specified by the PPN. The physical address specified by the PPN must be aligned on a boundary equal to the size of the region mapped by the PTE. For example, given a virtual address as follows:

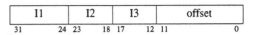

and given that the I2 entry of the appropriate Level-2 Page Table is a PTE (rather than a PTD) with a physical page number field containing the value PPN, the corresponding physical address is the bit-wise **or** of:

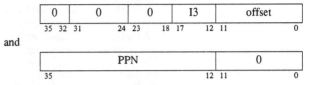

and

Note that the low-order 6 bits of PPN must all be zeros, to satisfy the alignment requirement on the region mapped by the PTE.

The sizes of the regions mapped by different levels in the page tables are summarized in the following table:

Table H-1    *Size of Region Mapped by MMU, by Page Table Level*

| Level | Mapping Size |
|-------|--------------|
| 3 | 4 Kilobytes |
| 2 | 256 Kilobytes |
| 1 | 16 Megabytes |
| Root | 4 Gigabytes |

Implementation Note    A Page Table Entry with an ACC field value of 6 or 7 represents a supervisor page. Translating supervisor addresses is more efficient if the Page Descriptor Cache ignores the context number used to fetch the PTE when matching cache tags for such references.

Implementation Note    The MMU should use one PDC entry for a Level-1 or Level-2 PTE to provide a large linear address mapping for busses, coprocessors, and kernels without requiring many translation cache entries.

**MMU Flush and Probe Model**    The privileged load and store alternate instructions are used to flush entries from the MMU's Page Descriptor Cache (PDC) and to probe for entries in the MMU. In an alternate address space used for flushing and probing, an address is composed as follows:

Figure H-9    *Flush/Probe Address, in Alternate Space*

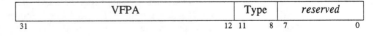

Field definitions:

**VFPA**    Virtual flush or probe address.

**Type**    The Type field indicates either the object(s) to be flushed from the PDC, or the object to be probed. Encoding of the Type field is described in the following table. (Note that Types 5-0xF are ignored. Probe Types 0-3, marked with a dagger in the table, are optional.)

| Type | Probe Object | Flush PDC Object(s) |
|------|------|------|
| 0  (page) | Level-3 entry † | Level-3 PTE |
| 1  (segment) | Level-2 entry † | Level-2 & 3 PTE/PTDs |
| 2  (region) | Level-1 entry † | Level-1, 2 & 3 PTE/PTDs |
| 3  (context) | Level-0 entry † | Level-0, 1, 2, & 3 PTE/PTDs |
| 4  (entire) | Level-$n$ entry | All PTEs/PTDs |
| 5 – 0xF | none (*reserved*) ‡ | none (*reserved*) ‡ |

† implementation is optional for this probe type.

‡ this probe/flush should be ignored in current MMU implementations.

*reserved*

This field is reserved and should be supplied as zero by software.

**Flush Operations**

A flush operation removes from the PDC a PTE or PTD that matches the criteria implied by the Type field [27]. A flush is accomplished by executing a store alternate instruction to the appropriate address (given by the VFPA field), with the appropriate type (given by the Type field), with the appropriate context (given by the Context register), and with the appropriate address space identifier (ASI), which is implementation-dependent. The data supplied by the store alternate instruction is ignored.

A flush operation removes the object(s) specified by the Type field from the PDC. The following paragraphs delineate the flush criteria. Since a flush operation in a particular implementation may remove more entries from the PDC than specified by the Type field, a "precise" flush is defined as one that removes the minimum number of entries implied by the Type field.

A page, segment, or region flush (Types 0-2) removes a PTE if the PTE's access code indicates a supervisor page (PTE.ACC = 6 or 7). A precise page, segment, or region flush removes a user page (PTE.ACC = 0 through 5) if the PTE's context tag equals the Context Register. Furthermore, a precise page, segment, or region flush removes a PTE if the PTE's address tag equals the corresponding bits of the VFPA field. Also, a precise page flush removes a PTE if the level tag indicates that the PTE was fetched from a level-3 page table; a precise segment flush removes a PTE with a level-2 or 3 tag; and a precise region flush removes a PTE with a level-1, 2, or 3 tag.

A precise context flush (Type 3) removes a PTE if its context tag equals the Context Register and the PTE's access code indicates a user page (PTE.ACC = 0-5). An imprecise context flush may also remove a supervisor entry. The PTE's address and level tags are ignored.

---

[27] It may remove more than one PTE or PTD, as long as it removes the indicated one.

An entire flush (Type 4) removes PTEs regardless of the values of their address tags, context tags, level tags, and ACC codes. In other words, the entire PDC is flushed.

A PTD is flushed if its context tag equals the Context Register and the level tag corresponds to the flush type. A precise segment flush removes a PTD with a Level-2 tag. A precise region flush removes a PTD with a Level-1 or 2 tag. A precise context flush removes a PTD with a Level-0, 1, or 2 tag. An entire flush removes all PTDs from the PDC.

The PTE flush match criteria are summarized in the following table.

Table H-2     *Page Table Entry Flush Match Criteria*

| VA[11:8] | Flush Type | Precise PTE Flush Match Criteria |
|---|---|---|
| 0 | Page | $((ACC \geq 6)$ **or** Contexts_equal) **and** VA[31:12]_equal |
| 1 | Segment | $((ACC \geq 6)$ **or** Contexts_equal) **and** VA[31:18]_equal |
| 2 | Region | $((ACC \geq 6)$ **or** Contexts_equal) **and** VA[31:24]_equal |
| 3 | Context | $(ACC \leq 5)$ **and** Contexts_equal |
| 4 | Entire | — |
| 5 – 0xF | *reserved* | — |

The PTD flush match criteria are summarized in the following table. Note that these criteria are the same as those for PTE's, except there are no access code checks.

Table H-3     *Page Table Descriptor Flush Match Criteria*

| VA[11:8] | Flush Type | Precise PTD Flush Match Criteria |
|---|---|---|
| 0 | Page | Contexts_equal **and** VA[31:12]_equal |
| 1 | Segment | Contexts_equal **and** VA[31:18]_equal |
| 2 | Region | Contexts_equal **and** VA[31:24]_equal |
| 3 | Context | Contexts_equal |
| 4 | Entire | — |
| 5 – 0xF | *reserved* | — |

## Probe Operations

A probe returns an entry from either the PDC or from a page table in main memory, or generates an error. A probe is accomplished by executing a privileged load alternate instruction with the appropriate address (given by the VFPA field), type (given by the Type field), context (given by the Context register), and address space identifier (ASI) — the last of which is implementation-dependent.

Two classes of errors may occur during a probe operation:

• An entry with ET ≠ 1(PTD) is encountered before the level being probed is reached.

• A memory error occurs. See Section H.5. No memory access exception is signaled to the processor, but the fault registers are updated.

SPARC International, Inc.

If either of the preceding errors occurs, the probe operation returns a zero value. If the probe operation succeeds, it returns the corresponding entry from a page table at the level implied by the Type field.

The value returned by a probe operation is specified in the following table. For a given probe type, the table is read left-to-right. "0" indicates that a zero is returned, "●" indicates that the page table entry itself is returned, and "⇒" indicates that the next-level page table entry is examined.

Table H-4    *Return Value from Reference MMU Probe*

| Probe Type | Upon a Memory Error | If No Memory Errors Occur | | | | | | | | | | | | | | | |
|---|---|---|---|---|---|---|---|---|---|---|---|---|---|---|---|---|---|
| | | Level-0 Entry Type | | | | Level-1 Entry Type | | | | Level-2 Entry Type | | | | Level-3 Entry Type | | | |
| | | 2 PTE | 3 res | 0 inv | 1 PTD | 2 PTE | 3 res | 0 inv | 1 PTD | 2 PTE | 3 res | 0 inv | 1 PTD | 2 PTE | 3 res | 0 inv | 1 PTD |
| 0 (page) | 0 | 0 | 0 | 0 | ⇒ | 0 | 0 | 0 | ⇒ | 0 | 0 | 0 | ⇒ | ● | 0 | ● | 0 |
| 1 (segment) | 0 | 0 | 0 | 0 | ⇒ | 0 | 0 | 0 | ⇒ | ● | 0 | ● | ● | — | | | |
| 2 (region) | 0 | 0 | 0 | 0 | ⇒ | ● | 0 | ● | ● | — | | | | — | | | |
| 3 (context) | 0 | ● | 0 | ● | ● | — | | | | — | | | | — | | | |
| 4 (entire) | 0 | ● | 0 | 0 | ⇒ | ● | 0 | 0 | ⇒ | ● | 0 | 0 | ⇒ | ● | 0 | 0 | 0 |
| 5–0XF | (undefined) | | | | | | | | | | | | | | | | |

Page, segment, and region probes should not update a PTE's Referenced bit, although an implementation can set the PTE.R bit for a Type 4 (entire) probe.

Probe types 5–0xF are reserved for future use. They return an undefined value. Also, the presence of page, segment, region, and context probes is implementation-dependent; that is, an implementation may not provide these probe operations. If not implemented, the value returned is undefined.

Implementation Note     It is recommended that probe operations check the PDC before walking the page tables in main memory. Also, it is recommended that a Type 4 (entire) probe bring the accessed PTE into the PDC. Updating the PDC is not recommended for probe Types 0 through 3.

## H.4. Hardware Architecture

### Accessing MMU Registers

This subsection describes the hardware architecture for the reference MMU.

Five internal registers are defined in the Reference MMU. The Control Register contains general MMU control and status flags. The current process identifier is stored in the Context Register, and a pointer to the base of the context table in memory is stored in the Context Table Pointer Register. If an MMU fault occurs, the address causing the fault is placed in the Fault Address Register and the cause of the fault can be determined from the Fault Status Register. All the internal MMU registers can be accessed directly by the CPU through peripheral accesses. The peripheral address map for the MMU is as follows. Note that the least significant 8 bits of the virtual address, VA[7:0], are unused; software should set these bits to zero.

Table H-5    *Reference MMU Internal Register Virtual Addresses*

| VA[31:0] | Register |
|----------|----------|
| 0X000000xx | Control Register |
| 0X000001xx | Context Table Pointer Register |
| 0X000002xx | Context Register |
| 0X000003xx | Fault Status Register |
| 0X000004xx | Fault Address Register |
| 0X000005xx to 0X00000Fxx | Reserved |
| 0X000010xx to 0XFFFFFFxx | Unassigned |

It is intended that the MMU be mapped via an Alternate Address Space of the CPU. See Appendix I, "Suggested ASI Assignments for SPARC Systems." However, the MMU definition only assumes the existence of a chip-select signal indicating that a peripheral access to the MMU is in progress.

**Control Register**

The MMU Control Register is defined as follows:

Figure H-10    *Reference MMU Control Register*

| IMPL | VER | SC | PSO | *reserved* | NF | E |
|------|-----|----|----|-----------|----|----|
| 31 | 28 27   24 | 23          8 | 7 | 6        2 | 1 | 0 |

**IMPL**    This field identifies the specific implementation of the MMU. It is hardwired into the implementation and is read-only.

**VER**    This field identifies a particular version of this MMU implementation, and is typically a mask number. It is hardwired into the implementation and is read-only.

**SC**    The System Control bits are implementation-defined. They may be reflected in a variable number of signals external to the MMU and need not all be implemented. If a bit is not implemented, it reads as zero and writes to it are ignored.

**PSO**    The PSO bit controls whether the memory model seen by the processor is Partial Store Ordering (PSO=1) or Total Store Ordering (PSO=0).

*reserved*
    This field is reserved and must be zero.

**NF**    NF is the "No Fault" bit. When NF = 0, any fault detected by the MMU causes FSR and FAR to be updated and causes a fault to be generated to the processor. When NF = 1, a fault on an access to ASI 9 is handled as when NF = 0; a fault on an access to any other ASI causes FSR and FAR to be updated but no fault is generated to the processor.

SPARC International, Inc.

If a fault on access to an ASI other than 9 occurs while NF = 1, subsequently resetting NF from 1 to 0 does not cause a fault to the processor (even though FSR.FT ≠ 0 at that time).

A change in value of the NF bit takes effect as soon as the bit is written; a subsequent access to ASI 9 will be evaluated according to the new value of the NF bit.

**E**    The Enable bit enables or disables the MMU and is defined as:

| E bit | MMU State |
|-------|-----------|
| 1     | Enabled   |
| 0     | Disabled  |

When the MMU is disabled:

- All virtual addresses pass through the MMU untranslated and appear as physical addresses

- The upper 4 of the 36 bits of the physical address are zero

- The MMU indicates that all virtual addresses are non-cacheable

- The E bit reads as 0

On MMU reset, the MMU is disabled and the PSO bit is set to 0.

**Context Table Pointer Register**    The Context Table Pointer Register is defined as follows:

Figure H-11    *Reference MMU Context Table Pointer Register*

| Context Table Pointer | reserved |
|-----------------------|----------|
| 31                    | 2  1  0  |

The Context Table Pointer points to the Context Table in physical memory. The table is indexed by the contents of the Context register (see below). The Context Table Pointer appears on bits 35 through 6 of the physical address bus during the first fetch occurring during miss processing. The context table pointed to by the Context Table Pointer must be aligned on a boundary equal to the size of the table.

For example, if number of bits used in the context register is 8, then the table must be aligned on a 1024-byte (that is, $2^{8+2}$-byte) boundary.

The *reserved* field is reserved and must be zero.

**Context Register**    The Context Register is defined as follows:

Figure H-12    *Reference MMU Context Register*

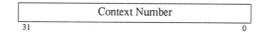

| Context Number |
|---|
| 31                                                                    0 |

The Context Register defines which of the possible process virtual address spaces is considered the current address space. Subsequent accesses to memory through the MMU are translated for the current address space, until the Context Register is changed. Each MMU implementation may specify a maximum context number, which must be one less than a power of 2.

**Diagnostic Registers**

A SPARC Reference MMU may provide access to diagnostic registers through an alternate address space See Appendix I, "Suggested ASI Assignments for SPARC Systems." If present, their operation is implementation-dependent; the following describes a suggested operation.

Accessing an MMU Diagnostic Register reads or writes a PDC entry or performs a diagnostic PDC hit/miss operation. Suggested decoding of the virtual address VA[31:0] presented to the MMU follows:

Table H-6    *Reference MMU Diagnostic Register Address Decoding*

| Bits | Decode as |
|---|---|
| VA[31:12] | Virtual address |
| VA[11: 4] | PDC entry |
| VA[ 3: 2] | Register *(See Table H-7)* |

Suggested further decoding of VA[3:2] follows:

Table H-7    *Reference MMU Diagnostic Register Selection*

| VA[3:2] | Register | |
|---|---|---|
| 0 | D[31:20]: context<br>D[19: 0]: address tag | |
| 1 | PTE | |
| 2 | control bits (e.g.: V, Level, LRU) | |
| 3 | Load: | Start compare in every PDC entry; if hit, return the PTE; if miss, return 0. |
| | Store: | For each PDC entry: if the contents of its LRU counter is less than the "stored" data value, increment its counter. Otherwise, leave the LRU counter unchanged. In any case, zero the LRU counter of the addressed PDC entry. |

## H.5. Fault Status Register

The Fault Status Register provides information on exceptions (faults) issued by the MMU. Since the CPU is pipelined, several faults may occur before a trap is taken. The faults are grouped into three classes: instruction access faults, data access faults and translation table access faults. If another instruction access fault occurs before the fault status of a previous instruction access fault has been read by the CPU, the MMU writes the status of the latest fault into the Fault Status Register, writes the faulting address into the Fault Address Register, and sets the OW bit (see below) to indicate that the previous fault status has been lost.

The MMU and CPU must ensure that if multiple data access faults can occur, only the status of the one taken by the CPU is latched into the Fault Status Register. If data fault status overwrites previous instruction fault status, the overwrite bit (OW) is cleared, since the fault status is represented correctly. An instruction access fault may not overwrite a data access fault.

A translation table access fault occurs if an MMU page table access causes an external system error. If a translation table access fault overwrites a previous instruction or data access fault, the OW bit is cleared. An instruction or data access fault may not overwrite a translation table access fault.

The MMU Fault Status Register is defined as follows:

Figure H-13    *Reference MMU Fault Status Register*

| reserved | EBE | L | AT | FT | FAV | OW |
|----------|-----|---|----|----|-----|-----|
| 31    18 | 17    10 | 9    8 | 7    5 | 4    2 | 1 | 0 |

**reserved**
This field is reserved and must be zero.

**EBE**    Bits in the External Bus Error field are set when a system error occurs during a memory access. The meanings of the individual bits are implementation-dependent. Examples of system errors are: timeout, uncorrectable error, and parity error. The MMU need not implement all the bits in **EBE**. Unimplemented bits read as zeros.

**L**    The Level field is set to the page table level of the entry which caused the fault. If an external bus error is encountered while fetching a PTE or PTD, the Level field records the page table level of the page table containing the entry. The Level field is defined as follows:

| L | Level |
|---|-------|
| 0 | Entry in Context Table |
| 1 | Entry in Level-1 Page Table |
| 2 | Entry in Level-2 Page Table |
| 3 | Entry in Level-3 Page Table |

**AT**    The Access Type field defines the type of access which caused the fault. (Loads and stores to user/supervisor instruction space can be caused by load/store alternate instructions with ASI = 8 or 9). The AT field is

SPARC International, Inc.

defined as follows:

| AT | Access Type |
|----|-------------|
| 0 | Load from User Data Space |
| 1 | Load from Supervisor Data Space |
| 2 | Load/Execute from User Instruction Space |
| 3 | Load/Execute from Supervisor Instruction Space |
| 4 | Store to User Data Space |
| 5 | Store to Supervisor Data Space |
| 6 | Store to User Instruction Space |
| 7 | Store to Supervisor Instruction Space |

**FT**  The Fault Type field defines the type of the current fault.  It is defined as follows:

| FT | Fault Type |
|----|------------|
| 0 | None |
| 1 | Invalid address error |
| 2 | Protection error |
| 3 | Privilege violation error |
| 4 | Translation error |
| 5 | Access bus error |
| 6 | Internal error |
| 7 | Reserved |

Invalid address, protection, and privilege violation errors depend on the Access Type field of the Fault Status Register and the ACC field of the corresponding PTE.  The errors are set as follows:

| AT | PTE.V = 0 | PTE.V = 1 PTE.ACC = 0 | 1 | 2 | 3 | 4 | 5 | 6 | 7 |
|----|-----------|-----|---|---|---|---|---|---|---|
| 0 | 1 | – | – | – | – | 2 | – | 3 | 3 |
| 1 | 1 | – | – | – | – | 2 | – | – | – |
| 2 | 1 | 2 | 2 | – | – | – | 2 | 3 | 3 |
| 3 | 1 | 2 | 2 | – | – | – | 2 | – | – |
| 4 | 1 | 2 | – | 2 | – | 2 | 2 | 3 | 3 |
| 5 | 1 | 2 | – | 2 | – | 2 | – | 2 | – |
| 6 | 1 | 2 | 2 | 2 | – | 2 | 2 | 3 | 3 |
| 7 | 1 | 2 | 2 | 2 | – | 2 | 2 | 2 | – |

A translation error is indicated if an external bus error occurs while the MMU is fetching an entry from a page table, a PTD is found in a level-3 page table, or a PTE has ET=3.  The **L** field records the page table level at which the error occurred, and the **EBE** field records the type of bus error (if any).  Access bus error is set when an external bus error occurs during memory access that is not a page table walk access. The **EBE** field records the type of bus error.

Internal error indications are set when the MMU detects an internal inconsistency. This should be considered a fatal error by software, requiring system reset.

**FAV**   The Fault Address Valid bit is set to one if the contents of the Fault Address Register are valid. The Fault Address Register need not be valid for instruction faults. The Fault Address Register must be valid for data faults and translation errors.

**OW**   The Overwrite bit is set to one if the Fault Status Register has been written more than once by faults of the same class since the last time it was read. If an instruction access fault occurs and the **OW** bit is set, system software must determine the cause by probing the MMU and/or memory.

If a single access causes multiple errors, the faults are recognized in the following order (from highest to lowest):

Table H-8    *Reference MMU Fault Priorities*

| Priority | Error |
|----------|-------|
| 1 | Internal error |
| 2 | Translation error |
| 3 | Invalid address error |
| 4 | Privilege violation error |
| 5 | Protection error |
| 6 | Access bus error |

The highest priority fault is recorded in the Fault Type field. Reading the Fault Status Register clears it. Writes to the Fault Status Register are ignored.

## H.6. Fault Address Register

The Fault Address Register is defined as follows:

Figure H-14    *Reference MMU Fault Address Register*

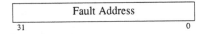

| Fault Address |
|---|
31                                           0

The Fault Address Register contains the virtual memory address of the fault recorded in the Fault Status Register. Fault addresses are overwritten according to the same priority used for the Fault Status Register. Writes to the Fault Address Register are ignored.

Implementation Note    It is not required that the MMU latch the full address. It need only latch the Virtual Page Number for which the fault occurred. In this case, the low-order address bits are set to zero.

In the case of a Translation Error, the contents of the Fault Address Register will be the original virtual memory address for which translation was requested.

Programming Note    After a Translation Error, the table can be walked by software to find the entry which triggered the fault.

## H.7. Operation

This subsection describes the operation of the reference MMU.

### Reset

Upon detection of a reset, the MMU sets the Enable and PSO bits in the Control Register to zero (that is, the MMU is disabled and Total Store Ordering is in effect). All other MMU state is unaffected.

### Miss Processing

If the MMU does not have the required information to perform a requested translation in the PDC, it initiates miss processing to retrieve the required Page Table Entry from the page tables. The retrieved Page Table Entry is then cached in the MMU, and the MMU completes the permission checking and address translation.

### Referenced and Modified Bit Updates

A successful translation, of any kind, results in the Referenced bit in the Page Table Entry being examined. If the Referenced bit (R) is zero, the MMU sets the Referenced bit of both the cached Page Table Entry and the Page Table Entry in memory to one.

A successful translation of a write operation results in the Modified bit in the Page Table Entry being examined. If the Modified bit (M) is zero, the MMU sets the Modified bit of both the cached Page Table Entry and the Page Table Entry in memory to one.

*Implementation Note*    The MMU must provide signals that make it possible for the Referenced and Modified bits in memory to be atomically updated with respect to other system accesses to the page tables. In addition, updating these bits must be synchronous with the access that caused the update.

Specifically, the Modified bit must be set before a store to a location in a page becomes visible. This applies equally to store, LDSTUB, LDSTUBA, SWAP, and SWAPA instructions.

SPARC International, Inc.

# I

I

# Suggested ASI Assignments for SPARC Systems

## I.1. Introduction

The SPARC architecture defines 4 of the 256 address space identifiers: user instruction, user data, supervisor instruction, and supervisor data. The remaining alternate spaces — only accessible via the privileged load/store alternate space instructions — are not explicitly assigned by the SPARC architecture.

This appendix suggests an Address Space Identifier (ASI) assignment for SPARC-based systems. Its goal is to discourage designers of SPARC-based systems from partitioning the ASI space into disjointed or overlapping regions that would lead to incompatible hardware or an unnecessarily large number of operating system/hardware interfaces. For example, a particular vendor could map its devices into the upper 4 ASI bits, restricting other companies to the lower 4 bits.

Ideally, all systems with similar architectures should conform to this assignment. As that may not be practical, these assignments are a suggestion only. However, the underlying philosophy is that ASIs should not be thoughtlessly consumed. In particular, half of the ASI space is reserved for future use.

ASIs are assigned herein for MMU operations, cache data/tag read/write operations and, in the case of a write-back cache, flush operations. Two ASIs have been selected for systems with memory block-copy and fill operations. The assignments also include a short description of how each space can be optionally subdivided.

It is a goal for the Reference MMU assignments that operating system routines that manipulate the MMU should be able to run properly, without change, on all systems based upon the Reference MMU.

Since SPARC only handles one fault or trap at a time, systems based on separate instruction and data caches with separate MMU chips should still present a single MMU interface to the operating system. Thus, separate alternate spaces have not been defined for separate instruction and data MMUs (except for diagnostic functions).

When new systems are designed with different functions than suggested below, it is not mandatory for the designer to assign new spaces for the new functions, particularly as an operating system cannot reasonably support all possible SPARC systems. Alternate spaces can be recycled, and assignments within a particular space can change. For future portability, all systems should decode all 8 ASI bits.

SPARC International, Inc.

**I.2. ASI Summary**

The following table summarizes suggested ASI assignments, and the text that follows discusses each assignment separately. Note that in the case of a separate or split instruction and data cache system, the following terms apply:

| Term | Description |
|---|---|
| Data PDC (TLB) | Data-stream MMU functions |
| Instruction PDC (TLB) | Instruction-stream MMU functions |
| Combined MMU | MMU that services both the instruction and data streams |
| Reserved | Reserved for future use |
| Unassigned | ASI that system designers are free to use |

Table I-1    *Suggested ASI Assignments*

| ASI | Function |
|---|---|
| 0 | *reserved* |
| 1 | unassigned |
| 2 | unassigned (system registers) |
| 3 | MMU flush/probe ‡ |
| 4 | MMU register ‡ |
| 5 | MMU diagnostic for instruction PDC (TLB) ‡ |
| 6 | MMU diagnostic for data or combined-I&D PDC ‡ |
| 7 | MMU diagnostic for I/O PDC (TLB) ‡ |
| 8 | user instruction space † ‡ |
| 9 | supervisor instruction space † ‡ |
| A | user data space † ‡ |
| B | supervisor data space † ‡ |
| C | cache tag for instruction cache |
| D | cache data for instruction cache |
| E | cache tag for data cache or combined-I&D cache |
| F | cache data for data cache or combined-I&D cache |
| 10 | flush combined-I&D cache line (page) |
| 11 | flush combined-I&D cache line (segment) |
| 12 | flush combined-I&D cache line (region) |
| 13 | flush combined-I&D cache line (context) |
| 14 | flush combined-I&D cache line (user) |
| 15 | *reserved* |
| 16 | *reserved* |
| 17 | block-copy |
| 18 | flush instruction cache line (page) |
| 19 | flush instruction cache line (segment) |
| 1A | flush instruction cache line (region) |
| 1B | flush instruction cache line (context) |
| 1C | flush instruction cache line (user) |
| 1D | *reserved* |
| 1E | *reserved* |
| 1F | block-fill |
| 20 – 2F | MMU physical address pass–through ‡ |
| 30 – 7F | unassigned |
| 80 – FF | *reserved* |

† Address Space Identifier required by SPARC architecture
‡ Address Space Identifier recognized by the MMU.

SPARC International, Inc.

## I.3. Detailed Descriptions

The following text presents a short summary of the function provided by each suggested alternate space assignment.

**ASI = 0 (reserved)**

### Reserved

This space is reserved and should not be used by the system designer.

**ASI = 1 (Unassigned)**

### Unassigned

This space is unassigned and can be used by the system designer.

**ASI = 2 (Unassigned sys regs)**

### Unassigned (system registers)

This space can be used to read or write a system status register. The assignments in this space are specific to a particular implementation.

**ASI = 3 (MMU flush/probe)**

### MMU flush/probe

This space is used for a flush or probe operation. Virtual Address bits VA[11:8] are decoded to determine the type of flush or probe. A flush is caused by a single STA instruction and a probe by a single LDA instruction. A flush results in the entire Page Descriptor Cache (PDC) being purged of the specified object.

In a system with separate instruction and data cache PDCs (TLBs), the applicable PDC should respond to a probe operation. Both PDCs should perform a flush operation.

An object is flushed if it meets certain comparison criteria. See Appendix H, "SPARC Reference MMU Architecture," for more detailed information about MMU flush and probe operations.

**ASI = 4 (MMU registers)**

### MMU registers

This space is used to read or write an internal MMU register, which is selected by decoding VA[11:8]. In a system with separate instruction and data cache PDC's, the applicable PDC should respond to a register read operation. Both PDCs should perform a register write operation. For example, the Fault Status Registers should be written to the same value in both PDCs.

Byte, halfword, and doubleword accesses can return undefined data (and should be flagged as an error). VA[7:0] are ignored.

See Appendix H, "SPARC Reference MMU Architecture," for further information.

**ASI = 5 (MMU I diagnostic)**

**MMU diagnostic for Instruction PDC**

This space is used to read or write a PDC entry or perform a diagnostic PDC hit/miss operation in an I-cache's PDC in a split-cache system. This alternate space is **not** to be used by normal supervisor software, only by diagnostic code. See Appendix H, "SPARC Reference MMU Architecture," for a suggested decoding of the virtual address presented to the MMU.

**ASI = 6 (MMU D/I&D diag)**

**MMU diagnostic for Data PDC or Combined MMU**

This space is used to read or write a PDC entry or perform a diagnostic PDC hit/miss operation in a D-cache's PDC in a split-cache system, or in the single MMU in a combined cache system. This alternate space is **not** to be used by normal supervisor software, only diagnostic code. See Appendix H, "SPARC Reference MMU Architecture," for a suggested decoding of the virtual address presented to the MMU.

**ASI = 7 (MMU I/O diagnostic)**

**MMU diagnostic for I/O PDC**

This space is used to read or write a PDC entry or perform a diagnostic PDC hit/miss operation in a DMA or I/O PDC. This alternate space is **not** be used by normal supervisor software, only by diagnostic code.

**ASI = 8 (User I)**

**User instruction**

This space is defined and reserved by the SPARC architecture as the address space in which user instructions are accessed.

**ASI = 9 (Supervisor I)**

**Supervisor instruction**

This space is defined and reserved by the SPARC architecture as the address space in which supervisor instructions are accessed.

**ASI = 0xA (User D)**

**User data**

This space is defined and reserved by the SPARC architecture as the address space in which user data is accessed.

**ASI = 0xB (Supervisor D)**

**Supervisor data**

This space is defined and reserved by the SPARC architecture as the address space in which supervisor data is accessed.

**ASI = 0xC (I-Cache tag)**

**Cache tag for instruction cache**

This space is used to read or write a tag entry from an I-cache in a split cache system.

Implementation Note
    If the width of the attached data bus does not equal the width of the tag entry, VA[3:2] can be used to select a tag subfield. Also, VA[31] can be used to select a dual physical address tag.

SPARC International, Inc.

**ASI = 0xD (I-Cache data)**    **Cache data for instruction cache**

This space is used to read or write an I-cache entry in a split-cache system.

**ASI = 0xE (D/I&D-Cache tag)**    **Cache tag for data cache or combined I&D cache**

This space is used for a cache tag, data PDC or combined MMU. It is used to read or write a tag entry from a D-cache in a split-cache system, or from a combined cache.

Implementation Note

If the width of the attached data bus does not equal the width of the tag entry, VA[3:2] can be used to select a tag subfield. Also, VA[31] can be used to select a dual physical address tag.

**ASI = 0xF (D/I&D-Cache data)**    **Cache data for data cache or combined–I&D cache**

This space is for cache data in a system data PDC or with a combined MMU. It can be used to read or write a data cache entry from a D-cache in a split-cache system, or from a combined cache.

**ASI = 0x10-0x14 (Flush I&D)**    **Flush I&D cache line; page, segment, region, context and user**

These spaces are used to flush single cache lines. A cache line flush is caused by a single STA instruction to one of these spaces, and results in a single line (possibly across multiple sets) being removed from both the instruction and data caches, or from the combined cache.

Spaces 0x10-0x14 apply to **both** the I-cache **and** the D-cache in a split-cache system, or to the combined I&D cache in a combined-cache system.

A cache line is flushed if it meets the minimum criteria given in the following table, where "S" is the supervisor tag bit, "U" = "not S", "CTX" is a comparison based on the context register, and VA[31:xx] is a comparison based on the virtual address tag.

Table I-2    *Flush Compare Criteria for ASI's 0x10 - 0x14 and 0x18 - 0x1C*

| ASI[2:0] | Flush Type | Compare Criterion |
|----------|------------|-------------------|
| 0 | Page | (S or CTX) and VA[31:12] |
| 1 | Segment | (S or CTX) and VA[31:18] |
| 2 | Region | (S or CTX) and VA[31:24] |
| 3 | Context | U and CTX |
| 4 | User | U |
| 5,6 | *reserved* | — |

**ASI = 0x17 (Block copy)**    **Block copy**

This space is used for block-copy read and block-copy write operations. A block-copy operation is a block-copy read, followed by a block-copy write that moves a source line to a destination line. The choice of instructions (e.g. LDA, STA, SWAPA) used to accomplish these operations is implementation-dependent.

SPARC International, Inc.

The source line for a block-copy read can be either main memory, or a line from a cache (possibly from a separate D-cache in a split-cache system). The destination line of a block-copy write is always main memory, although a destination line in a data cache might need to be invalidated also.

**ASI = 0x18 - 0x1C (Flush I)**

**Flush I-cache line; page, segment, region, context and user**

These spaces are used for a cache line flush which is caused by a single STA instruction. A cache line flush results in a single line, possibly across multiple sets, being removed from the Instruction cache in a split-cache system.

In a split-cache system, spaces 0x18 - 0x1C apply only to an instruction cache. The type of flush is specified the same as for ASIs 0x10 - 0x14.

Implementation Note
A split cache can be implemented on top of a combined I&D bus. For example, I/O can be routed through a data cache that is separate from an instruction cache.

**ASI = 0x1F (Block fill)**

**Block fill**

This space is for a block-fill operation, which is caused by a single instruction (typically STA or STDA). A "block-fill" causes a line to be written to a given value in main memory, and either written to that value or invalidated in a data cache.

**ASI = 0x20 - 0x2F (Pass-through)**

**MMU physical address pass-through**

These 16 spaces can be used to access an arbitrary physical address. They are particularly useful before the MMU or main memory have been initialized.

The low-order 32 physical address bits are set to the 32 virtual address bits, and the upper 4 physical bits are set to the low-order 4 bits of the ASI value: $PA[35:32] \leftarrow ASI[3:0]$, $PA[31:0] \leftarrow VA[31:0]$.

Note that when one of these ASI's are used, the MMU's Referenced and Modified bits in the Page Table Entry for the accessed location are not updated.

**ASI = 0x30–0x7F (Unassigned)**

**Unassigned**

These spaces are unassigned, and may be used by system designers. Designers are encouraged to coordinate their use of these spaces through SPARC International.

Implementation Note
Several existing implementations use ASI = 0x36 for a flash I-cache flush and ASI = 0x37 for a flash D-cache flush. At least one implementation uses ASI = 0x31 for flushing internal instruction buffers.

**ASI = 0x80–0xFF (Reserved)**

**Reserved**

These spaces are reserved, and should not be used by system designers.

SPARC International, Inc.

# Programming with the Memory Model

This appendix describes how to program with the SPARC Memory Model. An intuitive description of the model is provided in Chapter 6, "Memory Model." A complete formal specification appears in Appendix K, "Formal Specification of the Memory Model." In this section, general guidelines are given first, followed by specific examples showing how low-level synchronization can be implemented in TSO and PSO.

Note that all "Code for PSO" examples in this appendix will execute correctly at all times, on all SPARC implementations. "Code for TSO" examples will execute correctly only on machines that do not implement PSO, or on machines that implement PSO but have PSO execution mode disabled.

## J.1. Memory Operations

Programmers access memory via five operations: load, store, LDSTUB, SWAP, and STBAR. Load copies a value from a location into a register. Store copies a value from a register into a memory location. LDSTUB and SWAP are atomic load-store instructions that store a value into a memory location and return the old value in a register. STBAR ensures that all previous stores have been completed before subsequent stores and atomic load-stores are executed by memory.

FLUSH is not a memory operation, but it is relevant here in the context of synchronizing stores to instructions. When a processor wants to modify an instruction at address $A$, it does a store $A$ followed by a FLUSH $A$. The FLUSH ensures that the change made by the store will become visible to the instruction units of all processors in the system some time later.

## J.2. Processors and Processes

In the SPARC Memory Model, the term "processor" may be replaced systematically by the term "process" or "thread," as long as the code for switching processes or threads is written properly. The correct process switch sequence is given in Section J.6. If an operating system implements this process switch sequence, application programmers may ignore the difference between a process/thread and a processor entirely.

## J.3. Portability and Recommended Programming Style

Whether a program is portable across various memory models depends on how it synchronizes access to shared read-write data. Two aspects of a program's style are relevant to portability: **Good semantics** refers to whether the synchronization primitives chosen and the way in which they are used is such that changing the memory model does not involve making any changes to the code that uses the primitives. **Good structure** refers to whether the code for synchronization is encapsulated through the use of primitives such that when the memory model is changed, required changes to the code are confined to the primitives. Good semantics are a prerequisite for portability, while good structure makes porting even easier.

Programs that use single-writer-multiple-readers locks to protect all access to shared read/write data are portable across PSO, TSO, and Strong Consistency. The code that implements the lock primitives themselves is portable across all three models only if it is written to run correctly on PSO. If the lock primitives are collected into a library, then at worst only the library routines need to be changed. Note that mutual exclusion (mutex) locks are a degenerate type of single-writer-multiple-readers lock.

Programs that use write locks to protect write accesses but read without locking are portable across PSO, TSO, and Strong Consistency only if writes to shared data are separated by STBAR instructions. If the STBAR instructions are omitted, then the code is portable only across TSO and Strong Consistency, but it will not in general work with PSO. The code that implements the lock primitives is portable across all three models only if it is written to run correctly on PSO. If the lock routines are collected into a library, the only possible changes that are not confined to the library routines are the STBAR instructions needed to separate writes in user code.

Programs that do synchronization without using single-writer-multiple-readers locks, write locks or their equivalent are, in general, not portable across PSO, TSO, and Strong Consistency. More precisely, programs written for PSO work on TSO or Strong Consistency; programs written for TSO work on Strong Consistency, but may not work on PSO; programs written for Strong Consistency may not work either on TSO or PSO. Thus programs written for PSO are the most portable, those written for TSO are less so, and those written for Strong Consistency are the least portable. This general relationship between the three models is shown graphically in Figure J-1. Programs written for PSO are represented by the innermost area, those written for TSO by the next larger enclosing area, and those written for Strong Consistency by the outermost area.

Figure J-1    *Portability relations between PSO, TSO, and Strong Consistency*

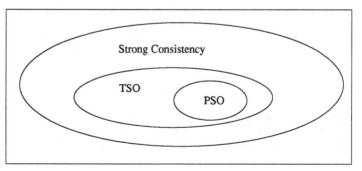

The style recommendations may be summarized as follows: Programs should use single-writer-multiple-readers locks, or their equivalent, when possible. If write locks must be used, writes should be separated by STBAR instructions. Other lower-level forms of synchronization (such as Dekker's algorithm for locking) should be avoided when possible. When use of such low-level primitives is unavoidable, it is recommended that the code be written to work on the PSO model to ensure portability. Additionally, lock primitives should be collected together into a library and be written for PSO to ensure portability.

**J.4. Spin Locks**

A spin lock is a lock for which the "lock held" condition is handled by busy waiting. Figure J-2 shows how spin locks can be implemented using LDSTUB. A nonzero value for the lock represents the locked condition, while a value of zero means that the lock is free. Note that the code busy waits by doing loads to avoid generating expensive stores to a potentially shared location. The STBAR in UnLock ensures that pending user stores are completed before the store that frees the lock.

Figure J-2    *Lock and Unlock using LDSTUB*

| Code for PSO | | | Code for TSO | | |
|---|---|---|---|---|---|
| **LockWithLDSTUB**(*lock*) | | | **LockWithLDSTUB**(*lock*) | | |
| retry: | ldstub | [*lock*],%l0 | retry: | ldstub | [*lock*],%l0 |
| | tst | %l0 | | tst | %l0 |
| | be | out | | be | out |
| | nop | | | nop | |
| loop: | ldub | [*lock*],%l0 | loop: | ldub | [*lock*],%l0 |
| | tst | %l0 | | tst | %l0 |
| | bne | loop | | bne | loop |
| | nop | | | nop | |
| | ba,a | retry | | ba,a | retry |
| out: | nop | | out: | nop | |
| **UnLockWithLDSTUB**(*lock*) | | | **UnLockWithLDSTUB**(*lock*) | | |
| | stbar | | | | |
| | stub | %g0,[*lock*] | | stub | %g0,[*lock*] |

Figure J-3 shows how spin locks can be implemented using SWAP. Again, a nonzero value for the lock represents the locked condition, while a value of zero means the lock is free (the advantage of this encoding is that the lock owner's name can be kept in the lock). Also, note that the code busy waits by doing loads, not SWAPs.

SPARC International, Inc.

Figure J-3    *Lock and Unlock using SWAP*

| Code for PSO | Code for TSO |
|---|---|
| **LockWithSWAP**(*lock*, *old*)<br><pre>retry:   mov     -1,%l0<br>         swap    [lock],%l0<br>         tst     %l0<br>         be      out<br>         nop<br>loop:    ld      [lock],%l0<br>         tst     %l0<br>         bne     loop<br>         nop<br>         ba,a    retry<br>out:     st      %l0,[old]</pre> | **LockWithSWAP**(*lock*, *old*)<br><pre>retry:   mov     -1,%l0<br>         swap    [lock],%l0<br>         tst     %l0<br>         be      out<br>         nop<br>loop:    ld      [lock],%l0<br>         tst     %l0<br>         bne     loop<br>         nop<br>         ba,a    retry<br>out:     st      %l0,[old]</pre> |
| **UnLockWithSWAP**(*lock*, *new*)<br><pre>         ld      [new],%l0<br>         stbar<br>         st      %l0,[lock]</pre> | **UnLockWithSWAP**(*lock*, *new*)<br><pre>         ld      [new],%l0<br>         st      %l0,[lock]</pre> |

## J.5. Producer-Consumer Relationship

In a producer-consumer relationship, a producer process generates data and puts it into a buffer, while a consumer process takes data from the buffer and uses it. If the buffer is full, the producer process stalls when trying to put data into the buffer. If the buffer is empty, the consumer process stalls when trying to remove data.

Figures J-4 and J-5 show the buffer data structure and the producer and consumer code for PSO and TSO. The code assumes the existence of two procedures Incr-Head and IncrTail which increment the head and tail pointers of the buffer in a wraparound manner and return the incremented value. **Note that these routines do not modify the pointers in the buffer.**

Figure J-4    *Data Structure for Producer and Consumer code*

Buffer data structure:

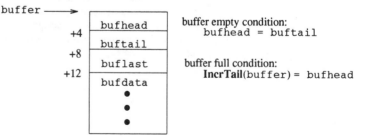

buffer empty condition:
```
bufhead = buftail
```

buffer full condition:
**IncrTail**(`buffer`) = `bufhead`

SPARC International, Inc.

Figure J-5    *Producer and Consumer code*

Register usage:

|  |  |
|---|---|
| %i0 and %i1: | parameters |
| %l0 and %l1: | local values |
| %o0: | result |

| Code for PSO | Code for TSO |
|---|---|
| **Produce**(*buffer*, *data*) | **Produce**(*buffer*, *data*) |
|     mov    %i0,%o0 |     mov    %i0,%o0 |
|     call   incrTail |     call   IncrTail |
| full: ld    [%i0],%l0 | full: ld    [%i0],%l0 |
|     cmp    %l0,%o0 |     cmp    %l0,%o0 |
|     be     full |     be     full |
|     ld    [%i0+4],%l0 |     ld    [%i0+4],%l0 |
|     st     %i1,[%l0] |     st     %i1,[%l0] |
|     stbar |     st     %o0,[%i0+4] |
|     st     %o0,[%i0+4] |  |
| **Consume**(*buffer*) | **Consume**(*buffer*) |
|     ld    [%i0],%l0 |     ld    [%i0],%l0 |
| empty: ld    [%i0+4],%l1 | empty: ld    [%i0+4],%l1 |
|     cmp    %l0,%l1 |     cmp    %l0,%l1 |
|     be     empty |     be     empty |
|     mov    %i0,%o0 |     mov    %i0,%o0 |
|     call   IncrHead |     call   IncrHead |
|     ld    [%i0],%l0 |     ld    [%i0],%l0 |
|     st     %o0,[%i0] |     st     %o0,[%i0] |
|     mov    %l0,%i0 |     mov    %l0,%i0 |

## J.6. Process Switch Sequence

This section provides code that must be used during process or thread switching to ensure that the memory model as seen by a process or thread is the same as that seen by a processor. The **HeadSequence** must be inserted at the beginning of a process or thread when it starts execution on a processor. The **TailSequence** must be inserted at the end of a process or thread when it relinquishes a processor.

Figure J-6 shows the head and tail sequences. The two sequences refer to a per-process variable *tailDone*. The value 0 for *tailDone* means that the process is running, while the value -1 (all ones) means that the process has completed its tail sequence and may be migrated to another processor if the process is runnable. The SWAP in the HeadSequence is required to be able to provide a switching sequence that ensures that the state observed by a process at its source processor will also be seen by the process at its destination processor. Note that since FLUSHes and stores are totally ordered, the head sequence does not need to do anything special to ensure that FLUSHes performed prior to the switch are visible at the new processor. Also note that the switch sequence works for FLUSHes when the new processor is the same as the old processor only because there are more than 5 instructions in the head sequence.

Figure J-6    *Process or Thread Switch Sequence*

| Code for PSO | Code for TSO |
|---|---|
| **HeadSequence**(*tailDone*) | **HeadSequence**(*tailDone*) |
| ```nrdy: ld      [tailDone],%l0``` | ```nrdy: ld      [tailDone],%l0``` |
| ```      cmp     %l0,-1``` | ```      cmp     %l0,-1``` |
| ```      bne     nrdy``` | ```      bne     nrdy``` |
| ```      mov     0,%l0``` | ```      mov     0,%l0``` |
| ```      swap    [tailDone],%l0``` | ```      swap    [tailDone],%l0``` |
| ```      cmp     %l0,-1``` | ```      cmp     %l0,-1``` |
| ```      bne,a   nrdy``` | ```      bne,a   nrdy``` |
| | |
| **TailSequence**(*tailDone*) | **TailSequence**(*tailDone*) |
| ```      mov     -1,%l0``` | ```      mov     -1,%l0``` |
| ```      stbar``` | ```      st      %l0,[tailDone]``` |
| ```      st      %l0,[tailDone]``` | |

## J.7. Dekker's Algorithm

Dekker's algorithm is the classical sequence for synchronization entry into a critical section using just loads and stores. The reason for showing this example here is to illustrate how one may ensure that a store followed by a load in issuing order will be executed by the memory system in that order. Dekker's algorithm is **not** a recommended synchronization primitive, because it requires a Strongly Consistent memory model to work. Dekker's algorithm (and similar synchronization sequences) can be coded on PSO and TSO simply by replacing all stores by SWAPs. The value returned by each SWAP is ignored.

Figure J-7 shows the entry and exit sequences for Dekker's algorithm. The locations *A* and *B* are used for synchronization; *A* = 0 means that process P1 is outside its critical section, while any other value means that P1 is inside it; similarly, *B* = 0 means that P2 is outside its critical section, and any other value means that P2 is inside it.

Figure J-7    *Dekker's Algorithm*

| Code for PSO | Code for TSO |
|---|---|
| **P1Entry( )** | **P1Entry( )** |
|       mov   -1,%l0 |       mov   -1,%l0 |
| busy: swap  [A],%l0 | busy: swap  [A],%l0 |
|       ld    [B],%l0 |       ld    [B],%l0 |
|       cmp   %l0,0 |       cmp   %l0,0 |
|       bne,a busy |       bne,a busy |
|       st    %g0,[A] |       st    %g0,[A] |
| | |
| **P1Exit( )** | **P1Exit( )** |
|       stbar |       st    %g0,[A] |
|       st    %g0,[A] | |
| **P2Entry( )** | **P2Entry( )** |
|       mov   -1,%l0 |       mov   -1,%l0 |
| busy: swap  [B],%l0 | busy: swap  [B],%l0 |
|       ld    [A],%l0 |       ld    [A],%l0 |
|       cmp   %l0,0 |       cmp   %l0,0 |
|       bne,a busy |       bne,a busy |
|       st    %g0,[B] |       st    %g0,[B] |
| | |
| **P2Exit( )** | **P2Exit( )** |
|       stbar |       st    %g0,[B] |
|       st    %g0,[B] | |

## J.8. Code Patching

The code patching example illustrates how to modify code that is potentially being executed at the time of modification. Two common uses of code patching are in debuggers and dynamic linking.

Code patching involves a modifying process *Pm*, and one or more target processes *Pt*. For simplicity, assume that the sequence to be modified is four instructions long: the old sequence is (*Old*1, *Old*2, *Old*3, *Old*4), and the new sequence is (*New*1, *New*2, *New*3, *New*4). There are two examples: **non-cooperative** modification, in which the changes are made without cooperation from *Pt*; and **cooperative** modification, in which the changes require explicit cooperation from *Pt*.

In non-cooperative modification, changes are made in reverse execution order. The three partially modified sequences (*Old*1, *Old*2, *Old*3, *New*4), (*Old*1, *Old*2, *New*3, *New*4), and (*Old*1, *New*2, *New*3, *New*4) must be legal sequences for *Pt*, in that *Pt* must do the right thing if it executes any of them. Additionally, none of the locations to be modified, except the first, may be the target of a branch. Figure J-8 shows the code for PSO and TSO. The code assumes that %i0 contains the starting address of the area to be patched and %i1, %i2, %i3, %i4 contain *New*1, *New*2, *New*3, and *New*4.

SPARC International, Inc.

Figure J-8     *Non-Cooperative Code Patching*

| Code for PSO | Code for TSO |
|---|---|
| **NonCoopPatch**(*addr*, *instructions...*) | **NonCoopPatch**(*addr*, *instructions...*) |

```
     st      %i4,[%i0+12]           st      %i4,[%i0+12]
     flush   %i0+12                 flush   %i0+12
     stbar                          st      %i3,[%i0+8]
     st      %i3,[%i0+8]            flush   %i0+8
     flush   %i0+8                  st      %i2,[%i0+4]
     stbar                          flush   %i0+4
     st      %i2,[%i0+4]            st      %i1,[%i0]
     flush   %i0+4                  flush   %i0
     stbar
     st      %i1,[%i0]
     flush   %i0
```

Note that the FLUSH instructions in the above code do not need to be followed by 5 delay instructions because the only assumption is that the modifications done by *Pm* happen in the correct order "some time later". This order is guaranteed even if a 5-instruction delay is not inserted after each flush.

The constraint that all partially modified sequences must be legal is quite restrictive. When this constraint cannot be satisfied, non-cooperative code patching may require the target processor to execute FLUSH instructions. One method of triggering such FLUSHes would be to send an interrupt to the target processor.

In cooperative code patching, changes to instructions can be made in any order. When *Pm* is done with the changes, it writes into a shared variable *done* to notify *Pt*. *Pt* waits for *done* to change from 0 to some other value as a signal that the changes have been completed. Figure J-9 shows the code for PSO and TSO. The code assumes that %i0 contains the starting address of the area to be patched, %i1, %i2, %i3, %i4 contain *New*1, *New*2, *New*3, and *New*4, and %g1 contains the address of *done*. The FLUSH instructions in *Pt* ensure that the instruction buffer of *Pt*'s processor is flushed so that the old instructions are not executed.

Figure J-9    *Cooperative Code Patching*

| Code for PSO | | Code for TSO | |
|---|---|---|---|
| **CoopPatch(***addr, instructions...***)** | | **CoopPatch(***addr, instructions...***)** | |
| st | %i1,[%i0] | st | %i1,[%i0] |
| st | %i2,[%i0+4] | st | %i2,[%i0+4] |
| st | %i3,[%i0+8] | st | %i3,[%i0+8] |
| st | %i4,[%i0+12] | st | %i4,[%i0+12] |
| mov | -1,%l0 | mov | -1,%l0 |
| stbar | | st | %l0,[%g1] |
| st | %l0,[%g1] | | |
| **TargetCode( )** | | **TargetCode( )** | |
| wait: ld | [%g1],%l0 | wait: ld | [%g1],%l0 |
| cmp | %l0,0 | cmp | %l0,0 |
| be | wait | be | wait |
| flush | A | flush | A |
| flush | A+4 | flush | A+4 |
| flush | A+8 | flush | A+8 |
| flush | A+12 | flush | A+12 |
| nop | | nop | |
| nop | | nop | |
| nop | | nop | |
| nop | | nop | |
| nop | | nop | |
| A: Old1 | | A: Old1 | |
| Old2 | | Old2 | |
| Old3 | | Old3 | |
| Old4 | | Old4 | |
| . . . | | . . . | |

## J.9. Fetch and Add

Fetch and Add performs the sequence $a = a + b$ atomically with respect to other Fetch and Add's to location $a$. Two versions of Fetch and Add are shown. The first uses the routine LockWithLdStUB described earlier, while the second uses LockWithSwapOnes, a version of LockWithSwap that uses the encoding all ones to mean lock held, and any other value to mean lock free. Note that index cannot have the value -1 since the lock routine uses this value to encode the lock-held state. The code for PSO and TSO is identical, so only one version is shown for the two models.

Figure J-10    *Fetch and Add using LDSTUB and SWAP*

```
/*Fetch and Add using LDSTUB*/
int Fetch_And_Add(Index, Increment, Lock)
        int *Index;
        int Increment;
        int *Lock;
        {
                int old_value;
                LockWithLdStUB(Lock);
                    old_value = *Index;
                    *Index = old_value + Increment;
                UnlockWithLdstUB(Lock);
                return(old_value);
        }

/*Fetch and Add using SWAP*/
int Fetch_And_Add(Index,Increment)
        int *Index;
        int Increment;
        {
                int old_value;
                int new_value;
                LockWithSwapOnes(Index,&old_value);
                    new_value = old_value + Increment;
                UnlockWithSwapOnes(Index,&new_value);
                return(old_value);
        }
```

**LockWithSwapOnes**(*lock*, *old*)
```
loop:   ld              [lock],%l0
        cmp             %l0,-1
        be              loop
        mov             -1,%l0
        swap            [lock],%l0
        cmp             %l0,-1
        be              loop
        st              %l0,[old]
```

**UnLockWithSwapOnes**(*lock*, *new*)
```
        ld              [new],%l0
        stbar
        st              %l0,[lock]
```

## J.10. Barrier Synchronization

Barrier Synchronization ensures that each of $N$ processes is blocked until all of them reach a given state. The point in the flow of control at which this state is reached is called the Barrier, hence the name Barrier Synchronization. The code uses the variable *Count* initialized to $N$. As each process reaches its desired state, it decrements *Count* and waits for *Count* to reach 0 before proceeding further. Two versions are shown, one that uses LockWithLdStUB, and the other that uses LockWithSwapOnes. The code for PSO and TSO is identical, so only one version is shown for the two models.

Figure J-11    *Barrier Synchronization using LDSTUB and SWAP*

```
/*Barrier Synchronization using LDSTUB*/
Barrier(Count,Lock)
   int *Count;
   int *Lock;
   {
        LockWithLdstUB(Lock);
           *Count = *Count - 1;
        UnlockWithLdstUB(Lock);
        while(*Count > 0)    {;/*busy-wait*/}
   }

/*Barrier Synchronization using SWAP*/
Barrier(Count)
   int *Count;
   {
        int current_value;
        LockWithSwapOnes(Count,&current_value);
           current_value--;
        UnlockWithSwapOnes(Count,&current_value);
        while(*Count > 0)    { ; /*busy-wait*/ }
   }
```

# K

## Formal Specification of the Memory Model

This Appendix provides a formal description of the SPARC Memory Model. The formal description is more complete and more precise than the intuitive description in Chapter 6, "Memory Model." It therefore represents the definitive specification. Implementations must conform to this model, and programmers must use this description in the case of ambiguity in the intuitive description.

The formal description specifies an interface between programs and hardware implementations that captures all information relevant to the functioning of memory operations. The goal of this specification is to allow programs and hardware implementations to be developed independently, while still allowing any program to run on any SPARC implementation. The axiomatic nature of the specification permits programmers to reason formally about whether critical program fragments satisfy desired properties. It also lets hardware designers use formal techniques to determine whether a given implementation conforms to the memory model.

**K.1. Notation**

Data loads and stores are denoted by $L$ and $S$, respectively. Atomic load-stores are denoted by $[L ; S]$, where [ ] represents atomicity. The instruction STBAR is denoted by $\check{S}$, and the instruction FLUSH by $F$. Instruction fetches are denoted by $IF$, and instruction loads by $IL$. Note that $L$ specifically excludes instruction loads. Superscripts on $L$, $S$, $\check{S}$, $F$, $IF$, and $IL$ refer to processor numbers, while subscripts on $L$, $S$, $F$, $IF$, and $IL$ refer to memory locations. $\check{S}$ does not carry subscripts because conceptually it applies to all memory locations. A $\#n$ after an $S$ refers to the value written by the $S$. Thus, for example,

$S_a^i \# 0$ denotes a store of 0 to location $a$ by processor $P^i$.

$L_a^i$ denotes a doubleword load from location $a$ by processor $P^i$.

$[L_a^i ; S_a^i \# 1]$ denotes an atomic load-store of 1 to location $a$ by $P^i$.

$\check{S}^i$ denotes an STBAR by processor $P^i$.

In the axioms that follow, $L$'s and $S$'s refer both to ordinary data loads and stores and those done as parts of atomic load-stores. The value returned by an $L$, $IF$, or $IL$, or stored by an $S$ is denoted by **Val**[ ]. **Val** is not defined for $[L ; S]$ as a whole, or for $\check{S}$. Thus,

**Val** $[L_a^i]$ denotes the doubleword value returned by $L_a^i$.

**Val** $[S_a^i]$ denotes the doubleword value in location $a$ immediately after $S_a^i$.

$SOp$ is used as shorthand for $S$ or $F$. $Op$ is used as shorthand for $L$, $S$, or $F$. Note that $Op$ specifically **does not** denote an atomic load-store. Finally,

$(Op;\ )\infty$ denotes the infinite sequence of $Op$.

A memory location is a container for a doubleword. Accesses to different bytes, halfwords, and words of a given doubleword are considered for ordering purposes as accesses to the same location.

Order relationships are fundamental to the formalism, so it is useful to define order.
A relation $\rightarrow$ is an **order** over a set $S$ if it is

  (i) **transitive** (a $\rightarrow$ b **and** b $\rightarrow$ c $\Rightarrow$ a $\rightarrow$ c)

  (ii) **reflexive** (a $\rightarrow$ a)

  and (iii) **antisymmetric** (a $\rightarrow$ b **and** b $\rightarrow$ a $\Rightarrow$ a = b).

Here a, b, and c are elements of $S$. The order is **total** if for all pairs (a, b) in $S$ either a $\rightarrow$ b or b $\rightarrow$ a; otherwise, it is **partial**.

The formalism uses two types of orders defined over the set of operations $\{L, S, F, IF, IL, S\}$ :

- A single partial order $\leq$ called the **memory order**. This order may be understood intuitively to conform to the order in which operations are performed by memory in real time. The order is partial because not all operations can be compared.

- A per-processor total order $;^i$ that denotes the sequence in which processor $i$ executes instructions. This is called the **program order**. The order is total because the instructions corresponding to **all** $L$'s, $S$'s, $F$'s, $IF$'s, and $S$'s of processor $i$ are related by $;^i$ . Note that $a;b$ does not mean that $a$ and $b$ are necessarily consecutive. Also note that unlike $\leq$ , this order is not defined directly over $\{L, S, F, IF, IL, S\}$ but over the instructions corresponding to these operations. Thus, the notation

$$S_a^i;\ S^i$$

means $P^i$ executed Instruction$[S_a^i]$ before it executed Instruction$[S^i]$. The superscript on $;$ is dropped when $i$ is obvious from context.

SPARC International, Inc.

## K.2. Total Store Ordering

Total Store Ordering (TSO) is the standard SPARC memory model. All implementations must support it. Programs written assuming TSO must not set the PSO mode bit in the MMU control register, because this may result in incorrect operation.

TSO guarantees that the store, FLUSH, and atomic load-store instructions of all processors appear to be executed by memory serially in a single order called the memory order $\leq$. It further guarantees that the sequence of these instructions for each processor $i$ is the same in the orders $;^i$ and $\leq$.

The complete semantics of TSO are captured by six axioms: Order, Atomicity, Termination, Value, LoadOp, and StoreStore. Note that the Value axiom applies only to those locations that behave like ordinary memory. The semantics of loads and stores to I/O locations are machine-dependent and therefore not covered by TSO. However, their **ordering** is as specified below. Additionally, loads and stores to I/O locations must be strongly ordered among themselves (this fact is, of course, not refelcted in the TSO axioms).

**Order** states that there exists a partial order $\leq$ over $\{L, S, F, IF, S\}$ that is total for all $S$'s and $F$'s; that is, all $S$'s and $F$'s must appear somewhere in this order.

$$(SOp_a^i \leq SOp_b^j) \ \lor \ (SOp_b^j \leq SOp_a^i)$$

**Atomicity** states that an atomic load-store issues the load before the store, that the $L$ part of an $[L ; S]$ appears before $S$ in $\leq$, and that between the $L$ and the $S$ there can be no other $S$'s in the memory order. Note that the axiom implies that the $L$ part of an atomic load-store is totally ordered with respect to $SOp$'s.

$$[L_a^i; S_a^i] \Rightarrow (L_a^i \leq S_a^i) \ \land \ (\forall SOp_b^j: \ SOp_b^j \leq L_a^i \ \lor \ S_a^i \leq SOp_b^j)$$

**Termination** states that all stores and atomic load-stores eventually terminate. This is formalized by saying that if one processor does an $S$, and another processor repeatedly does $L$'s to the same location, then there is an $L$ that will be after the $S$.

$$S_a^i \ \land \ (L_a^j; )\infty \Rightarrow \ \exists \ \text{an } L_a^j \text{ in } (L_a^j; )\infty \text{ such that } S_a^i \leq L_a^j$$

**Value** states that the value of a data load is the value written by the most recent store to that location. Two terms combine to define the most recent store. The first corresponds to stores by other processors, while the second corresponds to stores by the processor that issued the load.

$$\mathbf{Val}[L_a^i] = \mathbf{Val}[S_a^j \mid S_a^j = \underset{\leq}{\mathrm{Max}} \ [\{S_a^k \mid S_a^k \leq L_a^i\} \ \cup \ \{S_a^i \mid S_a^i; L_a^i\}]]$$

**LoadOp** states that any operation issued after an $L$ is later in the order $\leq$. This reflects the fact that a processor waits for a load to complete before issuing any subsequent operation.

$$L_a^i; Op_b^i \Rightarrow L_a^i \leq Op_b^i$$

**StoreStore** states that $S$'s and $F$'s issued by a processor appear in the same order in $\leq$. This reflects the fact that memory executes stores and FLUSHes in the order in which a processor issued them.

SPARC International, Inc.

$$SOp_a^i; SOp_b^i \Rightarrow SOp_a^i \leq SOp_b^i$$

Figure K-1 shows the intuitive model for comparison with the axiomatic specification.

Figure K-1    *Total Store Ordering Model of Memory*

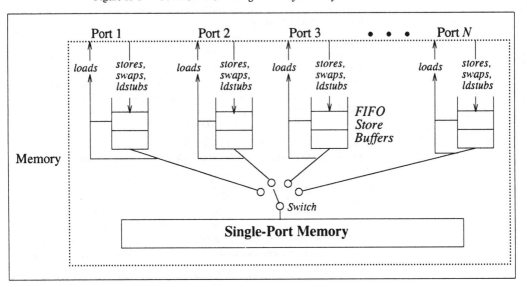

## K.3. Partial Store Ordering

Partial Store Ordering (PSO) is a performance-enhanced version of TSO which may be available via the PSO mode bit in the MMU control register. An implementation is not required to implement PSO, although use of this model is encouraged in high-performance machines. Programs written assuming PSO cannot detect any semantic difference between running with the PSO mode bit set to 1 or 0, although they may perceive significant differences in execution speed.

PSO guarantees that the store, FLUSH, and atomic load-store instructions of all processors appear to be executed by the memory serially in the memory order $\leq$. It further guarantees that the sequence of two $SOp$'s issued by any processor $i$ is the same in the orders $;^i$ and $\leq$ if the $SOp$'s are separated by $S$ in $;^i$ or if the two $SOp$'s are to the same location.

The complete semantics of PSO are captured by seven axioms: Order, Atomicity, Termination, Value, LoadOp, StoreStore, and StoreStoreEq. The first five axioms are identical to those for TSO, so they are not repeated here. Note that the Value axiom applies only to those locations that behave like ordinary memory. The semantics of loads and stores to I/O locations are machine-dependent and therefore not covered by PSO. However, their **ordering** is as specified below. Additionally, loads and stores to I/O locations must be strongly ordered among themselves (this fact is, of course, not reflected in the PSO axioms).

**StoreStore** states that $SOp$'s separated by $S$ in the execution order of a processor appear in the same order in $\leq$. This reflects the fact that memory executes stores and FLUSHes in the same order as a processor issues them only if the processor separates them by an $S$.

$$SOp_a^i; S; SOp_b^i \Rightarrow SOp_a^i \leq SOp_b^i$$

**StoreStoreEq** states that $S$'s and $F$'s issued to a given location by a processor appear in the same order in $\leq$. This reflects the fact that memory executes stores to the same location in the order in which they were issued by a processor, even if the processor did not separate them by an $S$.

$$SOp_a^i; SOp'^i_a \Rightarrow SOp_a^i \leq SOp'^i_a$$

Figure K-2 shows the intuitive model for comparison with the axiomatic specification.

SPARC International, Inc.

Figure K-2    *Partial Store Ordering Model of Memory*

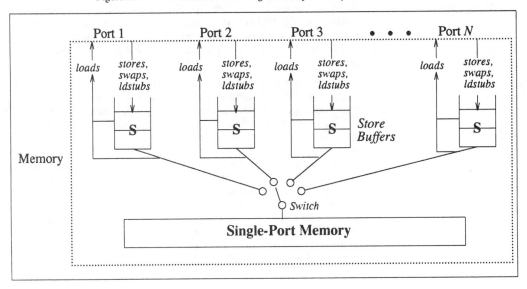

## K.4. FLUSH: Synchronizing Instruction Fetches with Memory Operations

The FLUSH instruction synchronizes the instruction fetches of the processor issuing the FLUSH to the loads, stores, and atomic load-stores of that processor, and forces the instruction fetches of all other processors to observe any store done to the FLUSH target prior to the FLUSH.

The semantics of FLUSH are expressed by three axioms: IFetchValue, FlushTermination, and IFetchIFetch. In IFetchValue, the symbol "<5>" is used to denote an arbitrary sequence of 5 or more instructions.

**IFetchValue** states that the value of an instruction fetch is the value written by the most recent $(S \; ; \; F)$ sequence to that location. Two terms combine to define the most recent such sequence. The first corresponds to sequences by other processors, while the second corresponds to sequences by the processor that issued the load. Note that in the first set of sequences, the store and the FLUSH may be issued by different processors. Also note that in the second set of sequences, the FLUSH must be followed by 5 arbitrary instructions before the instruction fetch to the FLUSH's target.

$$\mathbf{Val}[IF_a^i] = \mathbf{Val}[S_a^j \mid S_a^j =$$
$$\underset{\leq}{\mathrm{Max}} \; [\{S_a^k \mid S_a^k \leq F_a^l \leq IF_a^i\} \cup \{S_a^i \mid S_a^i; F_a^i; <5>; IF_a^i\}]]$$

**FlushTermination** states that an $S ; F$ sequence done by one processor will eventually be observed by the instruction fetches of all processors.

$$(S_a^i; F_a^i) \wedge (IF_a^j)\infty \Rightarrow \; \exists \; \text{an } IF_a^j \text{ in } (IF_a^j)\infty \text{ such that } S_a^i \leq IF_a^j$$

**IFetchIFetch** states that two instruction fetches issued by a processor appear in the same order in $\leq$.

$$IF_a^i; IF_b^i \Rightarrow \; IF_a^i \leq IF_b^i$$

Figure K-3 shows the intuitive model for comparison with the axiomatic specification.

Figure K-3    *Operation of the FLUSH Instruction*

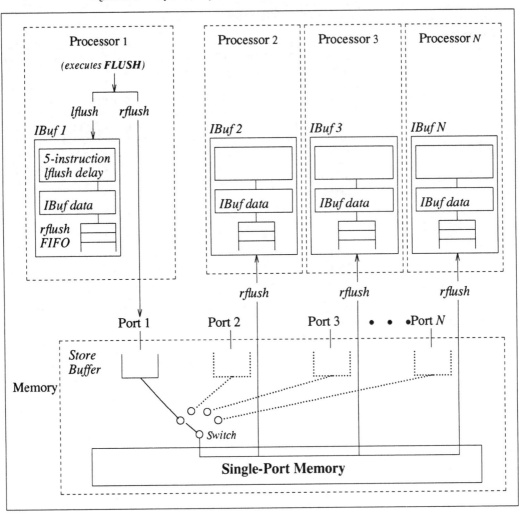

# L

# Implementation Characteristics

This appendix discusses implementation-dependent aspects of SPARC chip sets that are software visible. The appendix covers only IU and FPU implementations existing before December 1990. MMU implementations and ASI assignments are not covered. It is divided into three sections: (1) Processor State Register (PSR) *impl* and *ver* field values; (2) Floating-point State Register (FSR) *ver* field values; and (3) characteristics and limitations that are specific to the generally known IU and FPU implementations. Electrical characteristics and the timing constraints of the various implementations are available from the chip producers themselves. The third section also summarizes the cycle timing of the integer instructions, since this can affect the code generated by compilers.

## L.1. PSR *impl* and *ver* Values

The Processor State Register's (PSR) 4-bit PSR_implementation (*impl*) and 4-bit PSR_version (*ver*) fields are defined as "hardwired" values that are established when an IU implementation is designed and manufactured. A WRPSR instruction does not change or affect either of these fields.

Historically, a new PSR_implementation value was assigned when an IU implementation was significantly different from previous implementations. Such a difference might be due to additional instructions, a new instruction timing, new pipeline, etc. A new PSR_version value was assigned when a less significant change was made to the chip, such as a bug fix.

Table L-1 shows the assignment of PSR_implementation and PSR_version values to the five implementations publicly announced by December 1990. For the purposes of this appendix, the five implementations are labeled Fujitsu0, Cypress0, Cypress1, BIT0, and Matsushita0.

Parts that are second-sourced or cross-licensed typically follow the assignment of the original implementation. Thus, the L64801 and L64811 have the same PSR_implementation and PSR_version values as the MB86901A and CY7C601, respectively. Note that the CY7C611 is architecturally equivalent to the CY7C601, except for pinout differences. The implementation-dependent details of these chips are listed below.

SPARC International, Inc.

Table L-1    *PSR impl and vers Assignments to Processors*

| PSR *impl* | PSR *ver* | Company - Part Number | Label Used |
|---|---|---|---|
| 0 | 0 | Fujitsu - MB86900/1A  &  LSIL - L64801 | Fujitsu0 |
| 1 | 0,1 | Cypress - CY7C601  &  LSIL - L64811 | Cypress0 |
| 1 | 3 | Cypress - CY7C611 | Cypress1 |
| 2 | 0 | BIT - B5010 | BIT0 |
| 5 | 0 | Matsushita - MN10501 | Matsushita0 |

The current practice with respect to the assignment of PSR_implementation values is that a unique value is assigned to one or more sanctioned SPARC implementors by SPARC International. That value is then applied to all of its (their) future implementations. (Also, if necessary, a given licensee may request more than one PSR_implementation value.)

Each implementor or set of implementors, given its PSR_implementation number, has the freedom to assign the 16 possible PSR_version values as it deems necessary. PSR_version values can represent radically different IU implementations, or only minor changes. Note that the PSR_version field, however, **must not** be implemented as a general-purpose, read/write field.

Through December 1990, PSR_implementation values have been assigned to SPARC implementors according to Table L-2.

Table L-2    *PSR impl Assignments to SPARC Licensees*

| PSR *impl* | Implementor |
|---|---|
| 0 | Fujitsu Microelectronics, Inc. |
| 1 | Cypress Semiconductor Corp. & Ross Technology, Inc. |
| 2 | Bipolar Integrated Technology (BIT) |
| 3 | LSI Logic Corp. (LSIL) |
| 4 | Texas Instruments, Inc. (TI) |
| 5 | Matsushita Semiconductor, Inc. & Solbourne Computer, Inc. |
| 6 | Philips Corp. |
| 7 | Harvest VLSI Design Center, Inc. |
| 8 | Systems and Processes Engineering Corporation (SPEC) |
| 9 | Weitek |
| A-0xF | *reserved* |

## L.2. FSR *ver* Values

In addition to the PSR's *impl* and *ver* fields, the user-accessible Floating-point State Register (FSR) has a 3-bit FSR_version (*ver*) field. The FSR_version field is defined as a "hardwired" value that is established when an FPU implementation is designed and manufactured. An LDFSR instruction does not change or affect this field.

FSR_version values are interpreted relative to the IU implementation, given by the PSR_implementation and PSR_version fields. Thus, the interpretation of a particular FSR_version value depends on which IU implementation is involved.

A new FSR_version value is assigned when an FPU implementation differs from previous implementations. Such a difference might be due to additional instructions, new instruction timings, a new pipeline, or less significant changes such as bug fixes.

Through June, 1990, FSR_version values have been assigned to SPARC implementors according to Table L-3. Cypress0 and Cypress1 are equivalent in this table. Note that FSR_version = 7 always implies that there is no FPU hardware attached to the IU. (The operating system supplies this value when emulating an STFSR instruction that traps due to the lack of the FPU.) Note that the L64814, TMS390C602A, and WTL3171 FPU's are architecturally (and pin-) equivalent implementations.

Table L-3    *FSR ver Assignments*

| FSR ver | PSR.*impl*=0 (Fujitsu0) | PSR.*impl*=1 (Cypress0/1) | PSR.*impl*=2 (BIT0) | PSR.*impl*=5 (Matsushita0) |
|---|---|---|---|---|
| 0 | Fujitsu MB86910 (1-4) Weitek WTL1164/5 | LSIL L64812 TI ACT8847 | BIT B5010 BIT B5110/20 BIT B5210 | MN10501 |
| 1 | Fujitsu MB86911 (5-6) Weitek WTL1164/5 | LSIL L64814 | *reserved* | *reserved* |
| 2 | LSIL L64802 TI ACT8847 | TI TMS390-C602A | *reserved* | *reserved* |
| 3 | Weitek WTL3170/2 | Weitek WTL3171 Cypress 7C602 | *reserved* | *reserved* |
| 4 | LSIL/Meiko L64804 | *reserved* | *reserved* | *reserved* |
| 5 | *reserved* | *reserved* | *reserved* | *reserved* |
| 6 | *reserved* | *reserved* | *reserved* | *reserved* |
| 7 | No FPU | No FPU | No FPU | No FPU |

**L.3. Characteristics of Existing Implementations**

This section discusses how the existing implementations identified in Table L-1 handle some of the implementation-dependent aspects of the architecture. Implementations are referred to as they were in Table L-1: Fujitsu0, Cypress0, Cypress1, BIT0, and Matsushita0. This section is arranged according to the particular implementation-dependent architectural feature.

**Unimplemented Instructions**

Table L-5 shows which instructions are not implemented in the various IU's. An attempt to execute an instruction marked "unimp" in the table will cause an illegal_instruction trap on that implementation. An attempt to execute an instruction marked "cp_dis" in the table will cause a coprocessor_disabled trap on that implementation. Instructions marked "√" in the table are fully implemented in hardware in that implementation.

Table L-4    *Instructions Unimplemented in SPARC IUs*

| Instructions | Fujitsu0 | Cypress0 | Cypress1 | BIT0 | Matsushita0 |
|---|---|---|---|---|---|
| SWAP(A) | unimp | √ | √ | √ | unimp |
| (U/S)MUL(cc) | unimp | unimp | unimp | unimp | √ |
| (U/S)DIV(cc) | unimp | unimp | unimp | unimp | unimp |
| STDFQ(A) | √ | √ | √ | √ | √ |
| Coprocessor | √ | √ | cp_dis | √ | cp_dis |

FSQRTs and FSQRTd are not implemented by the Fujitsu MB86910 and MB86911 (WTL 1164/5), but are implemented by the remaining FPU's. None of the FPU implementations implements the quadruple-precision floating-point instructions, FsMULd, or FdMULq. An attempt to execute an instruction marked "unimp" in Table L-6 will set FSR.*ftt* to unimplemented_FPop and cause an fp_exception trap on that implementation. Instructions marked "√" in the table are fully implemented in hardware in that implementation.

Table L-5    *Instructions Unimplemented in SPARC FPUs*

| Instruction | Fujitsu0 | Cypress0,1 | BIT0 | Matsushita0 |
|---|---|---|---|---|
| FSQRTs, FSQRTd | unimp | √ | √ | √ |
| FsMULd, FdMULq | unimp | unimp | unimp | unimp |
| Quad-precision | unimp | unimp | unimp | unimp |
| all other f.p. instructions | √ | √ | √ | √ |

**FLUSH Instruction**

The FLUSH instruction acts as a NOP in the Cypress1 implementation. In the Fujitsu0 and Cypress0 implementations, FLUSH either acts as a NOP or causes an illegal_instruction trap, based on a signal from an external pin. In the BIT implementation, FLUSH either acts as a NOP or causes an illegal_instruction trap, based on the value of the IFT (Instruction Flush Trap) bit in its XCR register. FLUSH always causes an illegal_instruction trap in Matsushita0.

FLUSH does not clear the IU's pipeline in any of these five implementations. However, in each implementation the pipeline is clear of pre-FLUSH instructions by the time 5 instructions subsequent to the FLUSH have executed. See the FLUSH instruction description in Appendix B.

SPARC International, Inc.

**Integer Deferred-Trap Queue**

None of the existing implementations uses an Integer Deferred-Trap Queue.

**Floating-point Deferred-Trap Queue (FQ) and STDFQ Instruction**

A Floating-point Deferred-Trap Queue (FQ) exists and, except for the number of entries it may contain, is implemented identically in all five implementations.

The implemented FQ is a queue of doublewords that records the FPops that are pending completion by the FPU when an fp_exception occurs. After an fp_exception trap occurs, the first entry in the queue is the address of the FPop that caused the exception, together with the FPop instruction itself. Any remaining entries in the queue represent FPops that had not finished execution when the fp_exception trap occurred.

The store floating-point queue instruction (STDFQ) stores the front entry of the FQ into memory. The address part of the front entry is stored into memory at the effective address, and the instruction part of the front entry at the effective address + 4. The queue is then advanced to the next entry, or it becomes empty (as indicated by the *qne* bit in the FSR).

**FSR_nonstandard_fp**

The Fujitsu MB86910 and MB86911 (WTL 1164/5) and BIT B5010 implement the FSR_nonstandard_fp (NS or "fast") mode bit in the FSR. The MN10501 implements NS, but ignores it. The other implentations do not implement FSR.NS.

**FPU Exceptions**

A data_access_exception trap that occurs for a load floating-point instruction causes the destination *f* registers to be set to the constant value of all ones.

All five implementations implement deferred fp_exception traps. They delay the taking of an fp_exception trap until the next floating-point instruction is encountered in the instruction stream. The FPU implementations can be modeled as having 3 states: `fp_execute, fp_exception_pending,` and `fp_exception.`

Normally the FPU is in `fp_execute` state. It moves from `fp_execute` to `fp_exception_pending` when an FPop generates a floating-point exception. It moves from `fp_exception_pending` to `fp_exception` when the IU attempts to execute any floating-point instruction. At this time it also loads the FQ with the FPop and its address and generates an fp_exception trap. A fp_exception trap can only be caused while the FPU is moving from the `fp_exception_pending` state to the `fp_exception state.`

While in `fp_exception` state, only floating-point store instructions are executed (particularly, STDFQ and STFSR), which can not cause an fp_exception trap. The FPU remains in the `fp_exception` state until a STDFQ instruction is executed and the FQ becomes empty. At that time, it returns to the fp_execute state. If an FPop, floating-point load instruction, or floating-point branch instruction is executed while the FPU is in `fp_exception` state, the FPU returns to `fp_exception_pending` state and also sets the FSR *ftt* field to sequence_error. The instruction that caused the sequence_error is not entered into the FQ.

SPARC International, Inc.

**Trap Model and Trap Types**

None of the five implementations implements an enhanced trap model. They all implement the default trap model only.

Only BIT0 implements the instruction_access_error, r_register_access_error, and data_access_error traps. These correspond to a cache parity error on an instruction access, *r* register read, and load access, respectively. None of the chips implement the division_by_zero, data_store_error, unimplemented_FLUSH, or implementation-dependent exception (0x60-0x7F) traps.

The trap priorities of privileged_instruction and illegal_instruction traps are reversed in the Fujitsu0 implementation.

The data_access_MMU_miss, instruction_access_MMU_miss, and watchpoint_detected traps are implemented only by Matsushita0.

Matsushita0 causes error_mode to generate a reset trap with $tt = 0x20$ instead of $tt = 0x00$. In that implementation, the reset trap at $tt = 0x0$ is caused only by an external reset.

**Memory Model and STBAR Instruction**

All of the five implementations are capable of supporting a Strong Consistency memory model, depending on system implementation. Existing systems all implement a Strong Consistency memory model, thus support programs written assuming either Total (TSO) or Partial Store Ordering (PSO) memory models. However, none of these implementations has been designed to explicitly support either TSO or PSO memory systems.

All five implementations treat the store barrier instruction (STBAR) as a RDY with $rd = 0$.

**Ancillary State Registers**

None of the five implementations implements any user or privileged ancillary state registers. A WRASR instruction executed on any of them acts as a WRY instruction; the *rd* field is ignored.

**Width of Load/Store Effective Address**

Cypress1 only supplies to the memory the low-order 3 bits of the address space identifier (ASI[2:0]) and the low-order 24 bits of load/store and instruction access addresses. Matsushita0 supplies only the low-order 7 bits of the address space identifier (ASI[6:0]). The other four implementations supply the complete 8-bit ASI and 32-bit effective address to memory.

**Number of Windows**

Fujitsu0 and BIT0 implement 7 register windows. Cypress0, Cypress1, and Matsushita0 implement 8 register windows.

**Instruction Timing**

This section deals only with integer instruction timings, as measured in "cycles", or single ticks of an implementation's clock. These values assume a 0-wait state cache or memory system. Floating-point instruction timing is beyond the scope of this appendix.

Fujitsu0 is implemented for an external combined instruction and data cache/memory. Integer instruction timings are as follows:

Table L-6    *Integer Instruction Timings for Fujitsu0 Implementation*

| Cycles | Instructions |
|---|---|
| 1 | all integer instructions except those listed below |
| 2 | load single, untaken branch, taken Ticc, JMPL, RETT |
| 3 | load double, store single, untaken Ticc |
| 4 | store double, LDSTUB, SWAP |

Cypress0 and Cypress1 are also implemented for an external combined instruction and data cache/memory. Their integer instruction timings are equivalent to Fujitsu0 except that an untaken branch costs a single cycle, as follows:

Table L-7    *Integer Instruction Timings for Cypress0 and Cypress1 Implementations*

| Cycles | Instructions |
|---|---|
| 1 | all integer instructions except those listed below |
| 2 | load single, taken Ticc, JMPL, RETT |
| 3 | load double, store single, untaken Ticc |
| 4 | store double, LDSTUB, SWAP |

BIT0 is implemented for an external combined instruction and data cache/memory with a 64-bit bus, allowing it to normally execute a load single or load double in a single cycle. There are instruction-sequence-dependent exceptions to the following timings which are beyond the scope of this appendix.

Table L-8    *Integer Instruction Timings for BIT0 Implementation*

| Cycles | Instructions |
|---|---|
| 1 | all integer instructions except those listed below |
| 2 | load double, store single, JMPL, RETT |
| 3 | store double |
| 5 | taken Ticc |

Matsushita0 is implemented with internal, separate instruction and data caches with 64-bit busses. Note that the 64 bit internal cache busses on Matsushita0 allow loads and stores of any size to normally execute in a single cycle. The instruction-sequence dependent exceptions to the following timings are beyond the scope of this appendix.

Table L-9    *Integer Instruction Timings for Matsushita0 Implementation*

| Cycles | Instructions |
|--------|--------------|
| 1 | all integer instructions except those listed below |
| 2 | a store with the [*rs1* + *rs2*] addressing mode |
| 2 | RETT, STDFQ, taken Ticc |
| 5 | UMUL, UMULcc, SMUL, SMULcc |

# M

## Instruction Set Summary

This appendix provides a summary of the SPARC instruction set. Bold letters indicate the architectural names of instructions; for example, the architectural name of the "Floating-point convert from Single **TO** **D**ouble" is FSTOD.

Note that not all possible combinations in this summary map to actual instructions. For example, there is no "**Lo**a**D** single **C**oprocessor **Q**ueue" instruction.

- ## Data Transfer

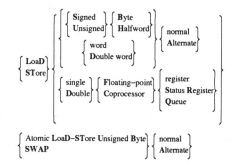

- ## Arithmetic & Logical Operations

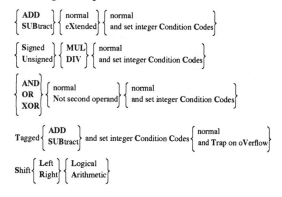

SPARC International, Inc.

- ## Control Transfer

  **CALL**
  JuMP and Link
  RETurn from Trap
  Trap on integer condition codes
  Branch on integer condition codes
  Floating-point Branch on floating-point condition codes
  Coprocessor Branch on coprocessor condition codes

- ## Miscellaneous

  No OPeration
  **SETHI**
  MULtiply Step and set integer Condition Codes
  **FLUSH** instruction memory
  STore BARrier

  $\begin{Bmatrix} \textbf{SAVE} \\ \textbf{RESTORE} \end{Bmatrix}$ register window

  $\begin{Bmatrix} \text{ReaD} \\ \text{WRite} \end{Bmatrix} \begin{Bmatrix} \text{Ancillary State Register} \\ \text{Processor Status Register} \\ \text{Trap Base Register} \\ \text{Y register} \\ \text{Window Invalid Mask} \end{Bmatrix}$

  UNIMPlemented (illegal) instruction

- ## Floating-point Operations

  Floating-point convert from $\begin{Bmatrix} \text{Integer} \\ \text{Single} \\ \text{Double} \\ \text{Quad} \end{Bmatrix}$ **TO** $\begin{Bmatrix} \text{Integer} \\ \text{Single} \\ \text{Double} \\ \text{Quad} \end{Bmatrix}$

  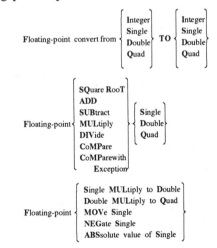

  Floating-point $\begin{Bmatrix} \text{SQuare RooT} \\ \textbf{ADD} \\ \text{SUBtract} \\ \textbf{MULtiply} \\ \text{DIVide} \\ \text{CoMPare} \\ \text{CoMParewith Exception} \end{Bmatrix} \begin{Bmatrix} \text{Single} \\ \text{Double} \\ \text{Quad} \end{Bmatrix}$

  Floating-point $\begin{Bmatrix} \text{Single MULtiply to Double} \\ \text{Double MULtiply to Quad} \\ \text{MOVe Single} \\ \text{NEGate Single} \\ \text{ABSsolute value of Single} \end{Bmatrix}$

SPARC International, Inc.

# SPARC IEEE 754 Implementation Recommendations

A number of details in ANSI/IEEE 754 floating-point standard are left to be defined by implementations, and so are not specified in this document. In order to promote increased portability among new SPARC implementations of programs such as instruction set test vectors, the following recommendations are designed to eliminate many uncertainties, especially with regard to exceptional situations. These recommendations, perhaps modified slightly in the light of subsequent experience, are intended to be incorporated as requirements in a future SPARC revision.

## N.1. Misaligned floating-point data registers

The effect of executing an instruction that refers to a misaligned floating-point register operand (double-precision operand in a register whose number is not 0 mod 2, or quadruple-precision operand in a register whose number is not 0 mod 4) is undefined in Section 4.3, "FPU *f* Registers." An fp_exception trap with FSR.*ftt* = 6 (invalid_fp_register) should occur in this case.

## N.2. Reading an empty FQ

The effect of reading an empty floating-point queue is not specified in Chapter 4, "Registers." A trap handler which attempts to read such a queue contains a software error. A sequence_error fp_exception trap occurs in this case.

## N.3. Traps inhibit results

To summarize what happens when a floating-point trap occurs, as described in Section 4.4, "FPU Control/Status Registers", and elsewhere:

- The destination *f* register is unchanged

- The FSR *fcc* (floating-point condition codes) field is unchanged

- The FSR *aexc* (accrued exceptions) field is unchanged

- The FSR *cexc* (current exceptions) field is unchanged except for IEEE_754_exceptions; in that case, *cexc* contains exactly one bit which is 1, corresponding to the exception that caused the trap

These restrictions are designed to ensure a consistent state for user software. Instructions causing an fp_exception trap due to unfinished or unimplemented FPops execute as if by hardware; that a hardware trap was taken to supervisor software is undetectable by user software except possibly by timing considerations. A user-mode trap handler invoked for an IEEE 754 exception, whether as a direct result of a hardware IEEE_754_exception or as an indirect result of supervisor handling of an unfinished_FPop or unimplemented_FPop, can rely on the following:

- Supervisor software will pass it the address of the instruction which caused the exception, extracted from a deferred trap queue or elsewhere
- The destination *f* register is unchanged from its state prior to that instruction's execution
- The FSR *fcc* field is unchanged
- The FSR *aexc* field is unchanged
- The FSR *cexc* field contains one bit set to "1" for the exception that caused the trap
- The FSR *ftt*, *qne*, *u*, and *res* fields are zero

Supervisor software is responsible for enforcing these requirements if the hardware trap mechanism does not.

### N.4.  NaN operand and result definitions

An untrapped floating-point result can be in a format which is either the same as, or different from, the format of the source operands. These two cases are described separately, below.

**Untrapped floating-point result in different format from operands**

F[sdq]TO[sdq], with quiet NaN operand: no exception caused; result is a quiet NaN. The operand is transformed as follows:

> **NaN transformation:** The most significant bits of the operand fraction are copied to the most significant bits of the result fraction. When converting to a narrower format, excess low order bits of the operand fraction are discarded. When converting to a wider format, excess low order bits of the result fraction are set to 0. The quiet bit (the most significant bit of the result fraction) is always set to 1, so the NaN transformation always produces a quiet NaN.

F[sdq]TO[sdq], signaling NaN operand: invalid exception, result is the signaling NaN operand processed by the **NaN transformation** above to produce a quiet NaN.

FCMPE[sdq] with any NaN operand: invalid exception, unordered *fcc*.

FCMP[sdq] with any signaling NaN operand: invalid exception, unordered *fcc*.

FCMP[sdq] with any quiet NaN operand but no signaling NaN operand: no exception, unordered *fcc*.

**Untrapped floating-point result in same format as operands**

No NaN operand: for an invalid exception such as sqrt(−1.0)  or  0.0÷0.0, the result is the quiet NaN with sign = 0, exponent = all 1's, and fraction = all 1's. The sign is 0 to distinguish such results from storage initialized to all '1' bits.

One operand, quiet NaN: no exception, result is the quiet NaN operand.

One operand, signaling NaN: invalid exception, result is the signaling NaN with its quiet bit (most significant bit of fraction field) set to 1.

Two operands, both quiet: no exception, result is the rs2 (second source) operand.

Two operands, both signaling: invalid exception, result is the rs2 operand with the quiet bit set to 1.

Two operands, just one a signaling NaN: invalid exception, result is the signaling NaN operand with the quiet bit set to 1.

Two operands, neither signaling NaN, just one a quiet NaN: no exception, result is the quiet NaN operand.

In the following tabular representation of the untrapped results, NaN$n$ means the NaN in rs$n$, Q means quiet, S signaling:

|  |  | rs2 operand | | |
|---|---|---|---|---|
|  |  | number | QNaN2 | SNaN2 |
|  | none | IEEE 754 | QNaN2 | QSNaN2 |
| rs1 | number | IEEE 754 | QNaN2 | QSNaN2 |
| operand | QNaN1 | QNaN1 | QNaN2 | QSNaN2 |
|  | SNaN1 | QSNaN1 | QSNaN1 | QSNaN2 |

QSNaN$n$ means a quiet NaN produced by the **NaN transformation** on a signaling NaN from rs$n$; the invalid exception is always indicated. The QNaN$n$ results in the table never generate an exception, but IEEE 754 specifies a number of cases of invalid exceptions and QNaN results from operands that are both numbers.

## N.5. Trapped Underflow definition (UFM=1)

Underflow occurs if the correct unrounded result has magnitude between zero and the smallest normalized number in the destination format. In terms of IEEE 754, this means "tininess detected before rounding".

Note that the wrapped exponent results intended to be delivered on trapped underflows and overflows in IEEE 754 aren't relevant to SPARC at the hardware/supervisor levels; if they are created at all, it would be by user software in a user-mode trap handler.

## N.6. Untrapped underflow definition (UFM=0)

Underflow occurs if the correct unrounded result has magnitude between zero and the smallest normalized number in the destination format, **and** the correctly rounded result in the destination format is inexact; that result may be zero, subnormal, or the smallest normalized number. In terms of IEEE 754, this means "tininess detected before rounding" and "loss of accuracy detected as inexact".

Note that floating-point overflow is defined to be detected **after** rounding; the foregoing underflow definition simplifies hardware implementation and testing.

The following table summarizes what happens when an exact **unrounded** value $u$ satisfying
$$0 \le |u| \le smallest\ normalized\ number$$
would round, if no trap intervened, to a **rounded** value $r$ which might be zero, subnormal, or the smallest normalized value. "UF" means underflow trap (with ufc set in *cexc*), "NX" means inexact trap (with nxc set in *cexc*), "uf" means untrapped underflow exception (ufc set in *cexc* and ufa in *aexc*), and "nx" means

untrapped inexact exception (nxc set in *cexc* and nxa in *aexc*).

| | underflow trap | UFM=1 | UFM=0 | UFM=0 |
|---|---|---|---|---|
| | inexact trap | NXM=? | NXM=1 | NXM=0 |
| $u = r$ | $r$ is minimum normal | none | none | none |
| | $r$ is subnormal | UF | none | none |
| | $r$ is zero | none | none | none |
| $u \neq r$ | $r$ is minimum normal | UF | NX | uf nx |
| | $r$ is subnormal | UF | NX | uf nx |
| | $r$ is zero | UF | NX | uf nx |

## N.7. Integer overflow definition

F[sdq]TOi: when a NaN, infinity, large positive argument $\geq 2147483648.0$, or large negative argument $\leq -2147483649.0$, is converted to integer, the resulting exception is invalid. If no trap occurs and the sign bit of the operand is positive (i.e., is 0), the numerical result is 2147483647. If no trap occurs and the sign bit of the operand is negative (i.e., is 1), the numerical result is $-2147483648$.

## N.8. Nonstandard mode

SPARC implementations are permitted but not encouraged to deviate from SPARC requirements when the nonstandard mode bit of the FSR is 1. Some implementations use that bit to provide alternative handling of subnormal floating-point operands and results that avoids unfinished_FPop traps with consequent poor performance on programs that underflow frequently.

Such traps could be avoided by proper system design. Cache misses in the CPU cause holds in the FPU, in order for extra cycles to occur to refill the cache, so that their occurrence is invisible to software and doesn't degrade performance in the normal cache hit case. Similarly "subnormal misses" in the FPU can be avoided by any of several better implementation techniques that avoid causing an unfinished_FPop trap or degrading performance in the normal case. One way is to cause subnormal misses in the FPU to hold the CPU, so that operand or result alignment can take a few extra cycles without any other effect on software. Another way to avoid extra cycles is to provide extra normalization hardware for operands and results.

So, the best implementation of nonstandard mode is for it to run identically to the standard SPARC mode. In such implementations the NS bit of the FSR always reads as 0, even after a 1 is written to it.

The next-preferred implementation of nonstandard mode is for subnormal operands and results to behave as outlined below (so that implementations operate uniformly):

Subnormal operands
> In nonstandard mode, operands are replaced by zeros with the same sign. An inexact exception always arises if no other exception would, and so traps if NXM=1.

Untrapped subnormal results
> In nonstandard mode, operands are replaced by zeros with the same sign. Underflow and inexact exceptions always arise. In terms of the previous table:

| | underflow trap<br>inexact trap | UFM=1<br>NXM=? | UFM=0<br>NXM=1 | UFM=0<br>NXM=0 |
|---|---|---|---|---|
| $u = r$ | $r$ is minimum normal<br>$r$ is zero | none<br>none | none<br>none | none<br>none |
| $u \neq r$ | $r$ is minimum normal<br>$r$ is zero | UF<br>UF | NX<br>NX | uf nx<br>uf nx |

SPARC International, Inc.

# Index